A Natural History of the Tahoe Sierra Soul

Including Desolation Wilderness and Fallen Leaf Lake

Trees, shrubs, ferns, flowers, birds, amphibians, reptiles, mammals and fishes inhabiting the Sierra Nevada watershed southwest of Lake Tahoe, California

CHARLES QUINN

with selected essays by
REBECCA CHAPLIN

Photographs by
David Cardinal, Christopher L. Christie, Dennis Deck, Steve Dowlan,
Dan Gleason, Tom Greer, Joyce Gross, Steve Matson, Gary Nafis,
Susan D. Prince, Charles Quinn, John H. Quinn,
California Academy of Sciences &
Stanford Sierra Camp Staff Photographers

CraneDance Publications
Eugene, Oregon

CraneDance Publications
PO Box 50535
Eugene, Oregon 97405
541-345-3974 or www.cranedance.com

© 2006 Charles Quinn
All rights reserved. No parts of this book may be reproduced in any form or by any electronic or mechanical means without permission of the author. Requests should be made to:

Charles Quinn c/o
Stanford Sierra Camp
P.O. Box 10618
South Lake Tahoe, CA 96158
530-541-1244
http://www.stanfordalumni.org/learningtravel/sierra/home.html
or email c.quinn@stanfordalumni.org

Library of Congress Cataloging-in-Publication Data
Quinn, Charles Patrick, 1972 -
  A Nature Guide to the Southwest Tahoe Basin Including Desolation Wilderness and Fallen Leaf Lake: Trees, shrubs, ferns, flowers, birds, amphibians, reptiles, mammals and fishes inhabiting the Sierra Nevada watershed southwest of Lake Tahoe, California / Charles Quinn.
  Includes bibliographic references.
  ISBN: 0-9708895-4-2
  1. Natural History—Lake Tahoe, California. 2. Natural History—Desolation Wilderness, California. 3. Natural History—Sierra Nevada, California.

First Edition

Book Design by BGleason Design & Illustration, LLC/CraneDance Publications, www.cranedance.com or www.bgleasondesign.com
Cover Photo by Lee Merrick/©2001 Stanford Sierra Camp:
  Sunrise over Fallen Leaf with Lake Tahoe in the background
Spine Photo ©2001 Stanford Sierra Camp: *Panorama, from top of Mt. Tallac*
Printed in United States of America

The author wishes to thank and gratefully acknowledge

Peter and Helen Bing

for their very kind, generous and complete support of this non-profit project through their Fund for Nature, Art & Education at Stanford Sierra Camp.

View of Fallen Leaf lake from Camp

This book is a non-profit project. Dozens of people volunteered their time and talent and all images were donated. The Peter and Helen Bing Fund for Nature, Art and Education at Stanford Sierra Camp sponsored the printing and production. Proceeds from book sales will be returned to the fund to enable future projects.

A Nature Guide to the Southwest Tahoe Basin

Full moon over the Crystal Range and Gilmore Lake, looking southwest from the top of Mt. Tallac

THIS BOOK IS DEDICATED TO

The diversity of life and the wonder it instills in all of us.

*My parents, John & Julie Quinn and my siblings, Willie and Katie:
thank you for making me who I am, in so many ways.*

*My grandparents:
Lady B. & Boogie (Edie & Dr. Thomas W. Bonynge),
Grandma Betty and especially Granddaddy (D. Ray Quinn),
who taught me to identify my first tree—
ponderosa pine—and was the last to leave us.*

*My best friend and wife, Dana Abel, and our children, Baird & Edie Abel Quinn:
thanks for putting up with me and this project—here's to the future!*

The Glen Alpine Watershed

Crystal Range from the southwest slope of Mt. Tallac

CONTENTS

Thank you iii
Dedication... v
Foreword ix
Preface xi
Acknowledgements xiii
Introduction xv
Quotes xvii
Maps of the Area .... xvi, xviii-xxi
Illustrated Glossary of Plant Parts xxii
TREES 1
Forest Fire Ecology 17
SHRUBS.. 25
Geology 32
FERNS & HORSETAILS...................................... 37
FLOWERS... 41
Edible & Medicinal Plants 79
AMPHIBIANS 87
REPTILES 95
Bird Species Checklist 103
BIRDS 106
MAMMALS 168
FISHES 200
Underwater: Lake Tahoe & Fallen Leaf Lake 201
Glossary of Terms... 212
Bibliography 218
About the Authors 224
Index 225

FOREWORD

I first met Charlie Quinn when I regularly visited Stanford Sierra Camp at Fallen Leaf Lake as a faculty lecturer in the '90s. The alumni families who are Camp regulars have a wide variety of interests, and hiking and learning about Sierra natural history are prominent among them. The Stanford undergraduates who compete actively to be staffers there bring a stunning variety of talents—some lead killer hikes, some coach volleyball, some wait tables, and some read to kids. In most past years, some have also been skilled and serious naturalists. Charlie and his colleague Jed Mitchell were the most recent of these experts, and they were nice enough to let me co-lead trips with them during a couple of summers.

I have to confess to being a bird-watcher. In Britain, such people—especially those who make lists and even convert list-making into a competitive sport—are derisively called "twitchers." Fortunately, most of my fellow birders avoid that extreme. Charlie and Jed were terrific bird-finders, and our forays into the field gave me a chance to experience the excitement of seeing a new species for the area every now and then. It was a treat to poach on their skill as field guides, and I was allowed to slip in an occasional extra bit of pedantry from some piece of research on bird behavior. What was particularly admirable about Charlie and Jed is that they were as interested in what the birds were doing as in how rare they were. On our trips, they would occasionally halt the group and make everyone listen for a while, and talk about bird vocalization and its role in their behavior. Not only did Charlie learn from field observation; he incorporated every bit of the new stuff he saw; he dove into the literature himself, well beyond my own depth. As this remarkable book indicates, he has become an unparalleled expert on the biology of the north Sierra. Thus this is much more than a manual for identifying the different kinds of birds, trees, reptiles, and so on. It links looking and knowing in an unexpectedly instructive way. One doesn't merely learn what a Clark's Nutcracker looks and sounds like; one comes to understand the co-evolutionary history that links its distribution to that of the whitebark pine.

It's no surprise that Quinn now works for The Nature Conservancy in Oregon, where he leads frequent trips into the Cascades and the High Desert. Those who have been in the field with him will understand the enthusiasm and intelligence with which he approaches creatures and the ecosystems they inhabit. Conservation biology is a new and exciting specialty, and the approach taken in this book is to connect species together in a functional way, not just to tell the reader how to identify them and add them to a list. The result is that it is possible to read it without going outdoors, and extract thought-provoking lessons about evolution and about ecosystems.

No account of the contemporary natural history of the Tahoe Sierra would be complete without some understanding of its geologic history. Becky Chaplin, a successor of Charlie's in the naturalist role at Sierra Camp and now a Ph.D. candidate, has supplied an authoritative account of that—along with a fine piece on fire ecology and fire suppression.

It is hard to imagine a better field companion for trips in the Tahoe Sierra than this book. Going with Charlie was an especially fortunate experience for me. I'd like to persuade him to guide me again, but since he's pretty busy doing that in Oregon, this guide will have to be his alter ego. It is a more than acceptable substitute!

Donald Kennedy, Ph.D.
Editor-in-Chief, *Science* magazine
President Emeritus, Stanford University

Twilight on Fallen Leaf Lake

Fallen Leaf Lake's southern end and the Glen Alpine Valley, viewed from the Angora Ridge fire lookout

PREFACE

Since childhood, Fallen Leaf Lake and Desolation Wilderness have provided solace for my mind, wonder for my senses and food for my body and soul. Appropriately, I first toddled onto Baby Beach as a one-year-old, although I only began what have become annual visits to Stanford Sierra Camp as an adolescent in 1984.

My curiosity about the natural world has its roots in my family: playing dinosaurs with my brother; stealing raspberries from our garden with my sister; my father showing me different constellations and birds; my mother and her mother unknowingly teaching me the names of plants through their conversations and gardens; Grandpa Bonynge teaching me how to draw; Granddaddy and Grandma Betty introducing me to the Sierras through hikes along the Stanislaus River near their Arnold home. My interest was further developed by spending time on Hope Ranch Beach with the Alexanders, sifting through tide pools, poking anemones, digging for sandcrabs, fishing with Uncle Tom and building sand sculptures of various creatures with my Dad. Classes at the Los Angeles County Museum of Natural History (i.e. "Creepy Crawly Critters") helped the rest of my childhood summers glide by in true little-boy fashion, pockets full of bugs.

Returning to the United States and Stanford University after having spent the latter half of my childhood in Tokyo, Singapore and Hong Kong, I was drawn to the Open Space Preserves of the Santa Cruz Mountains. When the necessity of a summer job loomed ahead, I was fortunate enough to be brought back into the fold of Camp as a legitimate "Stapher." Dr. John Thomas's class, *The Systematics and Ecology of Vascular Plants*, catapulted me onto the no-turning-back path of the avid nature hound. I majored in Human Biology with a self-designed focus on "Humans and Conservation Ecology." Eventually I became a docent and teaching assistant for Stanford's Jasper Ridge Biological Preserve and kept returning to Camp every summer during my undergraduate career. And I have returned almost every year since then.

I now work on behalf of The Nature Conservancy in Oregon. In 2004, for the first time, we had our own little Microbopper at Camp. With another on the way, I knew it was time to finally publish this book—ten years after I completed writing the first (much smaller) version.

In so many words, that is how this work came into being. It is far from perfect, complete, or final (Willis Jepson would be happy). My only hope is that someone, sometime, just might set this book down a little wiser, more interested, more knowledgeable, more inclined towards conservation or just plain happier than they were when they picked it up.

Charles Quinn

The author (on right) and his brother at Fallen Leaf Lake, 1973

ACKNOWLEDGEMENTS

In addition to those mentioned previously, I would like to thank the many other people who helped me both directly and indirectly with this production:

First and foremost, Helen Bing, without whose support and encouragement this nature guide would have been written on paper napkins and ended up as nothing more than a mouse nest.

My two Desolation Wilderness friends: Jed Mitchell—my best birding buddy, most helpful editor and a whole lot more—and Alex Lustberg, for always insisting, "Tell me something interesting about it." Amy Winkelman, for editing the very first draft. Dave Bunnett, Antja Thompson, Sam Hawkes Booth, Dave Dennis (for sustenance to hike the trails and at our wedding), Tim Varga, the Arps, Chris & Carol Thomsen, Chris Sauer, Desi Reyes, Rod Baker, Toby Juno, Barbara & Bill Craven and Mrs. Mel Hawley for their input and assistance. Ruth D'Anneo (as she was known back when I started this book) and John Rich for supplying invaluable advice—and running a great store and marina on Fallen Leaf Lake. My parents, for all their help and encouragement. My in-laws, David & Joan Abel, for helping look after Baird while I worked on this project. My supervisor at The Nature Conservancy, Carrie Walkiewicz, who understood my need to finally make this happen.

David Lukas, excellent trip leader, top-notch naturalist and author of the most recent revision of Storer & Usinger's classic, *Sierra Nevada Natural History*—thank you for all of your encouragement and assistance in reviewing this text. Suzy Lancaster, Wilderness Manager and Mike St. Michel, Director of Interpretive Services with the US Forest Service's Lake Tahoe Basin Management Unit. Gary Nafis, for his amazing photos and very useful website on California Herps. Dale Steele, for his wonderful website on Mountain Beavers. Dr. Gary Williams at the California Academy of Sciences for his help, photo and research on the jelly-ball protists. Marta Makarushka, who helped talk me through self-publishing. Russ & Blyth Carpenter, who helped me first start thinking seriously about publishing at all. And Barbara and Dan Gleason, who finally transformed it all into a real book!

The photographers who so generously donated their work for this project (see Bibliography for their websites and contact info): David Cardinal and

Lorrie Duval, Christopher L. Christie, Dennis Deck, Stephen Dowlan, Dan Gleason, Tom Greer, Joyce Gross, Steve Matson, Gary Nafis, Susan D. Prince, John H. Quinn, Randy & Peggy/Dale Steele, Gary Williams and all the Stanford Sierra Camp (SSC) Staff Photographers, 2001-2004: Lee Merrick, Tarmigan Casebolt, Dale Stahl, Leah Sullivan, Anna-Christina Douglas, and especially Tim Varga and Sam Hawkes Booth. Dan Gleason, for donating photos, scanning photos and editing the bird section. Many of the photographs were downloaded, with permission, from CalPhotos, a project of the University of California's Berkeley Digital Library Project. Many of those were donated by the California Academy of Sciences (CAS) from their Manzanita Project, including photographs by Gerald & Buff Corsi, Dr. Lloyd Glenn Ingles, Alden M. Johnson, Walter Knight, Robert Potts and Charles Webber.

All of Camp's Naturalists who came before me—and after me—and tried to leave something behind for those who followed, especially Mark Colt Whitley (my first "natural" mentor at Camp), DJ Dull and (most of all!) Becky Chaplin.

Mr. Squier, my seventh-grade life science teacher at The American School In Japan, who let me do my first animal report on the Echidna and sparked my first real academic interest in biology. Mr. Baker at Singapore American School, who let us camp on his Malaysian island. Wil Chan at Hong Kong International School who took me to India twice to see Bengal tigers, wild asses, Asiatic lions and many other amazing animals. The Stanford professors and post-docs who influenced me, especially all those at the Center for Conservation Biology and Jasper Ridge Biological Preserve: John Hunter Thomas, Carol Boggs, Alan Launer, Bill Durham, Rob Blair, John McLaughlin, Roman Dial, Paul Ehrlich, Gretchen Daily, Hal Mooney, Joan Roughgarden, Deborah Gordon, Robert Sapolsky, Peter Vitousek and many others.

And, last but certainly not least, Donald Kennedy, for helping me realize that bird walks could happen more than once a summer and providing me with the knowledge and confidence to make them happen twice a week.

There are many influential people who were not mentioned and I hope they know they are still an integral part of who I am and I thank them for it.

Finally, I recognize that none of this would be possible without all the authors, naturalists and scientists who preceded me and provided invaluable information on the nature of the area: I truly stand on their shoulders.

INTRODUCTION

This book was written for the 500,000 or so people who visit the area every year. Maybe one percent of you will actually encounter it, but it was written with all of you in mind, weekend naturalist, ornithologist and botanist alike.

The area covered by this book—the Fallen Leaf Lake watershed, southwest of Lake Tahoe, California—is often referred to as "our area" and the organisms found in it as "ours" as well. This is meant to imply familiarity only, not ownership. The map included in this book shows the primary area covered, but information has been gathered from as far north as Granite Chief Wilderness and as far south as Mokelumne Wilderness.

Throughout this work, some pronouns are used: "I" am the writer, "you" are the aforementioned audience or reader, "we" are those people wandering through the watershed today.

The capitalized word, Camp, is used to refer to Stanford Sierra Camp, a Stanford Alumni Association retreat at the end of Fallen Leaf Road on the southwest shore of Fallen Leaf Lake. It is used as a family camp for alumni during the summer and a conference center during the fall and spring. Camp is often mentioned as a place to find certain species because of my special familiarity with it and not because the species are lacking elsewhere in the watershed.

Terms and technical jargon that are either used in descriptions or commonly used in the discussion of environmental/wildlife issues are included in a Glossary. Every effort was made to keep the use of unfamiliar terms to a minimum.

I again stress that this work is far from complete or perfect and can only hope to continually strive towards that unattainable (but worthy) goal.

Please do not hesitate to send records of sightings, suggestions, comments, additions, or inquiries to the author (contact information at the front of this book).

Also, please alert the Forest Service to any unusual observations:

USDA Forest Service, Lake Tahoe Basin Management Unit
35 College Drive, South Lake Tahoe CA 96150
Phone: (530) 543-2600 Fax: (530) 543-2693
Email: mailroom_r5_lake_tahoe_basin@fs.fed.us
Website: http://www.fs.fed.us/r5/ltbmu/

Complete Map of the Southwest Tahoe Basin Area

Many people are more apt to conserve the things they know about than to conserve the things that are foreign to them. This flora will, I hope, acquaint at least a few more people with the plants around them and perhaps thus serve as a stimulus, however slight, toward more permanent protection of our environment.

—John Hunter Thomas (1928-1999), from the preface to his *Flora of the Santa Cruz Mountains of California*

The botanist's objective is a futherance of knowledge of living plants. He wishes by his investigations to discover new facts and establish new principles that will aid in promoting botanical research. If wise, he will never try to produce a work which is perfect, complete and final. Any such work would be a paradox and at cross-purposes with our concepts of living things and our ideas of endless evolution associated with them. Completion, perfection, finality represent an anomaly, a contradiction in the field of biology. The far-seeing botanist, on the contrary, will strive to do work which is inspiring, productive of thought and promoting the soundest progress, so that botanical science will ever advance into new and more fruitful fields. "There is something lost behind the ranges over yonder. Go you there."

—Willis Linn Jepson, the inscription in a friend's copy of his *Manual of the Flowering Plants of California*

A scientific interest in at least certain features of our natural environment, as for example trees, shrubs or herbaceous plants, directs one to useful and agreeable intellectual activity. Accurate and detailed knowledge of even a small area lifts the possessor out of the commonplace and enables him directly or indirectly to contribute to the well-being and happiness of his community.

—Willis Linn Jepson, 1909

This book is for the fourlegged people, the standing people, the crawling people, the swimming people, the sitting people and the flying people: that people walking with them may know and honor them.

—Daniel Mathews,
from his masterpiece:
Cascade-Olympic Natural History

Part 1 of 4 parts—NW quadrant detail

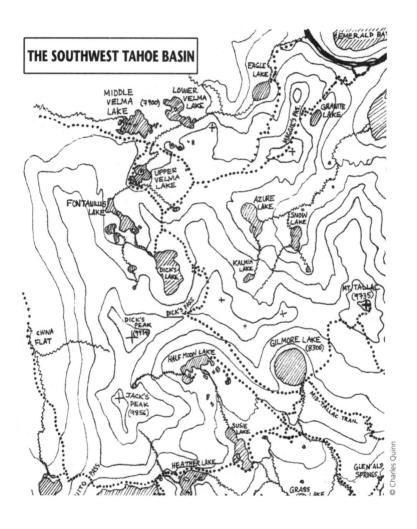

Part 2 of 4 parts—NE quadrant detail

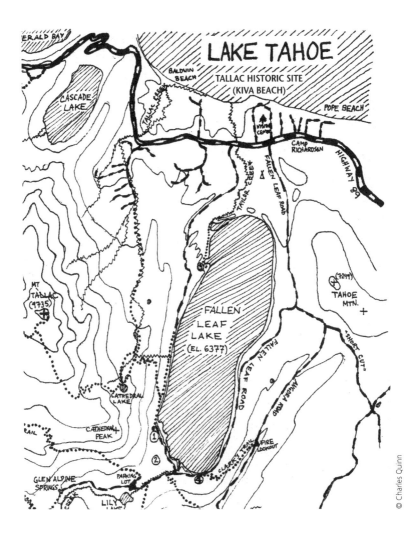

Part 3 of 4 parts—SW quadrant detail

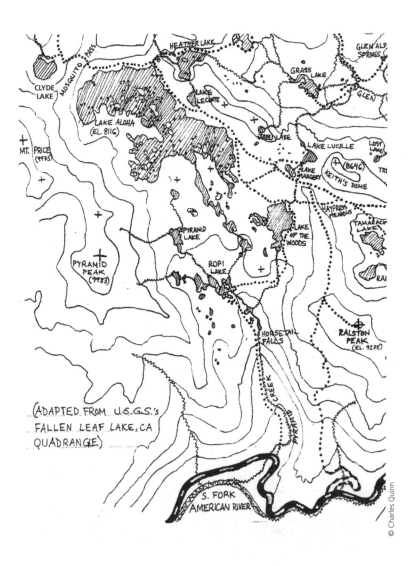

Part 4 of 4 parts—SE quadrant detail

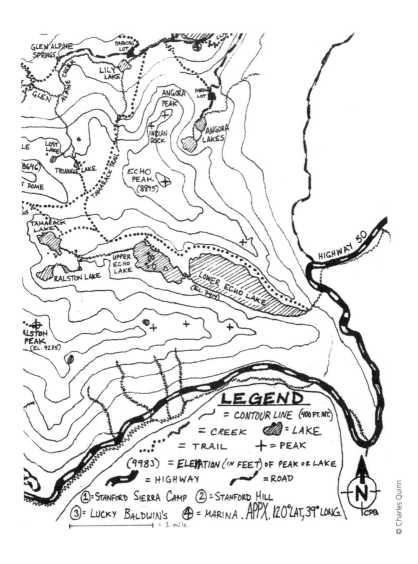

A Nature Guide to the Southwest Tahoe Basin

An Illustrated Glossary of Botanical Terms

General Flower Parts

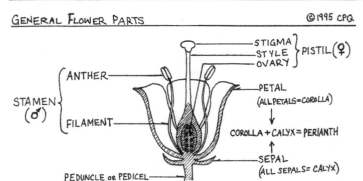

Sunflower Parts

Iris Parts

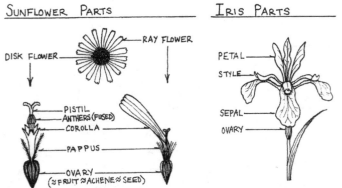

Pea Flower Parts

Orchid Parts

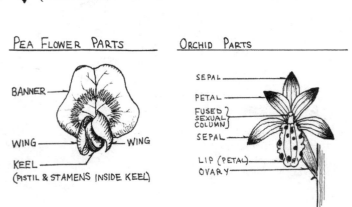

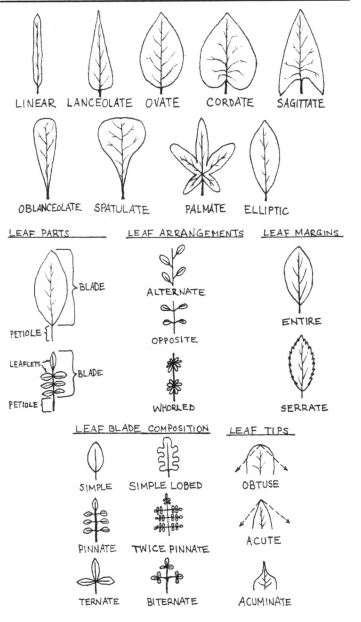

Fallen Leaf Lake from the Angora Trail.

TREES

Coniferous Trees
  Needles, single or in bunches
    One-needled
        Firs: *White Fir*
                             Red Fir
        Hemlocks: *Mountain Hemlock*
        False-Hemlocks: *Douglas-fir*
    Two-needled
        Pines: *Lodgepole Pine*
    Three-needled
                             Ponderosa Pine
                             Jeffery Pine
    Five-needled
                             Sugar Pine
                             Western White Pine
                             Whitebark Pine
  Scale-like leaves appressed to twigs
    Flat sprays
        Beautiful-Cedars: *Incense-cedar*
    Rounded bunches
        Junipers: *Western Juniper*

Broadleaf Trees
  Leaf edges smooth or mildly serrate
        Willow Family: *Quaking Aspen*
                             Black Cottonwood
                             Shining Willow
                             Scouler Willow
  Leaf edges strongly serrate
        Birch Family: *White Alder*
                             Mountain Alder
        Maple Family: *Mountain Maple*

Also see SHRUBS section for other small "trees."

TREE TALK: Conifer vs. Broadleaf

Conifers (Division Coniferophyta) are a subset of the old class *Gymnospermae* (*gymno* = naked, *sperm* = seed: seeds not enclosed by an ovary). A characteristic common to *most* conifers (all of ours) is that they bear their seeds in cones. Cones generally consist of seeds on scales, usually radiating outwards in a corkscrew-like spiral along a central columnar axis. Most conifers (again, all of ours) also have needle-like or scale-like leaves.

Broadleaf is a term used to refer to those trees that (in contrast with most conifers) have wide, flat, net-veined leaves and do not bear cones. They are a subset of the class Angiospermae (*angio* = vessel: seeds enclosed by an ovary), which includes all flowering plants.

Although often used interchangeably, the terms *conifer* and *broadleaf* are preferred over *evergreen* and *deciduous*. This is because there are deciduous conifers (i.e. Larches or Tamaracks) as well as evergreen broadleaves (i.e. Live Oaks and Eucalyptus), both of which do not normally fall within the average person's concept of what a "deciduous" or "evergreen" tree should look like.

CONIFEROUS TREES

ONE-NEEDLED

White Fir *(Abies concolor; Pinaceae) Plate 1.*

>   Leaves: single needles 1 1/2–2 in. long, flat. Petioles (leaf stems) bend and twist 180 degrees at base.
>   Cones: 3–5 in. long, sitting upright on upper branches like tiny barrels. Thin, fan-shaped scales.
>   Bark: gray, vertically furrowed
>   Height: 60–160 ft.
>   Altitudes: 3000–7000 ft.

The White Fir is the only single-needled tree around Fallen Leaf. There are no Red Firs below about 7000 feet and no Mountain Hemlocks until about 8000 feet. (The only Douglas-fir I have seen around Fallen Leaf is at Lucky Baldwin's on the northwest end of the lake—possibly planted there by humans.) In short, get to know the White Fir around Fallen Leaf so you can tell it apart from other trees when in more ambiguous, higher elevation territories.

True Firs (genus *Abies*) are second-rate lumber due to their soft, coarsely grained wood which warps easily. Up until the 1800s, pines dominated the Tahoe basin because they had evolved to deal best with long droughts and frequent ground fires. Firs were mostly understory trees that had adapted to germinate in the shade of the pines but not as well to fires and drought. When most of the pines were selectively logged out in the early part of this century, firs were left to do most of the re-seeding. Since then, fire-suppression has allowed the fir-dominated forest to continue —shading out pines, which need bare mineral soil and full sun to successfully sprout and grow. The resulting unprecedented concentration of firs has caused new problems. Without pines to provide shade, water loss through transpiration and evaporation increased dramatically. Compounding this was the increased density and therefore heightened competition for water. Years of substantial drought in the late 1980s and early 1990s made the White Firs even more water-stressed. So stressed, in fact, that the trees could no longer maintain enough sap tension (fluid pressure) to flush out pests like the Fir Engraver Beetle (Photo page 20). End result: a forest thick with so many dead trees that it might as well have been soaked in lighter fluid.

Red Fir *(Abies magnifica magnifica; Pinaceae) Plate 1.*

Leaves: single needles about 1 in. long. Rounded triangular- to diamond-shaped in cross section.
Cones: 5–8 in. long, sitting upright on upper branches like little barrels. Thin, fan-shaped scales.
Bark: deep reddish, vertically furrowed, rough bark
Height: 60–150 ft.
Altitudes: 6600–9000 ft.

As its Latin name attests, this is a truly magnificent tree. The Red Fir is the extreme-weather version of the White Fir. Both can be found in the transition zone (approx. 6500–7000 feet) but the Red Fir dominates the higher elevations. Even in the transitional zone, Red Firs are usually found in harsher, colder habitats such as north-facing slopes. The Red Fir's heightened resistance to frost-cracking is one reason it can out-compete the White Fir in colder areas. Another reason is that the smaller, more densely compressed needles of the Red Fir do not accumulate as much snow or lose as much water as the White Fir. However, the Red Fir is more predisposed to rotting—which cavity nesting wildlife routinely take advantage of by carving out their homes in its fungally-softened heartwood.

Red Firs are distinguished from White Firs by their reddish-purple bark, shorter untwisted rounded needles, larger cones and higher elevational occurrence.

Mountain Hemlock *(Tsuga mertensiana; Pinaceae)* Plate 1.

> Leaves: single needles less than 1 in. long, flat, blue-green anchored to woody pegs along branchlets.
> Cones: about 2 in. long, pendulous and purple, skinny and thin-scaled.
> Bark: reddish brown, grayer in younger trees.
> Height: 20–80 ft.
> Altitudes: 7500–9500 ft.

This is one tree you will not see around Fallen Leaf. The Mountain Hemlock is most populous around 8000 feet and surrounds many of the alpine lakes in Desolation Wilderness. The unique identifying factor of hemlocks is that their leaves attach to tiny protruding woody pegs that densely spiral along the length of its branchlets. The small and skinny purplish cones are also good indicators. A personal favorite, however, is their droopy, nodding tops—appearing as though Dr. Seuss himself had designed them.

This flexibility (also apparent in the tips of their limbs, especially when bearing cones) allows them to survive unimaginable snow packs and even landslides. During the spring thaw, they can be seen literally springing back to their (almost) upright positions.

The Hemlock tree is *not* the hemlock of poisonous, Socrates-killing infamy. Poison Hemlock (*Conium maculatum*) is an herb in the Celery and Carrot Family (*Apiaceae*) and the exact origin of the word hemlock is unknown.

The genus, *Tsuga*, is derived from the Japanese name of the tree. The specific epithet, *mertensiana*, is after Karl Heinrich Mertens who did a great deal of botanical exploration along the west coast of North America during the early 1800s.

Douglas-fir *(Pseudotsuga menziesii; Pinaceae)* Plate 1.

> Leaves: single needles about 1 in. long, deep green in color, spiralling around twig; pointed buds.
> Cones: about 3 in. long, pendulous, thin scaled, with conspicuous 3-pronged bracts protruding.
> Bark: reddish brown to gray, sometimes resembling White Fir bark.
> Height: 150–300 ft.
> Altitudes: 2500–6000 ft.

Although Fallen Leaf Lake is technically too high to have Douglas-firs, I have spotted one lone specimen growing just southeast of Lucky Baldwin's foundation (on the northwest side of Fallen Leaf Lake). I do not know its history, but it looks fairly young, maybe 50 years old and I would guess it was planted. I have never seen any others in our area, but they become quite abundant as one descends down highway 50 into the moister mixed conifer and broadleaf forests between 3000 and 5000 feet.

Douglas-fir is hyphenated because it is not a true fir (genus *Abies*). Instead, it is classified ambiguously as a "false-hemlock." It has gone through many botanical names and narrowly escaped being pigeon-holed as a spruce, fir, or hemlock.

The common name now honors David Douglas, one of the first European botanical backpackers to extensively explore what is now Washington and Oregon during the early 1800s. The scientific name comes from Archibald Menzies, a surgeon-naturalist on the 1792 voyage of the HMS Discovery under captain Vancouver. Keep in mind that neither really "discovered" the tree because, as Daniel Matthews so eloquently states, "It is chauvinistic and silly to call any paleface the discoverer of America or of any conspicuous feature on it..."(Matthews, p.17).

According to legend, the papery bracts are actually the hind feet and tails of greedy little mice trying to get at the Douglas-fir's seeds.

TWO-NEEDLED

Lodgepole Pine (*Pinus contorta murrayana*; Pinaceae)
Also **Tamarack Pine**. *Plate 1.*
Needles: two per bundle, twisted, usually about 2 in. long.

> Cone: about 2 in. long, almost spherical when open, some remaining attached for many years.
> Bark: Thin and scaly, resembling cornflakes.
> Height: 5-100 ft. (highly variable, dependent on conditions)
> Altitudes: 6000-10,000 ft.

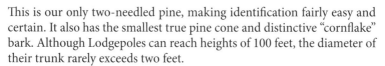

This is our only two-needled pine, making identification fairly easy and certain. It also has the smallest true pine cone and distinctive "cornflake" bark. Although Lodgepoles can reach heights of 100 feet, the diameter of their trunk rarely exceeds two feet.

The first common name originates from Lewis and Clark. The explorers apparently witnessed Native Americans of the Great Plains making special trips into the Rockies just to obtain these straight, thin trees for constructing lodges and tepees. However, not all individual trees grow particularly straight—especially near treeline. Some trees even have right-angles or "S" shapes in their trunk due to temporary periods of heavy snowpack.

The second common name is a true misnomer due to easterners like John Muir mistaking this pine for a tree of similar habit, the Eastern Larch or Tamarack (*Larix laricina*). Consequently, we have trails, lakes and cabins throughout the Sierra Nevada that are named after a tree that does not even grow here. *Contorta*, the specific epithet of the botanical name, may either refer to the manner in which its needles twist away from each other or the way weather-beaten individuals grow.

Fire has an especially beneficial effect on the Lodgepole Pine. Some cones, or the bases of some cones, remain unopened and attached for many years, sealed with a resin that has a melting point of 113 degrees Fahrenheit. The heat from a fire causes the resin to melt and the cones slowly open upon cooling. Because the seeds are released directly after the passage of fire, there are very few other species to compete with during the critical stages of germination and early growth. In places where an extensive fire is improbable or impossible (such as near treeline on any of our rocky peaks), animals perform an effectively similar service (see also Whitebark Pine and Clark's Nutcracker).

THREE-NEEDLED

Jeffrey Pine (*Pinus jeffreyi*; Pinaceae) Plate 2.

Needles: three per bundle, 5–9 in. long.
Cone: 5–12 in. long, prickles curved inward.
Bark: Large, thick reddish-brown plates composed of jigsaw puzzle pieces. Butterscotch odor.
Height: 60–180 ft.
Altitudes: 6000–8500 ft.

© Charles Quinn

Any three-needled Pine found in the vicinity of camp is 99 percent likely to be a Jeffrey. As it is exceedingly difficult to visually distinguish between Ponderosa and Jeffrey Pines, it is better to employ a couple of our other senses:

The first test entails touch. Pick up and feel the pine cone. If the cone is relatively small (3–5 in.) and its prickles penetrate your palm, causing intense pain, then it is the Ponderosa (prickly = Ponderosa). If it is relatively large (5–12 in.) and its prickles are gently curved inwards, away from your palm, it is a Jeffrey (gentle = Jeffrey).

The second (and less painful test) involves inserting your nose into a choice crevice in the bark of a mature tree. If odors reminiscent of butterscotch, vanilla, pineapple, or banana are encountered, then your nose is stuck in a gentle, kind and giving Jeffrey. If all you get is gooey sap stuck to the end of your nose, then it is probably that old, stingy, prickly Ponderosa again. Attaching these "personalities" to the trees is useful in remembering which traits go with which tree.

Native Americans (especially the Piute tribe) used to harvest not only seeds, but also Pandora Moth larvae from Jeffrey Pines. In order to harvest the larvae that feasted upon the Jeffrey's needles, trenches were dug around the perimeter of an infested tree. The descending caterpillars were then swept into these trenches. Fire-heated soil was then deposited on top, slowly roasting the larvae and transforming them into delectable little vittles. They were then dried and stored for wintertime use.

The Jeffrey Pine can also be rather dangerous. This is not due to any innate maleficence on the part of the tree itself, but a simple combination between the Jeffrey's heavy cones, the food-gathering strategies of the Douglas Squirrel and gravity. When the squirrel's sharp incisors cut dinner free, the cone suddenly becomes a gravity-powered missile, capable of inflicting considerable damage on individuals passing below.

Ponderosa Pine (*Pinus ponderosa; Pinaceae*)
Also **Western Yellow Pine.**

   Needles: three per bundle, 5–9 in. long.
   Cone: 3–5 in. long, prickles sticking straight out.
   Bark: Large, thick yellowish-orange plates composed of jigsaw puzzle pieces. Not sweet-smelling.
   Height: 70–200 ft.
   Altitudes: 2000–6500 ft.

David Douglas (of Douglas-fir fame) gave the name meaning "ponderous" or "heavy" to this tree because of its immense size (sometimes 200 feet tall and six feet across) and awe-inspiring presence.

Although Fallen Leaf Lake, at 6377 feet, is technically above the local elevational limit of the Ponderosa (most common along Highway 50 from Placerville up to Strawberry), it may be possible to find a few stragglers. However, do keep in mind that Ponderosas are rare in our area and are easily confused with the more abundant Jeffrey Pine. I am not aware of any individuals in our watershed.

See the preceding entry, Jeffrey Pine, for information on how to tell the two species apart.

FIVE-NEEDLED

Sugar Pine (*Pinus lambertiana; Pinaceae*) *Plate 2.*

Needles: five per bundle, about 3 in. long.
Cone: 10–20 in. long, 4–5 in. wide. Scales thin throughout.
Bark: Thick, vertically grooved, dark reddish-brown tending towards purple.
Height: 100–250 ft.
Altitudes: 6000–8500 ft.

This tree boasts the world's longest cones and is the tallest of the pines. These two factors combine to give the Sugar Pine its stereotypical silhouette: a tall, flat-topped tree that towers above the forest with long, pendulous cones hanging at the tips of extremely long branches which leave the trunk at right angles.

Sugar Pine is one of the most desirable lumber trees because of its clear, white, straight-grained wood. Unfortunately, this is the probably one reason why we do not see many large specimens left in today's forests. (In Camp, there is one on the uphill side of the road just northwest of the tennis courts.)

True to its name, the Sugar Pine has also been prized for its sweet and sticky sap. Native Americans throughout its range used the pitch as both a sugary treat and a strong adhesive. For a snack, they would pluck the clear orbs that ooze from wounds in the trunk and chew them as a pitchy gum. John Muir even wrote that he preferred it to maple sugar. Unlike maple sugar, however, it has a strong laxative effect when consumed in quantity. For use as a glue, it would be heated and used, for example, to attach feathers onto the shaft of an arrow.

Western White Pine (*Pinus monticola; Pinaceae*)
Also **Silver Pine** or **Little Sugar Pine.** *Plate 2.*

Needles: five per bundle, about 3 in. long.
Cone: 4–8 in. long, often slightly curved. Scales slightly thickened and upturned at outer tips.
Bark: Brownish-gray, broken into small rectangular plates.
Height: 50–150 ft.
Altitudes: 6300–9000 ft.

This "mountain-dweller," as its Latin name translates, superficially appears to be a scaled-down version of the Sugar Pine, hence one of its alternate names.

The best method of distinguishing between the two is to look at the cones. White Pine cones are usually well under a foot long and often have a banana-like curve. Sugar Pine cones usually surpass the one-foot mark and are relatively straight. A second method requires good eyesight and possibly the help of a magnifier. If one looks closely, white lines can be seen on all three sides of the Sugar Pine needle, but only on two sides of the White Pine needle. The bark on mature trees is another good indicator (see descriptions). Height can also help since White Pines in our area rarely surpass 150 feet and Sugar Pines routinely hit 200.

White Pines were devastated by demand in the earlier part of this century. Even the demand for re-planting exceeded North America's supply and foresters were forced to import from abroad. A French shipment in 1906 brought with it a fatal fungus: the white pine blister rust (*Cronartium ribicola*). American trees, without any evolutionary experience with this fungus, had no natural defense. Many efforts were made to halt the resulting destruction, from eradicating the fungus' alternate host (*Ribes* spp.) to chemical warfare, but all were in vain. Eventually, cross-breeding with the few naturally resistant strains came to surface as the only possible solution. This project was quite successful and the White Pine has made a substantial comeback as a result.

Whitebark Pine (*Pinus albicaulis; Pinaceae*)
Plate 2. Note: See also cone size contrast with Sugar Pine, plate 2.

    Needles: five per bundle, about 1–3 in. long, yellowish-green & stiff.
    Cone: 1–3 in. long, purple. Scales thick, with blunt tips. Never opens.
    Bark: Light gray, thin and scaly.
    Height: 5–50 ft. (highly variable, dependent on conditions)
    Altitudes: 8000–10,000 ft.

Whitebark Pine gets both its common and scientific name from its light-colored bark (*albi* = white and *caulis* = stem). This is probably the most common five-needled pine near our timberline. One of the best identifiers is its unique cones. The small, blunt, purple cones never open. Instead, they slowly decay and fall apart, scale by scale—if they last that long. Being one of the few trees able to grow in such harsh conditions, they are a cherished food source for animals that share this demanding habitat. These trees are common near Dick's Pass.

Clark's Nutcracker has most closely co-evolved with this tree. Without the help of this bird, Whitebark seeds would not travel far. Apparently, this pine has traded up from the small, stunted pair of "wings" that it used to attach to its seeds for the larger, more mobile pair of the nutcracker's. By not opening the way other cones do, the Whitebark effectively "reserves" most of its stock for its favorite customer. Clark's Nutcracker caches tens of thousands of pine nuts each year in order to make it through the bitter, high Sierran winters. Fortunately for the Whitebark, although the bird has an amazing memory, it is not perfect. Those seeds that escape the Clark's memory are able to germinate in the advantageous and sheltered position where the nutcracker hid them so well (see also Clark's Nutcracker).

LEAVES SCALE-LIKE, TWIGS IN FLAT SPRAYS

Incense-cedar (*Calocedrus decurrens*; Cupressaceae) *Plate 3.*

Leaves: small, scale-like, longer than wide, tightly compressed along twigs, forming flat sprays.
Cones: 1 in. long, resembling a trefoil after opening. Only two fertile scales.
Bark: fibrous, shreddy, reddish.
Height: 75–150 ft.
Altitudes: 2500–7000 ft.

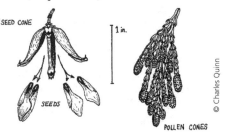
© Charles Quinn

Incense-cedar's bark causes some to mistake it for a redwood, but neither Giant Sequoias nor Coast Redwoods occur in the Tahoe region. The juniper is the only tree around with similar bark and is easily distinguished by inspecting any one of a number of other traits (see Western Juniper). (The Incense-cedar is not hard to find in Camp. The most obvious individual towers directly above the Fountain deck, its burned-out trunk a favorite among Munchkins and Snoopers alike.)

The botanical name likens this tree to a photosynthesizing waterfall: *Calo* = beautiful, *decurrens* = running down (referring to the drooping branches).

The common name is hyphenated because the Incense-cedar is not a true cedar. In fact, all our North American/Pacific Rim "cedars" are members of the Cypress Family and do not even remotely resemble true cedars (a member of the genus *Cedrus*) in appearance. The closest description of a true cedar, using North American trees, would be "an evergreen larch with fir cones." True cedars are native to the Middle East, North Africa and the Himalayas. In the U.S., they are widely planted as ornamentals (i. e. at the corners of the biology building and lining the road to the mausoleum at Stanford). Their similarly fragrant wood is the likely cause for the mix-up.

This fragrance is also what repels insects and fungi, making it excellent wood for moth-repellant closets, clothing chests and long-lasting coffins. The one fungus that has evolved to penetrate the Incense-cedar's volatile defense system is *Polyporus amarus*. Nick-named "pencil-rot," it riddles the wood with tiny holes supposedly rendering it only good for making pencils (which its soft, pliable and splinter-resistant wood is already ideally suited for). Enjoy the Incense-cedar's fragrance next time you sharpen your #2. Native Americans who lived among North American "cedars" used the bark extensively for constructing shelters and clothing. Its wood also made durable canoes.

LEAVES SCALE-LIKE, TWIGS IN ROUNDED BUNCHES

Western Juniper (*Juniperus occidentalis australis; Cupressaceae*)
Also **Sierra Juniper.** *Plate 3.*

> Leaves: small (1/8 in.) and scale-like, tightly compressed along round twigs, resinous pores at center.
> Cones: resemble berries 1/4–1/3 in., covered with a whitish powder. Green, ripening to dark blue.
> Bark: fibrous, shreddy, reddish.
> Height: 2–60 ft.
> Altitudes: 6400–10,000 ft.

The Western Juniper is unique among our conifers due to its small, fleshy, berry-like cones. As they ripen from their immature green to a dark bluish-black, the resemblance to berries is only strengthened. However, these juniper "berries" are actually (morphologically speaking) small, non-woody cones. Their fleshy scales overlap so tightly they resemble tiny, turgid spheres from a distance.

The bark is very similar to Incense-cedar and is responsible for confusing many tree-buffs. There are several ways to tell these two reddish, fibrous, shreddy-barked species apart: look at their twigs, habitat, height, or cones. The rounded bunches of juniper twigs contrast sharply with the flat sprays of Incense-cedar. Junipers are normally found on rocky, soil-less slopes and take on a gnarled, stunted appearance (less than 50 feet tall) whereas the Incense-cedar grows very tall (routinely over 100 feet) and erect, usually rooting in soil. The small cones of the Incense-cedar are also much more elongated than the spherical "berry" of the juniper.

Junipers are used by many animals and many animals are used by the juniper. It seems that natural selection has produced yet another win-win situation. Juniper "berries" ripen up in September and stay on the trees throughout the winter season, providing readily accessible food during an otherwise scarce season. The tiny seeds of the juniper have evolved not only to withstand the rigors of passing through an animal's digestive tract, but the acidic chyme found in the stomach actually helps prepare the seeds for germination by weakening their hard outer shells. The resultant "scat"-tering of seeds is far more wide-reaching than could be achieved by wind dispersal. In one experiment, a full two-thirds of seeding was thought to be bird-assisted.

Humans have also employed juniper "berries" in making menthol-like teas for the sick, preparing gourmet pasta sauces and flavoring alcohol— Gin, from the French word for juniper, *ginevre*. Like false cedar, juniper wood is aromatic and rot-resistant, making fine moth-repellant chests and long-lasting fence poles.

BROADLEAF TREES

Quaking Aspen (*Populus tremuloides; Salicaceae*)

Leaves: 1–3 in. long, round to broadly heart-shaped; flat stalked. Light dull green above, pale below.
Bark: light greenish-gray, almost white from a distance. Black branch scars at intervals.
Height: 10–60 ft.
Altitudes: 6000–9000 ft.

© Charles Quinn

Quaking Aspens owe their name to their uniquely flat leafstalks that cause their two-toned leaves to flutter and flash in even the slightest breeze. (Some have hypothesized that this action knocks insects off its leaves, but science has not yet determined this for certain.) In the fall, their appearance changes dramatically from bright green patches into brilliant gold splashes.

Aspens are also moisture-loving, frequently colonizing meadow margins and seepage patches. Since aspens have the ability to root-sprout, an entire patch of "individual" trees may actually be many vertical branches stemming up from the roots of a single, original, founder tree. These interconnected and genetically identical patches are called "clones." Individual patches are especially visible in the fall as each individual clone changes color at a slightly different time. (One clone in Colorado consisted of 47,000 trees—possibly the largest single living organism on earth, but some debate its validity as a "single" organism.)

The bark of the aspen contains just enough chlorophyll in order to allow it to start photosynthesis before it even leafs out, giving it a slight advantage over other deciduous competitors—especially at high altitudes with short growing seasons.

An important wildlife tree, beavers prefer the aspen's inner bark to any other food; deer, elk and pronghorn relish its leaves; grouse and pikas savor its buds; sapsuckers and woodpeckers nest in its fungally-softened heartwood.

Black Cottonwood
(*Populus balsamifera trichocarpa; Salicaceae*)

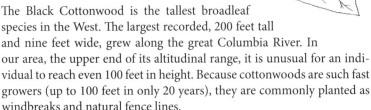

Leaves: 2–5 in. long, 2–3 in. wide, triangular with round stalks. Shiny dark green above, pale below.
Bark: gray to black, furrowed with age.
Height: 40–100 ft.
Altitudes: below 8,000 ft.

The Black Cottonwood is the tallest broadleaf species in the West. The largest recorded, 200 feet tall and nine feet wide, grew along the great Columbia River. In our area, the upper end of its altitudinal range, it is unusual for an individual to reach even 100 feet in height. Because cottonwoods are such fast growers (up to 100 feet in only 20 years), they are commonly planted as windbreaks and natural fence lines.

Cottonwoods require an abundant supply of water and are common stream associates, especially along the lower part of Glen Alpine Creek. The Latin term *trichocarpa* refers to the tree's "hairy fruits"—seeds which drift in the wind on cotton-like hairs, hence the common name as well.

The leaves can be told apart from Quaking Aspen leaves by their larger size, darker, shinier top surface and leaf stalks which are round in cross section—the aspen's are noticeably flattened.

Shining Willow
(*Salix lucida lasiandra; Salicaceae*) Also **Pacific, Yellow,** or **Red Willow.**

Leaves: 3–6 in. long, narrowly tapering, mildly serrate. Two glands on leaf stem just below blade.
Bark: light gray, smooth aging to rough with interconnecting ridges. Year old twigs yellowish.
Height: 3–30 ft.
Altitudes: below 8000 ft.

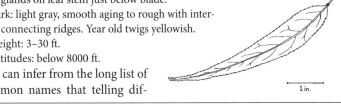

One can infer from the long list of common names that telling different species of willows (genus *Salix*) apart is no simple task. Two of the most readily identifiable species around Fallen Leaf are described here. The dozen other species that could be around are left up to only the most enthusiastic "salicophiles." (Under the heading of "SALIX," the Jepson Manual states, "Difficult, highly variable. Not all specimens will key easily…Studies of variation, hybridization needed.") The fact that willows have completely separate "male" and "female" plants (termed *dioecious*) only exacerbates the problem. Take heart and enjoy *all* willows indiscriminately! Almost all have long, thin leaves, pussy-willow-like catkins and grow in moist areas.

Willows seem to be favored nurseries for certain Cynipid wasps. Adult females use their ovipositor (modified into a stinger on other wasps) to inject eggs into young leaves and stems. It is hypothesized that the larvae secrete hormones that cause the galls to form around them. The galls then provide food and protection until the larvae metamorphose into adults and fly away to repeat the process. Huckleberry Oak (a shrub) also hosts Cynipids, but probably a different species.

Flexible willow twigs were often employed in basket making, willow bark for manufacturing twine and willow poles for shelter and fishing platforms. The seeds are so small and light (2–3 million per pound) they have never been collected for human food. Aspirin (acetylsalicylic acid) was first discovered in willow bark because of its use in traditional medicine.

Scouler Willow (*Salix scouleriana; Salicaceae*) Also **Nuttall Willow.**

Leaves: 2–5 in. long, wider and rounded at tip.
Bark: dull gray, smooth aging rougher, darker.
Height: 5–30 ft.
Altitudes: below 9000 ft.

This is one of the few willow species which is relatively easy to distinguish from its close relatives. It is the our only willow which has leaves that get wider towards the tip instead of tapering. This characteristic is more evident in some individuals than others, but if the leaf of a willow tree is not obviously skinny and tapering, it is probably a Scouler Willow.

Historically this species was known as *S. nuttalli*, hence the other common name. Both Nuttall and Scouler were botanists that roved the West in the early part of the nineteenth century.

Scouler Willows are exceptional members of this genus in that they can grow away from water courses. Their tiny wind-born seeds are frequently among the first to successfully germinate on recently burned soils.

White Alder (*Alnus rhombifolia; Betulaceae*)

Leaves: 2–4 in. long, ovate coming to a tip, serrated edges. Veination not indented.
Fruit: small (approx.. 3/4 in. long) woody "cones," persisting for several seasons.
Bark: whitish gray, smooth aging to rough with interspaced branch scars.
Height: 30–80 ft.
Altitudes: below 7800 ft.

The White Alder is a large streamside tree. It is easily confused with its smaller and more abundant relative, the Mountain Alder. If the size difference is not obvious, the leaves must be inspected carefully: if the midrib and prominent veins are not indented, it is the White Alder; if they are indented, its the Mountain Alder. This can be difficult to detect, so compare leaves of known species so that you will get an idea of what to look for. Measuring the cones is sometimes helpful, but size difference is so small that it is also difficult to detect. In our area, this species is quite rare in comparison to the Mountain Alder.

Both alders have small, cone-like fruiting bodies that stay attached to small twigs for several seasons after they ripen. Because of their miniature pine cone-like appearance they are commonly used in small holiday decorations, often spray-painted silver or gold.

Mountain Alder (*Alnus incana tenuifolia; Betulaceae*) Plate 3.

Leaves: 2–4 in. long, ovate coming to a tip, serrated edges. Veination indented.
Fruit: small (approx. 1/2 in. long) woody "cones" - persisting for several seasons.
Bark: gray, smooth.
Height: 10–25 ft, shrubby, often forming thickets.
Altitudes: 4000–8000 ft.

The Mountain Alder is a common tree often found in many moist areas around the lake (especially along the winding path up to Witch's Pond). Its small stature, serrated leaf margins and tiny cones make it relatively easy to identify. Its cousin, the White Alder, is much larger and less common in our area (see White Alder for other differences).

Periodically, alders and willows are infected by a virus that causes their leaves to develop reddish or yellowish wart-like protrusions on its leaves. These are sometime mistaken to be wasp galls, but if they are cut open, they are not hollow spheres nor do they shelter larvae.

Although alders are less famous than legumes (peas and beans), they too develop symbiotic associations with bacteria. The bacteria are harbored in root nodules and help the plant fix the readily available atmospheric nitrogen into other, often scarce, nitrogenous compounds that can be used by plants and kept in the soil. In this way, alders play a key role in enriching poor soil and preparing it to support other plants.

Mountain Maple (*Acer glabrum torreyi; Aceraceae*)
Also **Dwarf** or **Sierra Maple.** *Plate 3.*

> Leaves: 1–2 in. across, 3–5 lobed, central lobe largest. Thin and smooth. Twigs reddish.
> Fruit: pairs of winged seeds (*samaras*) spreading apart at about a 45 degree angle, found in clusters.
> Bark: gray, smooth.
> Height: 6–20 ft, shrubby.
> Altitudes: 4000–8000 ft.

This "tree" rarely exceeds twenty feet in height and has such small leaves that, from a distance, they can be mistaken for currant leaves. A quick feel tells them apart: the Mountain Maple has very smooth, thin leaves while the currant leaf is more glandular, bumpy and almost sticky.

Another way of telling them apart is that the Mountain Maples in our area frequently play host to a bright, blood-red blight (fungus) that encrusts parts of its leaves. Apparently the host-parasite relationship is so specific that the fungus cannot exist on any other kind of plant and certainly not currants. However, since the fungus only attacks a small percentage of a tree's total leaf surface and the tree itself is deciduous, the impact is relatively insignificant.

The seeds of the Mountain Maple are prized by many animals, Evening Grosbeaks in particular. The wings attached to the seeds help in wind dissemination—giving the seeds the common name of "helicopter" seeds. Throw one up to decide for yourself if the name is well-earned.

Forest Fire Ecology
by Rebecca Chaplin

You may have seen the sign on your way into the lake today. "Fire Danger: High." Or did it say "Extreme"? In recent decades, the Sierras and other Western forests have been ravaged by fires of an almost apocalyptic nature. Though Fallen Leaf itself hasn't suffered a wildfire since 1986, fires as close to us as Heavenly (670 acres) and Showers Lake (384 acres) should give even the most blasé visitor pause. The summer of 2002 was the third worst year for fires in history, after 2000 and 1988. Within months of each other were the 15,000 acre Humboldt-Toiyabe forest fire, the 466,000 acre fire in Rodeo-Chediski near Flagstaff and the 138,000 acre Hayman fire near Denver. These along with many other fierce and enormous fires contributed to a total seven million acres burned, 21 fire fighters dead and 2,000 structures destroyed. What is the cause of this recent trend of catastrophic fires?

Though forests in the West have always burned more frequently than anywhere else in the country, the kind of fires we see now are of our own making. For decades the prevailing view in forest management was that fires were destructive, not regenerative. Intending to protect humans and a valuable forest resource, the Forest Service suppressed fires for over a century. Smokey Bear became the icon for the Forest Service's crusade to prevent careless forest fires, but the message that spread through the national consciousness was that any fire was a bad fire. While this public prejudice largely remains, forest management has changed dramatically in recent years as ecologists learned about the essential role of fire in many ecosystems.

Succession and the Role of Fire

In order to understand how human intervention with natural fire regimes in the Sierras has affected the ecosystem function, it is necessary to understand the role fire historically played in these ecosystems. In order to understand the role of fire, a quick explanation of how succession operates in the Sierras is needed. Succession is the ordered progression of different types of communities in an area over time. The north end of Fallen Leaf Lake provides an excellent example of succession for our area. Grasses are often the first to fill in along the shoreline, followed by broadleaved trees such as willows, alders and aspens, then coniferous trees such as Jeffrey and Lodgepole Pine and finally White or Red Fir. This succession is perfectly illustrated if you look at the layers of vegetation moving outward from the shore over by the dam: a strip of grass, followed by a strip of willows and aspen, with conifers behind them. Presumably the shallow, flat area at that end of the lake is slowly filling in and could become forest by the end of the next century if left undisturbed.

The basic rule in succession is that each plant community both inhibits the growth of its predecessors and facilitates the invasion of its successors. Grasses, for instance, can inhabit very waterlogged, oxygen-deficient soils along a shoreline and, as they increase in abundance, draw down the amount of water in the soil until it can be colonized by trees. Willows, the trees most tolerant to excessive water, are usually the first to move in and on the sheer basis of height, can exclude the grasses by shading them out. Over time, willows continue to draw down the water and the alders that join them help fix nitrogen to enrich the soil, making it more hospitable to pine seeds that disperse into the area. Conifers can grow taller than the broadleaved trees and shade them out and the needles they shed also acidify the soil to prevent any non-coniferous plants from taking over the understory. Of the conifers, pines grow faster than firs and thus tend to dominate the canopy first. However, fir saplings outcompete their pine counterparts in the shade of a dense conifer canopy, so unless gaps are created through some means of disturbance, the firs will rise to eminence. Firs thus comprise what is known as the climax community, a community that is not replaced by any others unless disturbed by an exogenous force.

Disturbance can take the form of storms, floods, landslides, volcanic eruptions, droughts, clear-cutting, diseases, pests and fires. Depending on its extent, disturbance can prevent a community from yielding to its successor or can return the community to its primary stage of succession. In the Sierras, a mix of pines and firs has been historically maintained despite the firs being the climax community because of the frequent disturbance of fire. The natural fire frequency for this area was on an interval of 20 years and these fires served the important function of creating gaps in the forest for pines to maintain their population. In the absence of fire, firs have risen to much greater dominance in the Sierras than is natural. The consequences for this change in forest composition will be discussed in the next section. Fires offer the additional benefit of accelerating the nutrient cycling in a system where decomposition is extremely limited by lack of moisture and of keeping the forest at low enough density to prevent rapid spread of disease and reduce the competition for resources faced by the surviving trees.

The Effect of Fire Suppression

The suppression of fire in the West has led to disastrous consequences that we are only now beginning to understand. An area accustomed to burning every 20 years has missed at least the last four of its fire cycles. As ecologists and forest managers have learned about the importance of fire for maintaining general forest health as well as a diversity of species, the "any fire is a bad fire" policy has been largely abandoned. However, the best means of action is not as simple as standing back and letting fires run their natural course. We have already altered these forests too much through our years of fire suppression for the course to be "natural." Fires that occur in today's forests are hotter, taller and larger in extent than the fires that these forest communities are adapted to and have serious consequences for the future of forests as a result.

Hotter Fires

The most obvious effect of fire suppression on forests is the accumulation of biomass, in both the amount of dead trees and litter building up on the forest floor and in the unchecked growth of young trees at high densities. The forests look different than they did a century ago. John Muir wrote about riding horses through forests in the Sierras, a feat that would be impossible in today's thick forests. Our Western forests currently have densities similar to those in the East or Midwest and most of us expect that this is what a normal, healthy forest is supposed to look like. When viewed through Muir's eyes, however, these forests begin to look crowded, even cluttered. More biomass means more fuel for the fire. More fuel means a much hotter fire, especially when the fuel is smaller trees (with a much higher surface to volume ratio), or standing dead trees (with lower moisture contents), or trees closer together—all of which ignite more readily and burn faster. This can have many damaging effects. First, trees that have evolved in the presence of fire have thick bark that generally leaves large trees unscathed by flames, but when the fire is hot enough (or close enough because of over crowding) it can scorch and damage even the biggest trees. Additionally, a hot fire can sterilize the soil, destroying the seed bank and killing the microorganisms on which the plants depend for nutrient enrichment. Without these microorganisms, even seeds that disperse in after the fire will not fare well and few plants will be able to colonize the area until the microorganism populations have recovered. Finally, hot fires can volatilize nitrogen; when flames reach a certain temperature, this vital nutrient escapes the system as gas rather than being returned to the soil as ash. With less available nitrogen after the fire, surviving plants may be worse off than they were before, in spite of many of their competitors having been killed off.

The Fir Engraver Beetle

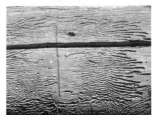

If you walk up Camp's Nature Trail from Witch's Pond, you'll come across an area with a lot of dead trees. This was a site of a beetle outbreak. You can see the scars on dead logs left by the beetle from when it burrows under the bark to lay its eggs and the swirled engravings in the wood left by the larvae as they eat their way out. By eating through the wood just under the bark, these larvae are cutting off the tree's transport systems to get oxygen and sugar from its leaves to its roots. If this happens around enough of the circumference of the trunk, the tree will die.

An additional result of the increase in biomass of living trees is increased susceptibility to pathogens. Population density is a major determinant of disease transmission for any organism and the higher densities of our modern forests put them at higher risk than would be the case under natural conditions. Additionally, as mentioned before, the absence of fire in the Sierras has changed the composition of the forest. Many forests, once well-mixed blends of pines and firs, now exist as fir monocultures. Their tolerance for shade enables these firs to grow at higher densities than pines and a community comprised of individuals of one species growing in close proximity to one another is ripe for an outbreak. We have witnessed just such an outbreak in the unprecedented attacks of the parasitic fir engraver beetle that have swept through many forests in our area. Recent estimates show that 25–30% of trees in the Tahoe Basin have been killed due to insect outbreak. The swath of dead trees we saw on Angora Ridge in the 1990s was the result of one of these beetle outbreaks. Such massive die-offs reduce the entire stand of trees to dry, dead wood, adding to the already increased fuel load of this system, creating an even greater fire hazard.

Taller Fires

Longer intervals between fires also substantially alters forest architecture. As young trees suffer a much higher mortality than older trees in a fire, the only intermediate-sized trees in a forest of high fire frequency will be the ones that grew fast enough between fires to reach a size refuge. Thus, there will be a higher proportion of intermediate-sized trees in areas where fire has been suppressed. This poses a significant threat to the forest because when a fire does come through such an area, the fire will be able to jump from the branches of a small tree to an intermediate-sized tree to a large tree (a phenomenon known as "fuel ladders"). While fires  in the Sierras historically were relegated fairly low to the ground in the absence of intermediate trees, fires in a fire-suppressed forest can reach the canopy, killing the tallest trees. A fire of this height is called a crown fire or a stand-replacing fire, because in reaching the crown or tops of the tallest trees it kills the entire stand of trees. In such a scenario, the process of succession will likely start all over (since grasses disperse and grow the fastest) and it could be many decades before the community that existed before the fire returns. Crown fires are becoming more and more common as a result of fire suppression, which is certainly not desirable from the standpoint of either conservation or resource management.

Larger Fires

The effects of hotter and taller fires are very serious, but do not explain why in recent years it has become more and more difficult to contain fires. Fires that spread throughout tens to hundreds of thousands of acres were once unheard of, but now loom as very real threats—as we have seen at Yellowstone and Los Alamos. This phenomenon is the result of the homogenizing effect of fire suppression on landscape ecology. In a large forest under a natural fire regime, different patches would burn at different times, creating a sort of mosaic of fire periodicities. In any given patch, the patch next to it may have burned ten years ago and the patch on the other side may have burned five years ago, so when enough fuel had accumulated in this particular patch to sustain a fire, the fire would naturally burn itself out when it reached the patches that burned more recently. By suppressing fire uniformly in all forests for the past century, we have destroyed this mosaic of natural firebreaks, such that the entire forest has now become one continuous patch at least four cycles overdue and raring to burn. Fires of unusually large extent face significant limitations in re-colonization, since seeds may not be capable of dispersing all the way from the edge of the burned area to the center of it. The center therefore may not recover until many generations later, as vegetation gradually fills in from the edges.

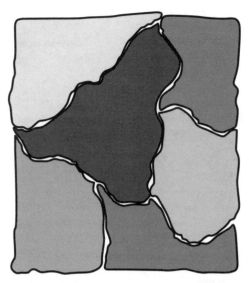

A mosaic of burned patches will keep a fire from getting out of control. In this figure, darkness corresponds to the number of years since the last burn. If the dark patch in the middle caught fire, the surrounding patches would not provide enough fuel for the fire to continue and the fire would naturally burn out.

The impetus for fire suppression in the first place was a deep-seated fear of wildfires encroaching upon human territory, destroying property and threatening lives. The irony is that the suppression has in fact increased this risk. Taller fires can jump over fire breaks and roads. Larger fires require many more fire-fighters and resources to contain them. Hotter fires are harder to put out. A century of fire suppression has made a veritable tinderbox of Western forests, which is as dangerous for humans as it is for the ecosystem itself.

Where Do We Go from Here?

Even if the Forest Service now recognizes the need to let natural fires burn, for the safety of those living near forests as well as for forest health, the fact remains that we are a long way from the conditions necessary for a natural fire. How can we return the system to its natural forest conditions? The most obvious way is to reduce the amount of fuel in the forest. But what is the best method to accomplish this to be consistent with the natural thinning effect of fire? Simply removing excess trees from the forest removes all the nutrients that have been locked up in those trees. As previously mentioned, fires play a very important role in nutrient cycling and thinning a forest through the removal of trees rather than burning breaks the cycle.

The products of thinning are likely more valuable in their contribution to soil enrichment if left in the forest than in any commercial uses we could derive from them. However, leaving the felled trees in the forest poses an even greater fire hazard than before thinning, as this wood will persist for decades before decomposing. How can the nutrients and carbon be returned to the system while still reducing the fire risk? One possible way would be to calculate the amount of total nutrients removed from the system along with the trees and then adding it back with fertilizers. This is an expensive and unnatural means of addressing the problem, however and has received little serious attention from forest managers.

The current preferred technique for correcting the problems caused by fire suppression is prescription burning. A prescribed or controlled burn is a small, well-contained fire that forest managers set themselves after a slight amount of thinning and other preparations. This closes the nutrient cycle and has the added benefit of returning the patchiness of fire intervals to the forest. Unfortunately, it is usually a very slow process, since the areas are usually small and each burn requires a great deal of planning and permitting as well as cooperation among a variety of public and private agencies. In addition, conditions for the day of the burn have to fit the "prescription" (the wind speed and direction, relative humidity, fuel moisture, temperature and weather forecasts have to fall within pre-determined ranges) and the containment of the burn requires a lot of manpower. The risk of an escaped fire resulting from prescription burning is very real; the 47,650 acre Los Alamos fire originated as a prescribed burn. The Forest Service in charge of Tahoe has been burning on the order of hundreds of acres a year, which is fairly pro-active compared to other areas. However, the Forest Service has over 150,000 acres in the Lake Tahoe Basin Management Unit under its jurisdiction—meaning that at the rate they're going it will take a thousand years to finish the job. (Although, the situation may be improving: in 2003 the Forest Service completed a total of 1000 acres of fuel reduction!) The forest will doubtlessly have corrected itself before we can. The only problem with that is it may be in the form of what we consider catastrophe. We probably need a more aggressive prescribed burning regime and that would take a lot of funding. This is a crisis that deserves national attention and the more informed citizens are about the issue, the more we can hold our representatives accountable to address it.

—Rebecca Chaplin

SHRUBS

Huckleberry Oak (*Quercus vaccinifolia; Fagaceae*) Plate 4.
Shrubby, 3–5 ft. tall.
Leaves about 1 in. long (± 1/2 in.), simple, margins smooth or slightly serrate.
Yellow staminate catkins 1–2 in. long, ovaries axillary.
Fruit a stubby acorn, about 1/2 in. long, maturing in 2 years.
Widespread, especially dry rocky slopes and open coniferous forests, 3000–9000 ft.

Although barely more than a bush, this plant is a true oak and produces acorns just like any other. Its common name is a literal translation of the Latin and refers to its huckleberry-like leaves. These generally smooth leaves help distinguish it from its low-altitude relatives Scrub Oak (*Q. dumosa*) and Leather Oak (*Q. durata*). Leaves are usually held vertically to decrease water loss. The Huckleberry Oak's acorns are an important food source for many animals, especially small rodents.

Bush Chinquapin (*Chrysolepis sempervirens; Fagaceae*) Plate 4.
Shrubby, 2–5 ft. tall, spreading.
Leaves about 2 in. long (± 1 in.), ovate, margins smooth, dark green on top, yellow underneath.
Yellow staminate catkins 1–2 in. long, ovaries axillary.
Fruit a spiny bur, about 1 in. across.
Open coniferous forests and rocky slopes, 3000–9000 ft.

This genus means "golden-scale" (a reference to the color of the underside of its leaves) and has fruits that are similar to those of its close relative, the chestnut (genus *Castanea*). Chinquapins can be found in the open coniferous forest mid-way up the Angora Trail.

Tobacco Brush (*Ceanothus velutinus velutinus; Rhamnaceae*) Also **California Lilac, Buckbrush, Deerbrush, Snowbrush** or **Ceanothus.** Plate 4.
Shrubby, 2–6 ft. tall.
Leaves 1–3 in. long, with three main veins, shiny green when young, dull in age, margins finely toothed. Not obviously thorny.
Flowers in dense elongated white conical clusters 2–5 in. long, fragrant. Individual flowers white, 1/4 in. across; 5 petaloid sepals curved inward; 5 thin petals with bulbous, hooded tips; 5 exserted stamens; cup-like hypanthium; flower center yellow.
Fruit a hard, 3-parted capsule.
Dry slopes, open forests, recent burns, 3200–10,000 ft.

This bush owes its primary name to the spicy scent of its crushed leaves, its second name to its fragrant flowers, the third and fourth name to animals that share its habitat and the last is derived from its misleading genus (meaning "thistle," probably from its thorny sister species). The specific epithet (and variety), *velutinus*, means "velvety," a reference to the softness of its leaves, especially in contrast with the hard leaves of most other chaparral shrubs. The fragrance of the blossoms is uniquely sweet and attracts people and bees alike.

The hard three-capsuled fruits protect seeds from most animals (except Fox Sparrows and very industrious chipmunks) for years to decades, awaiting a fire-induced release to insure a good, sunny spot for germination.

Mountain Whitethorn (*Ceanothus cordulatus; Rhamnaceae*). Also **Snowbrush.** *Plate 4.*

> Shrubby, 2–4 ft. tall.
> Leaves 1 in. long, with three main veins, dull grayish-green, margins smooth. Obviously thorny.
> Flowers in white conical clusters about 2 in. long. Individual flowers white, 1/4 in. across; 5 petaloid sepals curved inward; 5 thin petals with bulbous, hooded tips; 5 exserted stamens; cup-like hypanthium; flower center yellow.
> Fruit a hard, 3–parted capsule with crested valves.
> Dry rocky slopes, open forests, recent burns, 3000–9800 ft.

The thorns on this plant will let you know its identity if you happen to run into it. A white powdery substance lightly coats the surface of the plant, as if it was too close to a spray-painted house. (Above Camp one can be found on the right side of the Nature Trail just before it hits the Stanford Hill road on the way up from the Juniper Cabins.)

Sierra Coffeeberry (*Rhamnus rubra; Rhamnaceae*) *Plate 4.*

> Shrub or small tree, 4–8 ft. tall.
> Leaves 1–3 in. long, veins parallel, margins smooth.
> Flowers in small clusters. Individual flowers whitish, 1/3 in. across; 5 petaloid sepals curved inward; 5 thin petals with bulbous, hooded tips; 5 exserted stamens; cup-like hypanthium; flower center yellow.
> Fruit a ½–1in. long, black, 2–parted capsule with coffee-bean-like seeds.
> Dry rocky slopes, open forests, 3000–7000 ft.

Found in the Glen Alpine Watershed at the bases of rocky slopes with other shrubby species. Fruits can resemble small, purplish-black cherries.

Greenleaf Manzanita (*Arctostaphylos patula*; Ericaceae) *Plate 4.*
> 3–6 ft. Smooth reddish twigs, peeling bark on larger individuals.
> Leaves 1–2 in., roundish, held ± vertically with both sides alike, solid green, hardy.
> Flowers in groups of 4–8 hanging branchlets, 1/4–1/2 in. long, urn-shaped with 4–5 small lobes.
> Fruits vertically squashed spheres, resembling small green apples, ripening to a reddish-brown.
> Widespread, especially dry slopes. 3000–10,000 ft.

Arctos means "bear," *staphyle* is Greek for "a bunch of grapes," and *patula* refers to its habit of "spreading" out from its central burl.

It is no mistake that *manzanita* means "little apple" in Spanish. Several Native American tribes made use of the fresh green berries in a concoction resembling lemonade or hot cider. They would boil the berries in water, bruise them to extract the tart flavor and then add honey to sweeten it. The flavor of the unripe, seedy berries seems to be an astringent combination of a tart green apple and a lemon. When dried, these fruits were often pound into a fat-meat-meal mixture called *pemmican*. Birds, squirrels and bears relish manzanita berries.

Their dense rootstocks or "burls" allow for quick stump-sprouting after fires, giving it a formidable advantage on dry, frequently burned chaparral slopes. Because the underground burl can survive the fire with its root system intact and a store of food, it can quickly shade out seed-sprouting competitors while they are still in the early stages of germination. Due to its contorted, knotted and generally gnarly appearance, these burls have been used to fashion beautiful utensils, bowls and trays. During World War II, manzanita burls where carved into pipes because European briar was unavailable.

Pinemat Manzanita (*Arctostaphylos nevadensis*; Ericaceae) *Plate 4.*
> Low, prostrate, sprawling, 5–20 in. high. Smooth reddish twigs, peeling bark on larger individuals.
> Leaves 1/2–1 in., ovate, tips acutely pointed or obtusely rounded, held ± vertically with both sides alike, solid green, hardy. Young shoots of leaves dark red.
> Flowers in groups, white to pink, about 1/4 in. long, urn-shaped with 4–5 small lobes.
> Fruits vertically squashed spheres, resembling small green apples, ripening to a reddish-brown.
> Rocky slopes and open forests with granitic soil. 3000–10,000 ft.

This is a well-named manzanita, commonly forming a matted ground-cover under large pines. It seems to do well on sandy soils of granitic origin. Pinemat

Manzanita will often cover boulders as if they were bald heads with obvious comb-overs. The road from the parking lot to Angora Lake is an especially good place to see the creeping stems of this manzanita. Their berries are rumored to be tastier than those of the taller Greenleaf Manzanita.

Mountain Sagebrush (*Artemesia tridentata vaseyana; Asteraceae*)
Plate 5.

> Shrub with woody branches, 1–3 ft. tall.
> Leaves about 1 in. long, grayish-green, hairy, narrowly wedge-shaped, usually 3-toothed at tip, having a pungent aroma when rubbed.
> Flowers inconspicuous, yellow, lacking showy petals.
> Dry, sunny areas. 5,900–10,000 ft.

Sagebrush is common throughout the West in dry, inhospitable environments. Our subspecies of sagebrush grows on slopes in and around the Great Basin Desert. Although unrelated, the pungent, musky-minty-spicy smell of this plant earned it the common name "sage" and allows it to be used as a wild substitute for that cooking herb (culinary sage, *Salvia officinalis*, is a member of the Mint Family). This herb is at its best when served after a long hike with fresh fly-caught Golden Trout from Jabu Lake. Try using it in other savory camp dishes, too.

Other species of sagebrush in our higher elevations include: *A. rothrockii* (**Timberline**), *A. spiciformis* (**Snow**), *A. arbuscula* (**Low**).

Serviceberry (*Amelanchier utahensis & A. alnifolia pumila; Rosaceae*)
Plate 5.

> Shrub 2–8 ft. tall.
> Leaves round to oval, thin, 1/2–2 in. long, margins begin entire, becoming serrate about halfway to tip.
> Flowers in clusters of 3–9, each with 5 long, thin, white petals (appx. 1/8 in. wide by 1/2 in. long), small yellow centers.
> Fruit blue-black berries, about 1/2 in. across.
> Coniferous forests and open shrubland, 4900–8500 ft.

A tasty treat for late-summer hikers, this plant provides the "blueberries" of Desolation Wilderness. Native Americans also harvested these berries, eating them fresh as well as incorporating the dried fruits into winter pemmican (a mixture of jerky, fat, fruit and grains). It has been subsequently discovered that the antioxidants in the berries act as a preservative and helped to prevent the pemmican from spoiling too quickly.

The name "Serviceberry" is the result of a long, misguided game of "telephone." Originating due to confusion with the Mountain-ash (genus

Sorbus), "sorbus-berry" gradually changed into "sarvisberry." This word, in turn, mutated into today's accepted name of Serviceberry. One could argue that this resultant name (regardless of its haphazard origins) is an appropriate one for a fruit important in the diets of people, birds and beasts alike. The *utahensis* species is more common on the east slope and has minutely hairy leaves and stems. *Alnifolia* means alder-leaved and is glabrous, or hairless, on the upper surface (*pumil*a=dwarf).

Bitter Cherry (*Prunus emarginata; Rosaceae*) Plate 5.
 Shrub or small tree, 3–30 ft. tall, twiggy, often forming thickets.
 Leaves generally 1–2 in. long, elliptic with minute serrations.
 Flowers in groups of 3–12, each about 1/2 in. across with 5 white, rounded petals and many protruding stamens.
 Fruit smooth, bright red, shiny, ovoid spheres 1/4–1/2 in. long; bitterly astringent skin around a hard pit.
 Rocky slopes, avalanche tracks and forested areas up to 9500 ft.

This widespread shrub-tree thrives on rocky slopes frequented by avalanches, making the Bitter Cherry an especially familiar sight on the slopes of Cathedral Peak. Birds and beasts gobble up the ripening drupes in the late summer and fall. If you are curious as to the origin of this plant's common name, try nibbling on its fruit.

Western Choke-cherry, *Prunus virginiana demissa*, Plate 5, is a much larger tree with long, linear bunches of flowers (and later, fruits). Appropriately, there is one just north of Cherry House at Camp. Otherwise, this species is relatively rare in our area and is more common at lower elevations.

Mountain-ash (*Sorbus californica* & *S. scopulina; Rosaceae*) Plate 6.
 Shrub or small tree, 3–15 ft. tall.
 Leaves pinnate, up to 1 ft. long, with 7–13 leaflets. Leaflets 1–4 in. long, margins serrate.
 Flowers white, in clusters, each with five rounded petals, many protruding stamens.
 Fruits are apple-like, pithy, 1/2 in. across, orange to red.
 Moist forests and slopes, 4000–9000 ft.

These two species are included under one common name because they intergrade, making specific identification difficult. Generally, the more common *S. californica* is smaller (less than 7 ft. tall), usually has 7–9 leaflets per leaf and has smooth flower-stems. *S. Scopulina* can grow to 15 ft. tall, usually has 9–13 leaflets and has sparsely hairy flower-stems. Stick to the common name or genus and you will always be "right."

Mountain-ash is hyphenated because it is not a true Ash (genus *Fraxinus; Oleaceae*), but only superficially resembles one because of its pinnate leaves. These shrub-trees grow along the Tamarack Trail, among other places and provide fruit for many species of wildlife. Mountain-ash fruits remain on the tree throughout winter to provide resident birds with food during lean times. Because the fruits are sometimes sweet enough to ferment, drunken birds are sometimes observed flying away from these trees with unusually erratic flight patterns.

Red Elderberry (*Sambucus racemosa microbotrys; Caprifoliaceae*) Plate 6.

> 2–8 ft tall, usually shrubby.
> Leaves opposite, pinnate, with 5–7 narrowly elliptical leaflets. serrated margins.
> Flowers tiny (1/4 in.) white, 5–petaled flowers in dense, elongated racemose clusters appx. 2 in. wide and 3–5 in. long.
> Fruit in elongated bunches, bright red BB-sized berries.
> Moist places on rocky slopes, 6000–10,000 ft.

This alpine elderberry is easily distinguished from Blue Elderberry on the basis of its flower cluster shape and berry color. Not considered to be as good for eating since it often causes stomach discomfort.

Blue Elderberry (*Sambucus mexicana; Caprifoliaceae*) Plate 6.

> 3–26 ft tall, shrubby or tree-like.
> Leaves opposite, pinnate, 5–12 in. long with 3–9 narrowly elliptical leaflets with serrated margins.
> Flowers tiny (1/4 in.) white, 5–petaled flowers in dense, flat heads 9–10 in. across.
> Fruit in flat bunches of dark blue BB-sized berries covered with a white bloom (powder).
> Stream banks and forest openings, usually lower elevations.

Elderberries have been widely used in making wines, pies and preserves. Look for them in wet areas around Fallen Leaf and Glen Alpine. The berries are edible (and tart) when raw, but are more safely consumed in quantity when cooked.

Other parts of the plant have been boiled to make teas that were used to induce lactation, sweating and diarrhea as well as to reduce swelling, infection or diarrhea. Due to reports of possible toxicity and seemingly conflicting effects on the bowels, the reader is discouraged from experimentation.

The pithy stems can be hollowed out for use as straws, pea-shooters, pipe stems, elk-whistles and flutes. The genus is named after a Greek instrument made from its wood. There are some growing next to the Old Lodge at Camp.

Creek Dogwood (*Cornus sericea sericea; Cornaceae*). Previously *C. stolinifera*. Also **American, Silky,** or **Red-osier Dogwood**. *Plate 6.*

> Leaves: 2–5 in. long, elliptical and conspicuously veined.
> Flowers: loose heads (2-4 in. across) of many tiny (1/4 in.), four-petaled white flowers.
> Fruit: berry-like (1/4 in. across), green, in loose heads, whitish-blue at maturity.
> Bark: gray, smooth. Young twigs red.
> Height: 3–16 ft, shrubby.
> Altitudes: 4000–9000 ft.

Lacking the attention-grabbing white, petal-like bracts of the larger, more tree-like Pacific Dogwood (which grows below 5000 feet), many have a hard time accepting this species as a "true" dogwood. However, close inspection reveals typical dogwood leaves and a similar flowering structure —minus the large, white, subtending petaloid bracts.

Besides employing the bark in remedies for malaria, mange and constipation, dogwood was favored by Native Americans for drying racks and skewers. When early Scandinavian explorers witnessed this practice, they named the tree using their word for skewer—*dag*. "Dagwood" was then transformed into the common name used today, its connotation now far from the original. The genus, *Cornus*, is derived from the Latin word for horn due to its hard wood.

The common names refer to its habitat (creeksides) and its twigs (*osier*, French for "young stem"). The red stems are notably obvious in the fall and winter when they have no leaves to hide them. Another subspecies, *C. s. occidentalis* (**Western**) can also be found in our lower elevations. Its flowers are larger, leaves hairier below and its seeds are ridged.

Geology: A History of the Sierras, Tahoe and Fallen Leaf

By Rebecca Chaplin

The Uplift of the Sierra Nevadas

Our story begins 230 million years ago, when the North American geologic plate split off from Eurasia and headed westward on a collision course with the Pacific plate. The dense oceanic Pacific plate plunged beneath the lighter continental North American plate, forcing the uplift of what became the Sierra Nevada range over the next 200 million years. This process, known as subduction, gave rise to the incredible diversity of rock we see around Fallen Leaf. When the Pacific plate was thrust so deeply under the North American, an enormous amount of it melted due to the heat generated by the increased pressure. The resulting hot, molten magma rose to settle just below the surface, cooling into a series of solid granitic bubbles, or plutons, called the Sierra Nevada Batholith. Rock adjacent to the molten batholith was metamorphosed by the heat and pressure of the intrusion. The batholith and its metamorphic progeny remained underground until all the rock above was eroded away over time. To put this in a context relevant to us, the Sierra Nevada Batholith is the foundation of Desolation Wilderness. The vast majority of the rock back there is granite (more specifically, granodiorite) characterized by its light color and blocky structure (resulting from the way it fractures along its crystal faces). Mount Tallac and Angora Peak, along with the trails leading up to them, are metamorphic outcrops. You can tell this rock by the uniform or striped colors (as opposed to the speckled design of granite) and the sharp edges on fractured pieces.

> **Quick geology review**
>
> *When a rock melts and is completely reformed it's called igneous and when subjected to extreme temperature and pressure to the point of transformation, it's called metamorphic. Igneous rock can be extrusive (like basalt), cooling quickly at the surface, or can be intrusive (like granite) cooling much more slowly underground and yielding bigger crystals. Metamorphic rock types are largely determined by their parent rock types.*

The Formation of the Tahoe Basin

The Sierras were uplifted to their present glory because of subduction, but the Tahoe Basin would not exist as we know it without volcanism. The Pacific and North American plates shifted directions about 25 million years ago and started sliding past each other instead of butting heads. Volcanic activity increased along the plate boundary as a result and the earth's crust began to crack in places, forming faults. Most of the lava flows deposited by these volcanic activities were scoured away by the ensuing glaciers, but some still exist in areas nearby, such as Carson Pass and Castle Peak. You can recognize these formations from far away, since the rock is uncharacteristically dark for the Sierras and erodes away very smoothly. The most evident effect of volcanism from our perspective, however, is the formation of Lake Tahoe. This is a good trivia fact: Tahoe is the only natural lake in the area that is not the product of glaciation. The Tahoe Basin was formed from the uplift of two parallel faults (what is now the Sierra and Carson Range), which resulted in the subsidence of the crust between these two faults about 3 million years ago. Imagine a huge trough formed between two faulting mountain ranges. The trough was then plugged at both ends by molten lava, creating a giant hole resembling a crater, but not the remnants of an exploded volcano or asteroid impact. It took the unique combination of uplift and volcanic forces to create Lake Tahoe, the second deepest lake in North America (after Crater Lake in Oregon). Over the past few million years, water from the backcountry all around the Tahoe Basin slowly filled this giant void until it reached a level that could erode the lava plug and form an outlet, the Truckee River. The Truckee is the only outlet, but Tahoe is fed by 63 streams, encompassing a total area of 519 square miles that drain into the lake.

> **More Lake Tahoe Trivia:**
>
> –Maximum Depth: 1645 ft; Average Depth: 989 ft
> –22 mi long, 12 mi wide
> –The amount of water in Lake Tahoe could cover a flat area the size of California 14 inches deep. This is enough to supply everyone in the US with 50 gallons of water per day for 5 years. The water consumption of Los Angeles could be supported for 5 years on the amount of water that evaporates off Lake Tahoe every year! See http:// tahoe.usgs.gov/facts.html

The Formation of Fallen Leaf Lake

After the basic structure of the Tahoe Basin was established through the processes of subduction and volcanism, glaciers sculpted out the more intricate features, namely the valleys and many lakes of Desolation Wilderness. These features are much more recent in the grand scheme of things, as the last glaciers receded a mere 8,000 years ago. It's hard to imagine the dynamic power of glaciation while standing atop a snowfield in Desolation, which is the closest we can come to a glacier here. In geologic time, the effect of a glacier is better represented by a raging river (or colossal bulldozer) than the small, stationary snow masses we observe today. A glacier does everything a river does: just much, much more slowly. The same way a river deposits more sediment on the outside of a bend, so does a glacier. In glacial terms, these kinds of depositions are called moraines. The glacier that carved out Fallen Leaf Lake formed moraines on the east side (what we now know as Angora Ridge) and west side (what we call Cathedral Ridge). Normally these would be called lateral moraines, but because there were also glaciers on the other sides, they are technically medial moraines—formed between two glaciers. In fact, Angora Ridge is rumored to be one of the tallest medial moraines in North America. The one thing glaciers can do that rivers can't is retreat. "Retreat" is perhaps a misleading word, since glaciers don't actually back up, but essentially just start melting faster than they move forward so that the edge of the snow-pack effectively recedes. The deposition resulting from melting glacier edge is called a terminal moraine and such deposition may occur several times toward the end of an ice age, when the climate is fluctuating between warm and cold. The deepest terminal moraine deposits occur when the flow of the glacier is just balanced by the rate of melting,

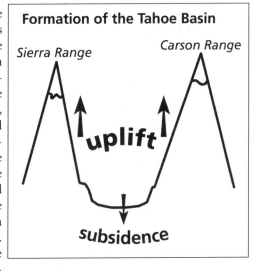

such that the end of the glacier is effectively pushing debris into the same pile for a long time. The strip of land between Fallen Leaf Lake and Lake Tahoe, for instance, contains at least two terminal moraines, indicating that glaciers retreated more than once. The shallow shore of the north end of the lake is one edge of the terminal moraine, in marked contrast to the south, which is essentially a sheer drop-off with depths exceeding 200 feet past Camp's buoys and reaching a purported 419 feet not far beyond that. The glacier that formed Fallen Leaf Lake stopped just short of Tahoe—if it had continued only half a mile further, Fallen Leaf would be a bay. (This, incidentally, is how Emerald Bay was formed.)

The Effect of Geology on Ecology in Tahoe

What does all this mean for the living environment? Geology plays a major role in the determination of vegetation type and the distribution of different plant communities directly affects the distribution of animal populations. The four major factors affecting vegetation are climate, biotic relationships, topography and soil type. (Time, or age of the soil, is a fifth factor.) While the last two items on this list are certainly mediated by the first two (climate governs the erosive forces that will continue to shape the topography and local biological processes have a strong effect on soil character which may overwhelm the initial parent rock material in the long term), geology is the main determinant for both topography and soil.

As far as topography is concerned, slope orientation and steepness are the important considerations for vegetation. The amount of light energy a hillside receives depends on the direction it is facing. In the northern hemisphere, southern facing slopes receive more sunlight that northern ones. While eastern and western facing slopes receive the same amount of sunlight, the western facing slopes receive it during the later, warmer part of the day. Therefore, southern and western slopes tend to dry out more quickly. In as dry a climate as the Sierras this translates into substantial differences in the vegetation that can be supported on these slopes. We should expect to see drier adapted species on southern and western facing slopes. We should also expect to see snow-pack lasting longer on northern and eastern facing slopes, which will dramatically affect the water availability later in the summer for seasonal vegetation like wildflowers. Indeed, this is why we see snow on the northeastern face of Mt. Tallac into July and why the meadow just below it boasts flowers that bloom much longer than others in the area.

The steeper the grade of a hillside, the thinner the layer of soil will be on that slope and the thicker the soil will be at the base of the hill. This phenomenon is especially pronounced around Tahoe due to the scouring action of the glaciers. Desolation Wilderness was scoured down to the bare bedrock in many places such that even now, several thousand years later, soil may be only an inch or two deep. (If soil is present at all—Desolation Wilderness, after all, earns its name from the dominance of bare rock throughout much of the area.) Additionally, the steeper the slope, the faster the run-off of snowmelt and the less time the soil has to absorb water. Steeper slopes are therefore drier and composed of thinner soils and often can only support small annual plants that can grow quickly enough to reproduce before what little soil moisture exists is depleted. Meanwhile, where sediment tends to accumulate, where terrain flattens out and at the lateral and terminal glacial moraines, the soil is much thicker and can support larger, slower growing plants such as trees. This, along with fire suppression and selective logging, is why moisture-loving White Firs cover our side of Angora Ridge; the depth of the soils of this lateral moraine prevent them from drying out too quickly despite the western exposure of the slope.

Regarding soil type, a fundamental determinant for vegetation is the composition of the parent rock. Because intrusive igneous rocks such as granite cool so slowly, resulting in a large individual crystal size as previously noted, the particle size of soils originating from these types of rocks is much larger than for soils originating from extrusive igneous (volcanic) or metamorphic rock. Granite is also composed of fairly inert minerals that do not contain many nutrients required for plant growth. The coarser, nutrient-poor granitic soils drain faster than fine soils, so vegetation will often be sparser in areas dominated by granitic soils. On the other hand, volcanic or metamorphic soils, which may have an average particle size one-hundredth of that of granitic soils, retain water so well they often get waterlogged from the early summer snowmelt. These soils also tend to be nutrient-rich because not only are they often composed of chemically active minerals, but their smaller particle size makes them more capable of absorbing nutrients dissolved in water. Volcanic and metamorphic soils are characteristic of bogs and meadows and the biggest problem faced by plants growing in these soils is poor diffusion of oxygen to the roots.

—Rebecca Chaplin

FERNS & HORSETAILS

Bracken Fern (*Pteridium aquilinum pubescens*; Dennstaedtiaceae)
Plate 7.

> 2–6 ft. Leaf stem 1/2–3 ft. long; leaf blade 1/2–5 ft. long, broadly triangular, usually 1–5 pinnate. Various habitats, usually below 9000 ft.

This fern is—paradoxically—toxic, carcinogenic a*nd* edible. As a young sprout of a leaf, it is tightly curled and eaten today as "fiddlehead" in areas such as the United States, Great Britain, Korea and Japan. Many Native American tribes ate the fiddleheads and rhizomes of the Bracken Fern. Its taste is apparently somewhere between asparagus and okra. Cooking, rinsing and drying breaks down the toxic thiaminase (an enzyme which breaks down vitamin B-1), but carcinogenic compounds may remain. Younger leaves are also less likely to have many of the unfavorable chemicals to begin with. There are not any records of humans consuming enough of the plant to break down all their B vitamins, but livestock are susceptible: 600 pounds over six weeks is enough to kill a horse (Daniels 1988, p. 241).

In 1981, the San Bernadino National Forest instituted a season and permits ($10/40lbs.) for bracken-picking due to the increased demand brought on by the growing Asian-American (especially Korean) population of Los Angeles. In 1992, 1,530 people harvested over 16,000 pounds. From 1981 to 1992, over 160,000 pounds were harvested—just one more way to enjoy the renewable resources of our public lands (LA Times, 4/25/93).

The scientific name of this species means "eagle feather," a reference to its great size and feathery shape. Our variety, *pubescens*, is named after the tiny hairs found on the underside of the leaves.

Leather Grape-Fern (*Botrychium multifidum*; Ophioglossaceae)
Plate 7.

> 6–18 in. Small, compact, fleshy fern with finely divided leaflets. Tiny ball-like sporangia clustered at the tips of erect fertile fronds. Moist habitats below 9000 ft.

This rarely-seen fern is named after the miniscule grape-like clusters of spore-bearing structures. Look for it under trees in moist woods and riparian areas.

Yosemite Moonwort (*Botrychium simplex*; Ophioglossaceae)

> 3–6 in. Very small, compact, fleshy fern with blunt, stubby, gingko-like leaflets (only twice-pinnate). Tiny ball-like sporangia clustered at the tips of erect fertile fronds. Moist meadows above 7000 ft.

A smaller, even rarer version of the leather grape-fern, this species grows in Haypress Meadows, between Echo Lakes and Lake Aloha. Keep an eye out for it in other wet meadows in our area.

Indian Dream (*Aspidotis densa; Pteridaceae*). Also **Dense Shield-bearer** or **Oregon Cliff-break.** Previously *Onychium densum* and *Cheilanthes siliquosa*. *Plate 7.*

> Leaves 3–12 in. long, stem a shiny chestnut brownish-red, fertile or vegetative, 3-pinnate, leaflets linear, light green, margins rolled under to protect lines of spores. Rocky slopes and crevices, 300–10,000 ft.

The second common name (a direct translation of the scientific name) refers to the way the leaflet edges curve inward to "shield" the reproductive spores, which are found in two dense, parallel lines on the underside of the fertile leaflets. Not your stereotypical shade-loving fern, this plant thrives on open rocky slopes like those found above Stanford Hill.

Five-finger Fern (*Adiantum aleuticum; Pteridaceae*) *Plate 7.*

> 1–2 ft. Can have more than five "fingers" at the end of a long, shiny, dark brown stem. Up to 8500 ft.

A rare fern that grows on wet cliff faces in our area. Branching pattern is reminiscent of a hand at the end of thin, polished, reddish-black lacquered stems (that were used to make beautiful tiny baskets). Close relative of the maiden-hair fern.

Bridge's Cliff-brake (*Pellaea bridgesii; Pteridaceae*) *Plate 7.*

> Leaves 5–14 in. long, stem a shiny reddish-brown; leaflets blue-gray-green, unlobed, roundly oval to chordate, almost 1/2 in. long, often folded lengthwise (like a clamshell) to protect the spores situated along the margins on the underside of the leaflet. Rock slopes and crevices, 4000–10,000 ft.

The genus name means "dusky," but there is debate about whether this is meant to apply to the blue-gray leaflets or the dark red stems. Nice crops of this species occur on the road cut just below Upper Falls.

American Parsley Fern (*Cryptogramma acrostichoides; Pteridaceae*). Also **American Rock-brake.** *Plate 7.*

> Sterile and fertile leaves distinctly different in appearance. Sterile leaves shorter (2–8 in. long), 2–4 pinnate, leaflets flat, margins mildly serrate. Fertile leaves about twice as long (4–12 in. long), erect; leaflets linear, margins rolled under to hide spores. Rocky slopes and crevices, 4600–10,000 ft.

Although it is a stretch to compare the sterile fronds of this fern to parsley, someone did it and the name remains. The two leaf types of this plant are so dissimilar that they appear to be different plants at first glance. This genus name translates as "hidden line," after the way the leaf margins roll under to cover the lines of spores. Found in rocky areas including Stanford Hill and the avalanche tracks between Mt. Tallac and Fallen Leaf Lake.

Lace Fern (*Cheilanthes gracillima; Pteridaceae*). Also **Lip Fern.**
Plate 7.

> Leaves 2–12 in. long, 1/2–1 in. wide, 2–pinnate; leaflets dark green, oval, tightly packed together, lower surfaces concave and densely rusty-brown wooly-hairy. Rocky places, 1500–10,000 ft.

This dark green fern has densely packed leaflets with hairy undersides which make it fairly easy to distinguish from our other small ferns. This genus means "lip flower" and is a reference to the location of its spores — along the lower "lip" of the leaflets. Lace Ferns are abundant in the rocky area at the north end of Camp's Nature Trail, south of Witch's Pond.

Common Horsetail (*Equisetum arvense; Equisetaceae*) *Plate 8.*

> Two kinds of stems. Sterile stems 1/2–2 ft. tall, ridged lengthwise, rough, regularly branched at the nodes, 6–16 segmented branches per whorl, leaves fused into a scale-like, toothed sheath that surrounds the stem above each node of branches. Fertile stems 4–13 in. tall, not branched, pale brown, fleshy, persisting only a few weeks in the spring, topped by a cone-like spore-bearing strobilus. Moist areas below 8000 ft.

The green bottle-brushes of the vegetative stems only vaguely resemble real horse tails, but are close enough for the name to stick (*equi*, "horse," and *setum*, "bristle"). What appear from a distance to be pine-needle-like leaves are actually branches, the leaves having been reduced to small, membranous sheaths. Common Horsetail grows along the tiny stream which runs through the forested section of Camp's Nature Trail.

The green, non-branched, taller persuasion also occurs in our area: **Common Scouring Rush**, *Equisetum hyemale affine.* This species is present in the wet seeps on the south slope of Stanford Hill that feed into Glen Alpine Creek. Common Scouring Rush generally has an acutely pointed cone tip and two dark bands around the leaf sheaths.

Members of the Horsetail Family draw significant amounts of minerals (mostly silica) out of the ground which they use to increase the rigidity and unpalatability of their stems. Due to the resulting roughness and coarseness of the stems, they are used like steel wool and sandpaper by traditional Native Americans, pioneers and backpackers. Nothing gets a pot cleaner than a handful of horsetails or "scouring rushes," as the non-branched species are called.

Other rarely-encountered ferns include:

Lady Fern, *Athyrium filix-femina cyclosorum*:
>moist woods at lower elevations. *Plate 8.*

Alpine Lady Fern, *Athyrium alpestre americanum*:
>wet rocky slopes at high elevations.

Holly Fern, *Polystichum lonchitis*:
>wet cracks in the Velma Lakes Watershed.

Kruckberg's Sword Fern, *Polystichum kruckebergii*:
>rock cracks near Echo Lakes.

Cliff Fern, *Woodsia scopulina*:
>Glen Alpine Watershed cliffs and near Ralston Peak.

Fragile Fern, *Cystopteris fragilis*:
>moist crevices in the Glen Alpine Watershed.

FLOWERS

The flower section has been organized first by flower color and then, within each color, increasing petal number. This method of organization was employed because it was deemed to be the most accessible to non-botanists. Although it is easy to comprehend in theory, it is far from perfect and will cause some frustration at times. For this unavoidable frustration, I apologize. Flower color varies and we all perceive color a bit differently. For example, your "pink" flower may be in the "red," "blue to purple," or even "white" section. Take heart, but also remember there is always the distinct possibility that I have neglected to include that particular species. This section purposefully describes only the most common and most asked-about species in our area.

Note: For those of you familiar with botanical floras and interested in a more complete treatment of our larger watershed, I highly recommend Michael Graf's Plants of the Tahoe Basin.

Flower Section Order:

    1. Blue-Purple   2. Pink   3. Red

    4. Orange   5. Yellow   6. White   7. Green

1. Blue to Purple Flowers

4 PETALS

Alpine Speedwell (*Veronica wormskjoldii; Scrophulariaceae*). Previously *Veronica alpina alternifolia* Also **Alpine Brooklime.** *Plate 9.*

> 4–12 in. tall, sprouting from hairy perennial rhizome. Leaves 1/2–2 in. long, elliptic, opposite, sessile. Flowers pale blue with yellow center, appear 4–petaled, top 3 similarly wide and roundish, bottom petal significantly smaller. Two obvious exserted stamens, pistil also exserted. Moist places, 6500–10,000 ft.

The Alpine Speedwell has a unique flower and, although it is in the Snapdragon (or Figwort) Family, it can be mistaken for a *Downingia* species (*Campanulaceae*) at a distance. (This species of Speedwell is *probably* the one I saw above Camp's water supply pond. I use a qualifier because I did not actually key it out, but have researched all the species of *Veronica* in California and feel fairly confident that this is the one.)

Other species of Speedwell in our area include: **American** (*V. americana*), **Cusick's** (*V. cusickii*), **Thyme-leaved** (*V. serpyllifolia humifusa*), **Purslane** (*V. peregrinus xalapensis*).

Mountain Jewelflower (*Streptanthus tortuosus* var. *orbiculatus*; Brassicaceae) Plate 9.

> 4–12 in. high. Flowers small (1/4 in.), purple urn-shaped sepals with four tiny, thin white petals protruding. Leaves varied: Lower, basal leaves serrated, with stems. Upper leaves (bracts) are smooth and clasping—making it appear as though the stem has pierced a rounded, almost heart-shaped leaf through the center. Leaves yellow with age. Fruit a long (1–4 in.), very skinny "bean." Found on exposed rocky slopes, 6200–10,000 ft.

Both parts of the botanical name for this species refer to the tiny, twisted petals that are only visible at close range. This particular variety probably gets its name from its conspicuously rounded, orb-shaped bracts.

5 PETALS

Explorer's Gentian (*Gentiana calycosa*; Gentianaceae) Plate 9.

> 2–18 in. tall, sprouting from a thick, root-like caudex. Leaves 1–2 in. long, opposite, ovate, sessile (without a stem-like base). Flowers indigo blue (rarely tending towards violet or white), upright, 1–2 in. long cups with 5 lobes. Tiny forked filaments found between each lobe. Moist seepages, 6000–10,000 ft.

This late-summer bloomer is a true delight to happen upon. Its common name stems from the fact that it is rarely found near human habitation. This may be a result of the gentian's habitat preference—cliff cracks or wet bogs where snow melt provides moisture through July and August. After climbing up the Tamarack Trail from Lily Lake, scrambling up the southeast bowl of Mt. Tallac or humping over the saddle between Boomerang and Tyler Lakes in the heat of late July, one gets a better understanding of why it was named "Explorer's Gentian."

Other members of the Gentian Family found in Desolation Wilderness include the cream-colored **Alpine Gentian** (*Gentiana newberryi*), the delicate purple **Hiker's Gentian** (*Gentianopsis simplex*) and **Green Gentian** or **Monument Plant** (*Swertia radiata*).

Alpine Blue Flax (*Linum lewisii alpicola*; Linaceae) Previously *Linum perenne lewisii*. Plate 9.

> 1/2–3 ft. Leaves linear, 1/2–1 in. long. Flowers 5–petaled, deep blue to light lavender, with yellow center. Streamsides, meadows and dry slopes, 6000–10,000 ft.

The stereotypical "flower" shape, blue color and long slender stem makes blue flax fairly easy to identify. A few usually grow right in the middle of Camp, near the stream south of the boat dock—possibly planted as part of a local native wildflower mix.

Another species in the same genus (*L. usitatissimum*) provides us with commercial linseed oil and linen (*linum* is Latin for "thread"). Native Americans also gathered the fibrous stems to twist into cordage. A red species native to North Africa (*L. grandiflorum*) is planted as an ornamental and thrives on the medians of Stanford's Palm Drive in the spring.

Small-flowered Stickseed (*Hackelia micrantha; Boraginaceae*). Previously *Hackelia jessicae*. Also **Jessica's Stickseed.** *Plate 9.*

> 1–3 ft. Leaves lanceolate, 2–9 in. long. Stem hairs sparse or absent. Flowers less than 1/2 in. across, blue petals with appendages at base forming a white circle with a yellow center. Fruits covered with lines of hook-like hairs. Meadows, rocky slopes, esp. near moisture. 2000–10,000 ft.

This plant has the stereotypical small blue flowers of the Forget-me-not Family. The name "stickseed" comes from the *Velcro*-like hooks that cover the seeds to aid in animal-assisted dispersal. If you brush past a stickseed in late summer you may be unwittingly enlisted to carry a few. Other stickseeds in our area include **Smooth** (*H. nervosa*), which has a longer corolla tube and **Velvet** (*H. velutina*) which has larger (2 1/2 in.) flowers.

Waterleaf Phacelia (*Phacelia hydrophylloides; Hydrophyllaceae*). Also **Ballhead Phacelia.** *Plate 9.*

> Stem 4–12 in. Leaf blade variously lobed, roughly in the shape of an elongated triangle, 1–3 in. long, on a petiole (leaf-stem) 1/4–2 in. long. Flowers in dense spherical heads, 5 purple reflexed petals, exserted stamens. Open woods, 4000–9500 ft.

This unassuming plant often hides its pale purple blooms under its leaves, making it even less likely to be noticed. The Waterleaf Phacelia is more often seen in Mokelumne Wilderness, but does occur in Desolation as well.

Purple Nightshade (*Solanum xanti; Solanaceae*) *Plate 10.*

> 1/2–3 ft. Leaves 1/2–3 in. long, ovate, often slightly wrinkled. Flower a purple pentagon formed from 5 fused petals. Five yellow stamens tightly clustered around central pistil. Fruit a tiny (1/4–1/2 in.) round green berry or "tomato." Open forests, woodlands and shrubby areas below 8500 ft. **POISONOUS.**

Don't try these little green tomatoes! The genus name, *Solanum*, means "quieting" and refers to the narcotic (and poisonous) properties of this plant. Southwestern tribes have used nightshade berries to dull pain and for curdling milk to make cheese, but a slight overdose can be lethal.

The Nightshade Family does include many important crops that were discovered in the New World: tomatoes, potatoes, chilies, eggplant and tobacco. Previously, Europeans had thought all members of this family to be poisonous because of experience with toxic species like our Purple Nightshade. I am eternally grateful that Native Americans introduced the world to the edible nightshades (for example, what would Italian cuisine be like without them?), but we probably could do without modern tobacco's problems. Guess you have to take the good with the bad.

Showy Penstemon (*Penstemon speciosus; Scrophulariaceae*) Plate 10.

> 5–20 in. tall. Low spreading stems bending upwards to expose flowers. Leaves lanceolate, 1–4 in. long, often folded lengthwise. Flowers pot-bellied trumpets, 1–2 in. long, tube violet-purple changing to blue on the reflexed lobes (2 upper, 3 lower). Dry rocky areas, Great Basin to Alpine environments, often sharing habitat with Mountain Sage. 4000–10,000 ft.

The blue lobes of the Showy Penstemon complement its violet-colored tubes to create a truly "showy" spectacle. This penstemon is relatively rare since we are at the western margin of its range, but I have seen it near the Fallen Leaf fire lookout on Angora Ridge. Showy Penstemons are fairly populous in Mokelumne Wilderness near Frog Lake.

Rydberg's Penstemon (*Penstemon rydbergii oreocharis; Scrophulariaceae*) Plate 10.

> Stem smooth, 1/2–2 ft. tall. Leaves lanceolate, opposite, 1–3 in. long. Flowers in distinct axial whorls. Flower a violet tube about 1/2 in. long with 5 blue lips, inner throat white-hairy. Moist meadows, 4000–10,000 ft.

A delicate plant with separate circular whorls of violet-blue flowers. Note: there are also a handful of other purple penstemon species in the region.

Towering Larkspur (*Delphinium glaucum; Ranunculaceae*) Also **Giant Delphinium** or **Sierra Larkspur**. Plate 10.

> 3–9 ft. tall. Leaves large mostly basal, deeply palmately lobed, tips jaggedly pointed. Flowers about 1 in. across, generally more than 50, purple, 5-petaled with rear spur, on long, indeterminate vertical spikes (often branched). Wet thickets, 5000–9500 ft. **POISONOUS.**

If you run into a giant herbaceous plant that towers over your head, chances are it is the Mountain Larkspur. These large members of the Buttercup Family are widespread and common in moist stream-side habitats. The genus name, *Delphinium*, refers to the dolphin-like shape of the flower buds (yes, this is a stretch). "Larkspur" is after the resemblance of the flower to a birds' foot—especially the long rear claw of the lark. Delphiniums are toxic and implicated in many instances of livestock poisoning.
Mountain Larkspur (*D. polycladon*) is slightly smaller (2–4 ft.), leaf lobes more rounded and has leaves on the lower fifth of the stem. **Nuttall's Larkspur** (*D. nuttallianum*), Plate 10, and—rarely—**Dwarf Larkspur** (*D. depauperatum*) are smaller (<2 ft.) species also found in our area.

Monkshood (*Aconitum columbianum;* Ranunculaceae) *Plate 10.*

> 1–6 ft. tall. Leaves large mostly basal, deeply palmately lobed, tips jaggedly pointed. Flowers about 1 in. long, purple, 5–petaled with large upper petal hood-like; on long, indeterminate vertical spikes (often branched). Wet thickets, 1800–9800 ft. **POISONOUS.**

The distinctive hooded flowers make this plant an easy identification when close-up, but it can be confused with larkspur at a distance. The flowers make perfect little hats for your finger or thumb—try drawing a face on your finger pad to enhance the imagination. Highly toxic.

Mountain Pennyroyal (*Monardella odoratissima pallida;* Lamiaceae) Also **Coyote Mint, Aromatic Monardella.** *Plate 11.*

> 1/2–2 ft. Stem square in cross-section, plant green with grayish cast. Leaves opposite, 1/2–2 in. long, ovate to lanceolate, strong minty odor when rubbed. Flowers in dense terminal heads about 1.5 inches across. Flowers white to light pinkish-purple, tiny (1/4–3/4 in. long) trumpets with two thin upper lobes and three thin lower lobes, 4 exserted stamens, calyx wooly. Dry montane forests and rocky slopes. 3300–10,000 ft.

The intense minty odor that emanates from the crushed leaves of this small plant makes it almost impossible to confuse it with any other.

Pennyroyal tea is an excellent accompaniment to sunrise over the Glen Alpine Valley. The tea is simple to make: simply use an entire stalk (or bouquet, depending on your desired strength) of pennyroyal to stir a mug of hot water for a minute, adding sugar if you like. When added to hot cocoa, this plant makes a mint-chocolate "nectar-of-the-gods." Pennyroyal leaves can also be stripped from the stalks and dried for future use. Only pick a few stalks where the plants are visibly thriving to keep your impact to a minimum. Never pick more than you will use. Keep in mind that harvesting plants is illegal in wilderness areas.

*WARNING: Pennyroyal tea is delicious, harmless, restorative and even promotes digestion and alleviates cold symptoms when used in moderation. However, it has been known to reduce milk flow and cause spontaneous abortions when taken in quantity (i.e. 20 cups a day).

Nettle-leaf Horsemint (*Agastache urticifolia;* Lamiaceae) Also **Giant Hyssop.** *Plate 11.*

> Usually many plants growing in close proximity, erect stems 2–4 ft. high. Dense terminal spikes of white to lavender, tubular, bilaterally symmetric flowers, each cupped by a purplish calyx. Four exserted stamens in two pairs, lower pair noticeably longer and spreading apart. Leaves opposite, angularly

heart-shaped with serrated margins, 1–4 in. long. Stems clearly four-sided (square in cross section). Crushed leaves have an earthy-musky mint odor. Widespread, esp. dry roadsides. Below 9,000 ft.

This plant displays the Mint Family's characteristics with exceptional clarity. The four-sided stem, opposite leaves and minty smell are all well-defined and conspicuous. The flowers are also typical: light-colored, tubular, bilaterally symmetrical and clustered in dense terminal heads.

The deeply serrated leaves and erect stems superficially resemble those of the Stinging Nettle, so be careful not to confuse the two. Nettle stems are covered in tiny hair-like needles and do not have obvious flowers. Horsemint stems are completely smooth. The largest patch around was formerly found on the east side of the road behind the Fallen Leaf Marina, right near the top of the hill.

This mint makes a fair addition to an herbal tea, but its smaller cousin, Pennyroyal, is far superior in both flavor and strength.

Lupine (*Lupinus* spp.; *Fabaceae*) Plate 11.

Bushes 1–5 feet tall with long spikes of purple-blue pea flowers. Widespread. **POISONOUS.**

As much as I would love to delve into the nearly thirty species of Lupine in the region, I am going to leave that to another flora. These plants owe their name to the misinformed notion that they robbed nutrients from the soil like a wolf (lupus). This idea could not be more incorrect: legumes colonize poor soils because they can obtain their own nitrogen through symbiotic associations with bacteria in their root nodules—and leave the soils richer than they were to start with. Lupines could be more accurately compared to wolves in that they both have the ability to kill livestock. Toxins present in lupines have earned some species the common name of "locoweed," because animals go crazy and die after eating them.

6 "PETALS" or "TEPALS" (petals & sepals which look the same)

Western Blue Flag (*Iris missouriensis; Iridaceae*) Plate 11.

1–2 1/2 ft. tall, perennial evergreen. Leaves parallel-veined, 1–3 ft. long. Flowers blue-purple-white-yellow, 3 sepals (lower "petals") & 3 erect petals alternating w/ shorter, 2–lobed petal-like styles which cover the stamens. Moist meadows up to 9000 ft.

Our only native iris, strikingly graceful and easy to identify. Appropriately, the genus is Greek for "rainbow." Although too bitter for even cattle to eat, iris leaves are very fibrous and tough and are used by many cultures for weaving strong baskets and other useful items.

Camas Lily (*Camassia quamash; Liliaceae*) *Plate 11.*

> 1/2–3 ft. tall. Perennial bulb. Leaves parallel-veined, 6–20 in. long. Flowers blue-purple (albinos possible), 6 "tepals." Moist meadows up to 8000 ft.

Camas and *quamash* are both translations of Native American words for one of the most important food plants for many Northwest tribes, including our local Washoe. The right to harvest certain fields of camas was often passed down matrilineally and these important sources of calories were carefully maintained by weeding out Death Camas and prescribed burning. The starchy bulbs were harvested in the fall and usually baked in underground rock-heated ovens overnight before being eaten, made into traveling cakes or bread, or dried for later use. Camas Lilies are not common in our watershed, but can be found in some of the lower, moister meadows.

MANY "PETALS"

Western Aster (*Aster occidentalis occidentalis; Asteraceae*) *Plate 11.*

> 1/2–2 ft. Leaves linearly obovate, 1–5 in. long. Composite flower with yellow disk flowers (center) and light lavender ray flowers (petal-like), one to a few "flowers" per plant. Open woods, alpine meadows, 4200–9000 ft.

Other species in our area include **Oregon Aster** (*Aster oregonensis*) and **Ascending Aster** (*Aster ascendens*). Members of the genus *Erigeron* are especially easy to confuse with Asters (see Wandering Daisy). If you find a mature plant, look at the pappus (the "parachute" of the seed): Asters have a single pappus, Erigerons have both an outer and inner pappus.

Wandering Daisy (*Erigeron peregrinus callianthemus; Asteraceae*)
Also **Fleabane Erigeron.**

> 1/2–2 ft. Leaves oblanceolate, 2–8 in. long, subclasping. Flower heads 1–4, flat-topped, yellow centers, light lavender ray flowers (petal-like). Alpine meadows, slopes, clearings. 4000–10,000 ft.

Other possible species of Erigeron include: **Sierra Daisy** (*E. algidus*), **Shining Daisy** (*E. barbellatus*), **Brewer's Daisy** (*E. breweri*), **Cut-leaf Daisy** (*E. compositus*) and **Coulter's Daisy** (*E. coulteri*).

2. Pink Flowers

4 PETALS

Fireweed (*Epilobium angustifolium circumvagum; Onagraceae*) Also **Willow-herb.** *Plate 12.*

> Widespread. Single erect reddish stem, 2–7 ft. high. Deep pink to purplish flowers bloom indeterminately all summer. Four-petaled with four linear bracts subtending. Stigmas appear as a curled white "X" on four fused styles, conspicuously longer than stamens and petals. Leaves 4–8 in. long, lanceolate.

Linear, 2–4 inch long fruits composed of four sections which split and curl upon maturity, releasing tiny seeds with small cottony tufts. Below 9000 ft.

Fireweed is an adept colonizer, its many tiny tufted seeds allowing for maximal wind dispersion. Somehow these tiny seeds are also extremely hardy—growing just about anywhere. Recently burned areas are often covered almost exclusively in thick stands of Fireweed, lending credibility to its common name. Fireweed, however, is not restricted to burned areas and commonly grows along roadsides, trail sides, mountain slopes and marshy areas.

The second common name refers to the willow-like leaves of the plant. These leaves turn bright red in the autumn as the plant casts its last seeds.

Survival books and edible plant manuals liken the stem to celery, but I have found it much too fibrous to be satisfying. The texture is more akin to a bundle of toothpicks and not something I would spread peanut butter on.

Smooth-stemmed Fireweed (*Epilobium glaberrimum glaberrimum; Onagraceae*) Also **Willow-herb.** *Plate 12.*

> 1–3 ft. Leaves 1/2–3 in. long, clasping, lanceolate. Flower <1/2 in. across, light pink-purple, 4 notched petals. Fruit a skinny capsule, 1–3 in. long, developing underneath flower. Gravely areas, 1800–9000 ft.

This is a scaled-down, leafier version of the previous fireweed. A few plants usually grow above Camp's lodge in the gravel drainage on the uphill side of the road. Other small fireweeds include: *E. ciliatum ciliatum, E. ciliatum glandulosum E. halleanum*, and *E. hornemannii hornemannii*.

Rockfringe (*Epilobium obcordatum; Onagraceae*) *Plate 12.*

> 3–8 in. Leaves 1/2–1 in. long, clasping, nearly round, grayish-blue-green. Flower 2 in. across, rosy-purple, 4 broad, notched (obcordate) petals. Fruit a skinny capsule, 1–2 in. long, developing underneath flower. Rocky slopes, 6000–10,000 ft.

These striking, showy flowers appear as bursts of color from beneath the rocks. Look for late in the season where the trail climbs up the talus bowl southeast of Mt. Tallac. The heart-shaped and Valentine-colored petals earn its specific epithet, *obcordatum*. A larger, leafier and rarer relative, **Broad-leaved Willow-herb**, *Epilobium latifolium*, also occurs in the wet, rocky seeps at our high elevations—its petals are not notched.

5 PETALS

Interior Rose (*Rosa woodsii ultramontana; Rosaceae*) Also **Mountain Rose.** *Plate 12.*

> Shrub with scattered prickles, 2–9 ft. tall. Leaves pinnate, leaflets usu. 5, elliptic, toothed, 1/2–2 in. long. Flower pink to white, about 2 in. across, 5 petals, many stamens. Fruit a reddish rose "hip," about 1/2 in. in diameter, 5 sepals still attached to top. Moist places. 2500–10,000 ft.

This is just about the only species of rose that one will run into in Desolation Wilderness. Among other places, these roses can be found along the Glen Alpine Trail north of Lily Lake. Wild roses always have five petals (cultivated varieties have been artificially bred and genetically altered to have many times that). The hips of all roses are edible and excellent sources of vitamin C. Because they are seedy, not too sweet and somewhat dry, these fruits are usually cooked, strained and made into jelly or tea.

Sierra Gooseberry (*Ribes roezlii roezlii; Grossulriaceae*) *Plate 12.*

> 1–3 ft. high. Flowers and spiny fruit (1/2–1 in. in diameter, green, ripening red) hang, often singly, on the underside of spiny stems. Sepals purple, reflexed; petals white. Leaves palmate, 3–5 lobed, smooth. Dry slopes, 3300–8000 ft.

Recently separated from the Saxifragaceae, the Gooseberry Family has only a single genus which now includes both gooseberries and currants. The basic distinction between the two is that gooseberries have spines and currants do not. We have about a half-dozen species of this family in our area.

The Sierra Gooseberry is our only common gooseberry, so if you stick your hand into a bush and get pricked, chances are you've found it. Red-tipped spines cover fruits that start green and ripen to dark red. The dried flowers often persist, hanging from the bottom of fruits. The berries are edible, but certainly hard to get into—this is one berry that is best left to the birds. (There is one plant in front of Spruce Cabin and a few more near the archery range and tennis courts.)

Sierra Currant (*Ribes nevadense; Grossulariaceae*)
Also **Mountain Pink Currant.** *Plate 13.*

> 2–7 ft. high. Flowers deep pinkish-red, bell-shaped, five-lobed, clustered in groups of 8–20, often nodding. Sepals pink as well. Fruit dark blue-black, 1/4–1/2 in., covered with a whitish bloom and scattered glandular hairs. Leaves palmate, 3–5 lobed, with veins indented, making the surface slightly bumpy. Streambanks and forest margins, 3300–9000 ft.

This species is one of our most prolific berry-producers. The berries ripen in August and September, offering themselves to animals of all kinds—humans included. After the white powder (a.k.a. "bloom") and glandular hairs are rubbed off the dark blue berries they make a nice little treat, albeit quite seedy.

In Europe, their dried currant (less seedy than our wild variety) often takes the place of our raisin and is commonly found in baked goods such as scones. Currant juice is also heavily marketed in Europe under the trade name of *Ribena* (after its Turkish genus name *Ribes*) and is very tasty—similar to our sweet, dark, cherry juice. Think about this plant next time you have a "black currant"-flavored soda or mineral water drink.

Sticky Currant (*Ribes viscosissimum; Grossulariaceae*). *Plate 13.*

> 1–4 ft. high. Flowers a light pink, tubular with five lobes, clustered in groups of 3–15, usually somewhat erect. Sepals greenish-yellow to pinkish. Mature fruit blue-black, 1/2 in. Leaves fuzzy, sticky, palmate, 3–5 lobed, with veins indented, making the surface slightly bumpy. Dry slopes, 4000–9000 ft.

Far less abundant around Fallen Leaf than the Sierra Currant, I have only encountered this species at the trail junction north of Cathedral Lake. Its sticky, glandular leaves and drier habitat make it easy to distinguish it from its relatively smooth-leaved and wet-footed cousin.

Pink Pyrola (*Pyrola asarifolia asarifolia; Ericaceae*). Also **Bog** or **Liverleaf Wintergreen.** *Plate 13.*

> Single straight stem, 6–20 in. high. Flowers pink, five-petaled, with conspicuously bent pistil extending well beyond petals. Flowers hang alternately from small pedicels along top half of stem. Leaves only at base of plant, round and leathery. Wet shady wooded areas, 3300–9000 ft.

This is one of the rare exotic-looking plants that cause fascination in even the most jaded hiker. The leaves are vaguely reminiscent of wild-ginger, hence *asarifolia*. Their pendulous pink blossoms often create polka-dot patterns under the shimmering shade of Quaking Aspens near Lily Lake.

Whisker Brush (*Linanthus ciliatus; Polemoniaceae*). Also **Linanthus.** *Plate 13.*

> Erect stems 2–8 in. high, covered with barely visible soft white hairs. Dense terminal head looks like a hairy white sphere with protruding green, linear, spikes. Flowers five-petaled, pink with yellow and white centers; reddish purple spots near each petal base. Tube 1/2–1 in. long, petal lobes appx. 1/4 in. long. Leaves (1/4–3/4 in. long) appear as regularly spaced linear whorls, but are in fact pairs of opposite, highly divided sessile leaves. Widespread, esp. open rocky fields. Below 9,000 ft.

Another belly-plant, the Whisker Brush is worth getting down for. The delicate pink flowers appear to be stuck into a ball of spikes, creating an incongruous image. If a magnifying glass is available, explore the patterns of pink, white, yellow and purple near the flower's center.

Whisker Brushes bloom late in the summer and are fairly common in the dry, rocky clearing at the highest point on Camp's Nature Trail.

Spreading Dogbane (*Apocynum androsaemifolium; Apocynaceae*)
Also **Bitter Dogbane.** *Plate 13.*

> 6–20 in. high. Many-branched prostrate plant with small clusters of pink, cup- or bell-shaped flowers with five reflexed lobes. Flowers 1/4–1/2 in. Leaves opposite, about 2 in. long, oval to roundly heart-shaped, tip sometimes with a small, spine-like projection. Milky sap. Found on forest floors and rocky open spaces. 4000–10,000 ft.

"Dogbane" is almost a direct translation of *Apocynum* (away-dog), referring to the historical use of this plant family as a canine poison. Even this species can prove to be a painful, purgative diuretic. The urban ornamental Oleander, Vinca and the tropical Plumeria (Frangipani) are also members of this toxic family.

Not being all bad, stems of this genus (esp. Indian Hemp, *A. cannabinum*) are exceptionally fibrous and were used extensively by Native Americans to make cords, nets and cloth. (**Important Note to the Experimentally-inclined**: the common name of "hemp" and the specific epithet, *cannabinum*, refer to the *fibrous* properties of these plants and <u>not</u> hallucinogenic ones. *Do not attempt to smoke this plant.* It is not at all related to *Cannabis sativa*: it will certainly not get you high and its toxins may even kill you.

Pink Alumroot (*Heuchera rubescens glandulosa; Saxifragaceae*). Also **Jack o' the Rocks**. *Plate 13.*

> Plants in clumps with numerous flowering stalks 6–20 in. high. Tiny white flowers with pink bases hang loosely around a central stalk. Leaves basal, lobed, roundish, 1/2–3 in. wide, on stalks 1/2–6 in. long. Dry rocky slopes. 5000–10,000 ft.

Alumroot gets its name from its bitter, astringent rhizomes. Touching your tongue to a cut root, this becomes readily apparent. These astringent properties allow it to be used as a styptic, helping to stop cuts from bleeding.

H. micrantha, more common at lower elevations, has also been documented in the Glen Alpine watershed.

Elephant's Head (*Pedicularis groenlandica; Scrophulariaceae*)
Plate 13.

> 3–24 in. high. Leaves mostly basal, 1–10 in. long, pinnately divided, serrate, dark green fading to red. Flowers pink, roughly shaped like an elephant (a curvy, tubular "trunk" flanked by 2 ear-like lobes), in spike-like racemes. Wet meadows and streamsides, 3200–10,000 ft.

Quite possibly the most intriguing flower shape found in our watershed, Elephant's Head is well-named. The flowers are shaped to accommodate a certain species of bumblebee which they depend upon for pollination. The upper stretch of the Tamarack Trail (between Lily and Triangle Lake) provides a good crop, but Mokelumne Wilderness has many more on the way to Winnemucca Lake. This plant has been used as a sedative, tranquilizer and muscular relaxant (read: danger) as well as an astringent and antiseptic for wounds.

Keep an eye out for **Little Elephant's Head** (*P. attollens*) too, which is hairier as well as smaller, with shorter trunks.

Mountain Pride (*Penstemon newberryi newberryi*; Scrophulariaceae) Also **Pride of the Mountain.** *Plate 14.*

> 5–12 in. high. Deep rosy pink, tubular flowers bloom June through July. Flower bilaterally symmetric, five-petaled: three lower, two upper. Flower tube floor short-hairy. Leaves oval, dark green, margins serrated. Rocky granitic slopes in clumps or mats. 4200–10,000 ft.

Mountain Pride, when seen from a distance, is often confused with California Fuchsia (Red, 4-petaled) since they both grow on dry slopes, form mats and have a reddish, trumpet-shaped flower. However, if you know what month it is, a lot of the guesswork disappears: Mountain Pride flowers in June and July while California Fuchsia does not bloom until mid-August. There are many ways to tell them apart if you are close up, but using the calendar is sufficient 99 percent of the time—and even works from the car.

This clear division of flowering times for these two plants is not as random as one may think. They are similar-looking for one very good reason—they both use the same pollinators. If both plants flowered at the same time, there would be a lot of pollen wasted on the wrong species when the hummingbirds went back and forth between the two species. Having each species flower at a totally separate time eliminates this competition and benefits both species equally, as well as their common pollinator: hummingbirds.

Note: it is possible to find other species of less-common penstemons in Desolation Wilderness—do not try to force all of them to fit this description.

Lewis's Monkeyflower (*Mimulus lewisii*; Scrophulariaceae) *Plate 14.*

> 1–3 ft. high. Light pink, trumpet-shaped, bilaterally symmetric flowers, 1–2 in. long. Five squarish lobes with darker pink central lines—two lobes bent up above center, three bent down below. Throat hairy, yellow. Leaves elliptic, 1–3 in. long, 3–5 main veins, clasping stem. Streamsides and seeps. 4000–9000 ft.

Possibly one of the most delicate flowers of Desolation Wilderness, Lewis' Monkeyflower is most abundant on wet, rocky cliffs. Accordingly, the Tamarack Trail is consistently the best place to encounter it.

This genus, *Mimulus* (mime or mimic), as well as its common name, Monkeyflower, refer to the flat, face-like corolla of the blossoms. (Few people are able to see this resemblance, so if you can, count yourself as gifted.)

Brewer's Monkeyflower (*Mimulus breweri*; *Scrophulariaceae*) *Plate 14.*

> Masses of tiny plants, 1–3 in. high. Tiny purple-pink, trumpet-shaped, bilaterally symmetric flowers, appx. 1/4 in. long. Five notched lobes—two lobes bent up above center, three bent down below. Purple spot on tube edge of lower middle lobe. Throat hairy, yellow. Leaves linear, 1/4–1 in. long. Wet soils and seepage areas. 4000–9000 ft.

This Monkeyflower is a true "belly-plant," meaning you have to get down on your belly to see it. The only patch of these I have noticed is at the north end of the Nature Trail (where the boat trailers are kept near Witch's Pond). Bring a magnifying glass—it's neat to see a Monkeyflower on such a miniature scale.

Mountain Spiraea (*Spiraea densiflora*; *Rosaceae*) *Plate 14.*

> 1–3 ft. Flowers pink, in flat-topped, fuzzy-looking terminal umbels. Individual flowers tiny, five-petaled, stamens exceeding petals (creating fuzzy appearance). Leaves ovate, slightly toothed at apex, alternate along smooth green to red stems. Coniferous forests and rocky areas, 2000–10,000 ft.

One might not believe that these fluffy pink masses on smooth stems belong to the Rose Family, but closer examination reveals the typical characteristics of wild roses: five petals and many stamens. This genus has been in cultivation for quite a while and nurseries sell many cultivated varieties as ornamentals.

Sierra Shooting Star (*Dodecatheon jeffreyi*; *Primulaceae*) *Plate 14.*

> 1/2–1 ft. Leaves oblanceolate, basal, 3–15 in. long. Flowers nodding, 5 petals reflexed backwards: petals yellow at base, white in the middle and pink at the tips. Stamens in a tight, exserted cluster with style protruding from center. Stem covered with glandular hairs. Moist meadows and streambanks, 1800–9000 ft.

This large shooting star intergrades with its smaller (2–6 in. tall), hairless relative the **Alpine Shooting Star** (*D. alpinum*), which also occurs in Desolation Wilderness above 7800 feet. The genus means "twelve gods," apparently implying the flower's beauty makes it fit for not one, but twelve Olympian gods.

Mountain Snowberry (*Symphoricarpos rotundifolius* var. *rotundifolius*; *Caprifoliaceae*) Also **Waxberry.**

> 1–4 ft. high. Flowers elongated bells (1/4–1/2 in. long) with five round lobes: deep pink as buds but blooming whitish pink; hanging in pairs from leaf axils. White berries 1/4–1/2 in. across. Leaves opposite, 1–2 in. long, elliptic to a rounded diamond-shape, sometimes mildly lobed. Rocky slopes and forest openings, 4000–10,000 ft.

Sometimes approaching a small shrub in shape and size, the Mountain Snowberry is a little more noticeable than its vine-like relatives. Both flowers and fruit can catch the eye of the wary hiker. Snowberries have been likened to popcorn, but only in appearance: their taste is repugnant and may have adverse health effects. Birds and rodents, however, eat them with regularity.

Creeping Snowberry (*Symphoricarpos mollis; Caprifoliaceae*). Also **Waxberry** or **Trip Vine**. *Plate 14.*

> 1/2–1 ft. high, sprawling. Flowers bells (≤1/4 in. long) with five round lobes: deep pink as buds but blooming whitish pink; hanging from leaf axils. White berries about 1/4 in. across. Leaves opposite, 1/4–1 in. long, elliptic to a rounded diamond-shape, sometimes mildly lobed. Slopes and woodland openings, up to 8000 ft.

Very similar to Mountain Snowberry, but is smaller, has a more prostrate creeping habit and much shorter flowers: lobes = 1/2 of tube length (compared to 1/4–1/3 in *S. rotundifolius*).

Alpine Laurel (*Kalmia polifolia microphylla; Ericaceae*) *Plate 14.*

> 3–9 inches tall, perennial evergreen. Leaves ovate, margins in-rolled, <1 in. long. Flowers pink, 5 petals fused into a shallow cup-like pentagram, <1 in. across, 10 stamens. Bogs & sheltered rocky areas above 8000 ft.

One of our most precious alpine plants, these tiny flowers have a friendly, disarming quality about them. This must help lure in insects which either do not suspect or do not care that the blossoms are booby-trapped. The shallow bowls of these pink pentagrams hold their stamens cocked back in tiny pockets, ready to spring forward at the slightest disturbance and shower the visitor with pollen.

Red Heather (*Phyllodoce breweri; Ericaceae*) *Plate 14.*

> 5–9 inches tall, perennial evergreen. Leaves needle-like, < 1 in. long. Flowers pink, 5 petals, < 1 in. across, 10 stamens are much longer than petals. Moist & shaded rocky areas above 6000 ft.

Another darling plant that forms mats in our higher elevations, this species is notable because of its strongly exserted stamens—they stick out way beyond the petals, and there are twice as many of them. From a distance, this makes the flowers look like they have special halos, similar to the way children draw the sun with rays of straight lines radiating outwards.

White or **Alpine Heather** (*Cassiope mertensiana*) is also in this family but in a completely different genus. It is of similar size, stature and habitat, but has tiny white bells with red caps (formed by the calyx) that hang from red pedicels above almost moss-like stems with tiny, scale-like leaves.

6 "PETALS" or "TEPALS" (petals & sepals which look the same)

Swamp Onion (*Allium validum; Liliaceae*) *Plate 15.*

> 1–3 ft. high. Dense terminal heads of pinkish purple six-petaled flowers. Stamens longer than petals. Leaves long (1–3 ft.) and flat, smelling of onion when crushed. Grows in thick stands on wet soils, 4000–10,000 ft.

The Swamp Onion's name is well-deserved: it is an onion and it lives in swampy environs. While lacking the large bulb of a stereotypical "onion," this onion is a superior substitute for our market-variety green onion. The Swamp Onion leaf has a much more delicate, nonintrusive flavor and is a welcome addition to salads, trout and vegetable dishes while on the trail. The flower clusters also serve as beautiful edible garnishes. The Swamp Onion is prolific and hardy (especially along Camp's Nature Trail), so don't hesitate to sprinkle a chopped leaf or two on your baked potato.

Sierra Onion (*Allium campanulatum; Liliaceae*) *Plate 15.*

> 2–6 in. high. Loose spheres of pink-tipped, six-petaled flowers on thin stalks. Stamens about equal to or shorter than petals. Leaves basal. Only one pair of long (3–8 in.), flat leaves that dry up almost before flowering. Found singly or in loose groups on dry, rocky soils. 2000–9,000 ft.

This plant grows from a miniature version (1/4–1/2 in. across) of our typical onion bulb. It definitely tastes like an onion, but it would take about a hundred of these to equal the mass of a single grocery store variety. Unlike the Swamp Onion, harvesting the edible portion of this plant ends its life. Therefore, I urge restraint in collecting.

The Sierra Onion is also favored as a tasty treat by rodents, raccoons and other animals. They are good sources of vitamin C (if you weigh less than a pound).

MANY "PETALS" (or number of petals difficult to determine)

Pink Pussy-toes (*Antennaria rosea rosea; Asteraceae*)
Also **Rosy Everlasting.** *Plate 15.*

> 4–16 in. tall. Leaves basal and along stem, linear to spoon-shaped, 1/4–2 in. long, grayish with hair. Flower heads elongated, red-edged with white white centers, appx. 6–20 clustered at the end of each stem. Open woods, meadow edges and rocky areas. 3900–10,000 ft.

Pussy-toes are so named because their upright, elongated flower heads resemble small feline digits. The term "everlasting" refers to the non-wilting quality of their papery petal-like structures. These two species are fairly easy to tell apart because of their differently colored heads.

Pussypaws (*Calyptridium umbellatum; Portulacaceae*) *Plate 15.*

> 1-6 in. high. Dense terminal heads of pinkish-white flower clumps. Hard to single out any one flower (need 20X magnification). Leaves in basal rosettes, oblanceolate to spoon-shaped, 1-3 in. Open sandy to rocky soils, 5000-10,000 ft. (At 300-600 ft. and 3X larger in the San Francisco Bay area).

A common "weed," Pussypaws can be seen from the rocky prominence at the mouth of Glen Alpine Creek all the way up to Dick's Pass. Just because it is considered a weed by some does not mean it is boring.

This plant actually has a daily cycle of movement. The flower clusters and leaves rise and fall with the sun: the closer to noon, the more vertical the plant. During the night the plant lies prostrate against the ground. This movement depends on turgor pressure: the hotter it is, the more the internal liquids expand, the more rigid the stem becomes. Probable benefits from this action include less water loss through the leaves during the hottest part of the day (since the sun's rays do not intersect perpendicularly with the leaf and they are raised above the hot surface), as well as increased visibility of the blossoms to better attract diurnal insect pollinators.

Anderson's Thistle (*Cirsium andersonii; Asteraceae*) *Plate 15.*

> 2-4 feet tall, perennial. Leaves lanceolate, dentate, spiny, 3-12 in. long. Stems gen. lacking spines. Flower heads purplish-pink, columnar. Dry slopes and open forests. 4500-9500 ft.

Unlike most thistles, Anderson's purplish-pink flower heads appear columnar or test-tube shaped, with nearly straight sides, even when in full bloom. Another native thistle that can be seen all the way up to near the top of Mt. Tallac is Elk Thistle (*Cirsium scariosum*)—usually a ground-hugging rosette of leaves with pale cream-colored flower heads in the middle, appearing like furry eggs in a spiny nest. The non-native Bull Thistle (*Cirsium vulgare*) has more hemispherical purple flowers, spiny stems and could be found in disturbed areas or along roadsides at our lowest elevations.

3. Red Flowers

5 PETALS

Snow Plant (*Sarcodes sanguinea; Ericaceae*) *Plate 15.*

> Flowering stalk thick, deep red, 4-12 in. high. Flowers in a dense raceme, each flower having five petals. Coniferous forest floors with deep duff, 3300-10,000 ft.

The botanical name describes the Snow Plant quite well: *Sarcodes* means fleshy and *sanguinea*, blood, after its blood-red, fleshy flowering stalk. This member of the Heath Family approaches life from a unique angle. Instead of relying on photosynthesis to manufacture its food, it is saprophytic. A saprophyte [*sapro* = rotten, *phyte* = plant] is often described as a vascular plant that lives off of decaying organic matter much like a mushroom.

However, the truth of the matter is that most saprophytes do not just act like fungi, they are actually connected to fungi—technically making them more of a parasite. The fungi, in turn is connected to at least one larger photosynthetic plant (such as a tree). The end effect is that the "saprophyte" uses the fungi as a kind of straw—siphoning nutrients from the tree's root system (making the "saprophyte" actually more of an epi- or hyper-parasite). (*Keep in mind this three-tiered model is an extremely over-simplified model of a vast mycorrhizal network involving hundreds to billions of organisms and not just three.*)

Popular thought is that, in the original arrangement, all three organisms benefited from each other. Then, over a very long period of time, evolutionary mutations caused the small plant to "realize" that it could freeload off the fungi and tree without paying for the ride. Consequently, the plant "lost" chlorophyll, functional leaves, root hairs and other no longer necessary organs, becoming a pale (or red) blob. Another sad victim of TV, you might think. But some scientists are currently researching possible stimulatory effects of non-green plants on fungi—it may be that these unusual plants are contributing members of society after all...(as if feeding hummingbirds was not enough already).

The Snow Plant's unusual lifestyle affords it a couple of formidable advantages:

- Since no chlorophyll is necessary, the whole plant can be red—a much more visible and attractive beacon for pollinators such as hummingbirds. This is especially important because the plant would otherwise be difficult to spot on the shadowy forest floor.

- As the snow plant does not rely upon sunlight for growth, it can sprout up through the snow in the early spring before there is enough light for most other plants to begin growing (hence the common name). Being one of the first flowers to bloom in early spring greatly decreases the competition for pollinators—effectively forming a monopoly on nectar and increasing the chances for successful inter-individual pollination.

Pine Drops (*Pterospora andromedea; Ericaceae*) *Plate 15.*

Flowering stalk brown to red, 1/2 in. thick, 1–5 ft. high. Flowers in a raceme, cream-colored, urn-shaped, pendant, with five lobes. Coniferous forest floors below 10,000 ft.

As the common name implies, this saprophyte grows under conifers. The reason for its close association with these large trees is that it taps into the same mycorrhizal/root network mentioned in the discussion of the Snow Plant. The genus name is a reference to its large-winged seeds. Pine Drops are commonly found on coniferous forest floors, especially on the way up to Angora Lakes.

California Fuchsia (*Epilobium canum latifolium; Onagraceae*). Also **Hummingbird's Trumpet** or **Zauschneria**. *Plate 16.*

> 5–20 in. high. Leaves elliptical, dull grayish-green, covered with tiny hairs. Bright scarlet flowers bloom mid-August to late September. Four-petaled, each one notched. Stigma conspicuously longer than styles and petals. Found on dry slopes, forming clumps or mats. 1600–10,000 ft.

The California Fuchsia does share the Evening Primrose Family with the popular tropical fuchsias, but is more closely related (same genus) to our Fireweed. Historically this plant was placed in its own genus, *Zauschneria*, but recent studies have placed it in the genus *Epilobium*.

From a distance, this flower can be easily confused with the Mountain Pride. (See Mountain Pride, page 52, for distinguishing factors.)

The California Fuchsia's other common name, Hummingbird's Trumpet, is well deserved for four distinct reasons:

- The color of the flower is arguably the best shade of red for attracting hummers (compare it with commercial feeders).
- The shape of the flower—a long, narrow tube—excludes most other nectivores (i. e. bumblebees) from accessing its sweet juice.
- It blooms in late summer, a time when very few other species are still flowering.
- This time also corresponds to the hummingbirds' fall migration—when they need calories the most.

Not only do these four factors help the birds, but they also help the plant —yet another example of cooperation in nature. The many limiting factors decrease competition and basically assure the plant that the same pollinator will go to the same species of plant, one after another, pollinating each flower in the right place with the right kind of pollen.

Traditional medicine used this plant to make a wash which was applied to cuts and bruises to promote healing.

Scarlet Gilia (*Ipomopsis aggregata; Polemoniaceae*) *Plate 16.*

> 1–3 ft. high. Flowers deep scarlet red (Fallen Leaf) or light pink (Winnemucca), trumpet-shaped (tube about 1 in. long) with five acutely pointed petals. Stamens and style are significantly longer than the tube. Leaves 1–2 in. long,

skinny and pinnate: 9–11 lobed at base of plant, 5–7 lobed along stem. Open montane shrublands, 4000–9000 ft.

A separate and distinct salmon to purplish-pink population, recently elevated to its own species, **Lavendar Gilia**, *I. tenuituba*, has stamens and a style that are fully contained within the tube. These species were historically included in the *Gilia* genus and members of *Ipomopsis* are still (now erroneously) referred to as "Gilias."

Crimson Columbine (*Aquilegia formosa*; Ranunculaceae) Plate 16.

1–3 ft. high. Leaves in threes, those most heavily lobed at the base of the plant. Flower pendulous and nodding: five reddish-orange hollow spur petals point straight up, yellow-tipped underneath; five reddish-orange petal-like sepals radiating out in the horizontal plane from between spurs; many stamens protruding out of bottom, clumped into a column. Moist meadows and shady areas below 10,000 ft.

This genus owes its name to the hollow spurs which give the flowers and "inside-out" type of appearance. The taxonomist who first named the genus thought they resembled the talons of an eagle (in Latin, *Aquila*).

The unique appearance of this flower makes it readily identifiable and hard to confuse with anything else. The young leaves of the columbine are supposedly edible as a boiled green, but toughen and turn distasteful with age.

Rosey Sedum (*Sedum roseum integrifolium*; *Crassulaceae*). Also **Rosewort**. *Plate 16.*

Succulent, 2–12 in. high; many erect, fleshy and leafy stems. Leaves succulent, obovate, mildly serrated distal end, sometimes with red tip. Flowers densely clumped at the tops; tiny (1/4 in.), red, five-petaled with conspicuous stamens. Dry rocky areas, 5900–10,000 ft.

The Stonecrop Family is aptly named as its succulent species are well-adapted to growing in the dry microhabitats of rocky crevices. Their simple survival strategy involves hoarding. They only grow during the brief period in the spring when they get doused with snowmelt and their leaves and stem swell to store water. When the available water runs out, the plant stops its vegetative growth and uses the stored water to bloom and fruit during the summer. Evaporation would pose a grave threat if other plants attempted this. Stonecrops, however, have a very thick, waxy coating on their leaves which acts as an almost impenetrable barrier to water vapor. Additionally, the general plumpness of the stems and leaves minimize the surface to volume ratio, further decreasing the rate of possible transpiration.

Most other stonecrops are yellow, so this species is relatively easy to identify.

6 "PETALS" or "TEPALS" (petals & sepals which look the same)

Spotted Coralroot (*Corallorhiza maculata*; Orchidaceae) *Plate 16.*

> 6–22 in. tall. Stems red to yellow or brown, Flowers in a raceme, each with six "petals:" upper five alike, reddish-brown, darkest at tips; lower "lip" largest, pale with maroon spots. (see Illustrated Glossary, Orchid Parts).

Another common saprophyte, this orchid owes its common name to the spotted lower lip of its flowers and its coral-like root structure. Orchid seeds are so small (i.e. Vanilla "bean" seeds) that they require fungal assistance and nurturing just to germinate. (One Spotted Coralroot sometimes grows across the road from the Lodgepole Pine cabins at Camp.)

4. Orange Flowers

Giant Paintbrush (*Castilleja miniata miniata*; Scrophulariaceae). Also Indian Paintbrush or Castilleja. *Plate 16.*

> Several unbranching stems, 1–3 ft. high. Leaves green, lanceolate, clasping reddish-brown stem of plant, becoming orange to red-tipped and rarely three-pronged when subtending flowers. Bracts usually reddish-orange and acutely tipped; often mistaken for petals. Flower hidden, yellow, tubular. Open meadows and moist areas, 5000–10,000 ft.

At least a half-dozen species of paintbrush grow in our area, but this is the most common around Fallen Leaf. Other species include: **Applegate's Paintbrush**, *Plate 16,* (*C. applegatei*, with oranger, more rounded bracts), **Small-flowered Paintbrush** (*C. parviflora*, a mini version of Giant), **Alpine Paintbrush** (*C. nana*, a small, greenish-yellow, owl-cloverish one) and **Hairy Paintbrush** (*C. pilosa*, with rounded, white-rimmed purple bracts). A couple of the rarer species in our area are **Frosty Paintbrush** (*C. pruinosa*, very hairy and orange-bracted) and **Lemmon's Paintbrush** (*C. lemmonii*, a small reddish-purple or fuchsia-colored one).

The genus Castilleja is named after Domingo Castillejo, a Spanish botanist, and is usually pronounced "cast-eh-lay-ha" (some people even retain the "ll" = "y" pronunciation). Many wildflower enthusiasts use this genus as a common name. This practice is common because the genus as a whole is easily recognizable, but the individual species (± 200) are incredibly difficult to tell apart. (Unless you have masochistic tendencies and a lot of extra time on your hands, I highly recommend the genus-oriented approach.)

Many species of the Snapdragon (or Figwort) Family are hemi-parasites on other plants, and the Giant Paintbrush is no exception. Paintbrushes appear to favor tapping into the roots of grasses and members of the Sunflower Family (i.e. sagebrush) in particular.

6 "PETALS" or "TEPALS" (petals & sepals which look the same)

Sierra Tiger Lily *(Lilium parvum; Liliaceae).* Also **Alpine Lily** or **Little Tiger Lily**. *Plate 16.*

> Erect, 2–6 ft. high. Leaves lanceolate, in whorls of about 2–6. Flower buds nodding, raising to horizontal or erect when in bloom. "Petals" (tepals) are deep orange at the tips, fading to yellow, then green at the base; scattered with small dark spots. Stamens six, anthers brownish with pollen. Streamsides, wet meadows. 6000–9000 ft.

This lily has many common names, all of them somewhat inappropriate. It is not striped like a tiger nor is it restricted to alpine habitats. If one were to compare it to a big cat, a cheetah might be the closest (another species, not in our area, is named Leopard Lily: also closer). At any rate, our orange lilies with dark spots have been traditionally been called tiger lilies. They are abundant in the marshy areas along Camp's Nature Trail and other wet areas.

Although somewhat bitter, the bulbs of tiger lilies were common in the diet of many Native American tribes.

5. Yellow Flowers

4 PETALS

Hooker's Evening Primrose *(Oenothera elata hirsutissima; Onagraceae).* Previously *O. hookeri angustifolia. Plate 17.*

> Single stem, 3–6 ft. tall. Leaves lanceolate, 2–8 in. long. Flower 3–4 in. across, yellow, 4 petals, 8 stamens, X-shaped stigma, inferior ovary tube and sepals reddish. Moist places below 9000 ft.

Due to a scientific name change, the common name "Hooker's Evening Primrose" is no longer proper and should be changed to "Wine-scented Tall Very Hairy Evening Primrose." On second thought, maybe the late botanist Hooker deserves the continued honor.

Sierra Wallflower *(Erysimum capitatum perrene; Brassicaceae).* Previously *E. perrene* Also **Western Wallflower**. *Plate 17.*

> Erect stem 1/2–2 ft. tall. Leaves linear to spatulate, 1–4 in. long. Flowers yellow, 1/2–1 in. across, 4 petals, bunched at the top of the plant. Rocky slopes, 6300–10,000 ft.

One of the more well-known denizens of the Sierra Nevada, this Mustard Family member is a beautiful sign that you are in the high country.

5 PETALS

Shrubby Cinquefoil *(Potentilla fruticosa; Rosaceae).* Also **Bush Cinquefoil**. *Plate 17.*

> 1–4 ft. tall. Leaves pinnate, <1in. long; leaflets 3–7 narrow, hairy, appx. 1/2 in.

long. Twigs reddish. Flowers about 1in. across, solid yellow, 5 petals, many stamens. Rocky environments, 6500–10,000 ft.

This is the only member of the *Potentilla* genus that has an almost woody, bush-like growth form. This genus shares the same Latin root with our word "potent," a reference to the medicinal value of some of its European species. "Cinquefoil" is French for "five-leaf" and also describes European species (our cinquefoils do not always have five leaflets). The Shrubby Cinquefoil is hard to miss when sprinkled with its definitively yellow blooms. Tamarack Trail has a pretty healthy population on the rocky ledges about a third of the way up.

Sticky Cinquefoil (*Potentilla glandulosa; Rosaceae*) Plate 17.

1/2–2 ft. Leaves pinnate, 1–12 in. long; leaflets 3–11 (usually 5–9), obovate, toothed, 1/4–3 in. long, tip leaflet largest. Flowers generally <1 in. across, 5 petals, white to yellow, center darkest yellow. Widespread below 10,000 ft.

The sticky, glandular hairs earn this species its specific common & scientific names. See Shrubby Cinquefoil for generic information. Although common in many habitats and elevations, the individuals at the north end of Camp's Nature Trail get the most attention.

Graceful Cinquefoil (*Potentilla gracilis; Rosaceae*) Plate 17.

1/2–2 ft. Leaves palmate; leaflets 3–7, oblanceolate, toothed, 1/2–5 in. long. Flowers generally <1in. across, solid yellow, 5 petals. Widespread, 500–9000 ft.

This plant's palmate leaves are similar in appearance to those found on hemp hats, shirts with "Maui Wowie" on them and "Legalize Pot!" bumper stickers. Do not, however, judge a book by its cover—this leaf has no known hallucinogenic properties, nor is it related to *Cannabis sativa*.

A related plant, *Potentilla diversifolia diversifolia*, is also found in Desolation Wilderness above 8000 feet.

Bird's-foot Lotus (*Lotus oblongifolius oblongifolius; Fabaceae*) Plate 17.

Erect or sprawling stems 1–3 ft. long. Leaves pinnate, leaflets 7–11, narrowly oblong to elliptic, 1/4–1 in. long, tips acutely pointed to spinescent. Flowers in half-circle groups of 2–6, typical Pea Family shape, about 1/2 in. long, upper banner solid yellow, lower wings and keel mostly white. Fruit long, thin beans (1/16–1/8 in. wide, 1–2 in. long). Open forests and streamsides, 1000–8500 ft.

This charming member of the Pea Family owes its common name to the unique shape and grouping of its fruit: the long, thin, mature pea-pods radiate outwards in a horizontal plane to create a pattern similar to that of a bird's foot. The striking yellow and white blossoms may catch your eye as you pass above Camp's main lodge.

A similar small, low, prostrate species is **Sierra Nevada Lotus** (*Lotus nevadensis nevadensis*), which has solid yellow petals backed with red.

Seep-Spring Monkeyflower (*Mimulus guttatus*; Scrophulariaceae)
Plate 17.

> 1–15 in. tall. Leaves opposite, elliptic, 1/4–3 in. long. Flower yellow, bilaterally symmetric: two upper lobes, three lower; throat hairy, often red-spotted; stigma divided into two lobes which slowly fold together when touched. Intergrades with **Mountain Monkeyflower** (*Mimulus tilingii*). Wet places, 5000–10,000 ft.

This common yellow snapdragon inhabits numerous seeps, streamsides, waterfalls and meadows throughout the mountains of western North America. One of the more interesting experiments to perform on this plant is to tickle its stigma (the small, pale, bi-lobed apparatus residing directly below the middle of the upper two lobes of the flower). In response to this tactile stimulation (normally performed by a pollen-bearing insect), the lobes begin to fold together. By closing its pollen-receiving apparatus directly after the incoming insect brushes it, the plant lowers the likelihood of self-pollination when the insect emerges from the throat of the flower bathed in that plant's own pollen. Cross-pollination is often more evolutionarily advantageous than self-pollination, especially in constantly changing environments.

Plantain Leaf Buttercup (*Ranunculus alismifolius*; Ranunculaceae)
Plate 18.

> 3–5 stems from base, 2–8 in. tall. Leaves lanceolate, 1–5 in. long. Flower petals usually 5, but can have as many as 8, shiny yellow; stamens and pistils many. Wet places, meadows and coniferous forests. 4000–10,000 ft.

The linear leaves of this buttercup resemble those of the Water Plantains (genus *Alisma*), providing both the common and scientific names. Since few other buttercups share this trait, identification is fairly straightforward. The shiny golden petals help place it into the *Ranunculus* genus right off the bat. The genus is literally translated as "little frog," after the moist habitats in which most of its species thrive.

Western Sweet Cicely (*Osmorhiza occidentalis*; Apiaceae).
Also **Western Sweet Root.** *Plate 18.*

> 1–4 ft. Leaves pinnately compound (2–pinnate or ternate), 1/2–2 ft. long; leaflets 1–4 in. long, ovate, serrate, often irregularly cut or lobed, aromatic. Flowers in delicate, spacious umbels; tiny yellow-green flowers. Forests and woodlands, 1000–9000 ft.

A somewhat delicate-looking member of the Celery/Carrot Family, the aromatic leaves of Western Sweet Cicely are often its best identifier. Found along at the first bend of Angora Trail, just above the church. The name Sweet Cicely was originally given to an aromatic European plant, *Myrrhis odorata*, but is now used to refer to species of the genus *Osmorhiza* as well.

Sulfur Flower (*Eriogonum umbellatum polyanthum; Polygonaceae*)
Low shrub or spreading mat, 4–24 in. high. Leaves spatulate, 1/4–2 in. long, covered in tiny white hairs. Flowers yellow (aging reddish), on the end of erect stalks in umbel-like heads 1–3 in. across; each flower 1/8–1/4 in. across, 6 lobes, 9 exserted stamens. Rocky slopes, 1000–10,000 ft.

Eriogonum is Latin for "wooly knees" and refers to the hair at the nodes of some species. The common name is a result of the bright yellow flowers. This species of wild buckwheat is common, especially on the rocky talus slopes on either end of Camp's Nature Trail.

Sierra Stonecrop (*Sedum obtusatum obtusatum; Crassulaceae*)
Plate 18.

2–8 in. tall. Leaves thick and succulent, about 1/4–1 in. long, often tinged red, covered with white powder, along stems and in basal rosettes 1/2–3 in. in diameter. Flowers clustered on erect stalks, usually 5 petals (sometimes with red centers or midveins. Rocky outcrops, 4000–10,000 ft.

Stonecrops are aptly named, almost always growing in a rocky crevice. Their succulent, tough-skinned leaves allow them to miraculously store water under both extremes of temperature without significant evaporation or crystallization.

Woolly Mullein (*Verbascum thapsus; Scrophulariaceae*) Plate 18.
3–6 feet tall, biennial. Leaves furry, soft, broadly lanceolate, 2–18 inches long. Flowers yellow, 5–petaled, 1 in. across, blooming randomly within a densely-packed raceme. Roadsides and disturbed areas below 8000 ft.

This Eurasian weed is commonly found along dusty roadsides and disturbed gravelly areas. In Latin, mullein means "soft," *Verbascum* means "bearded" and *thapsus* is the name of the plant. It has a long history of use by humans as medicine (often for treating ailments of the airways) and the absorbent leaves were used as wicks for candles or torches.

Pine Violet (*Viola pinetorum pinetorum; Violaceae*) Plate 18.
2–5 in. high. Leaves basal, blades ovate to linear, 2–6 in. long, slightly toothed or at least wavy-margined, scattered with minute white hairs. Flowers held singly on an erect stalks. Flowers with 5 yellow petals: top pair, side pair, single lower lip; bottom 3 purple-veined. Dry coniferous forests. 5000–9000 ft.

This cheery species is found in the dry, shady forests throughout our watershed, but it is not the only one possible. A couple other options are **Baker's Violet** (*Viola bakeri*) which has smooth leaf margins and **Mountain Violet** (*Viola purpurea*) which has dark, purple veins on its leaves and all petals. In lower, wetter, shadier riparian areas, look for the common yellow **Stream Violet** (*Viola glabella*) which has smooth, heart-shaped leaves with serrated margins.

6 "PETALS" or "TEPALS" (petals & sepals which look the same)

Prettyface (*Triteleia ixoides anilina; Liliaceae*). Also **Golden Stars**. *Plate 18.*

> 3–12 in. high. Leaves thin, basal, grass-like, 8–16 in. long, often withered before flowers bloom. Flowers yellow, in umbels, each appearing six-petaled with purple lines running down the center of each petal. Forest edges, in sandy soils, below 10,000 ft.

These striking little flowers are often seen while hiking the Mid-Tallac Trail in July and August, scattered throughout the dry, open woods southeast of Gilmore Lake.

MANY PETALS, SEPALS or TEPALS

Yellow Pond-lily (*Nuphar polysepala; Nymphaeaceae*).
(Previously *Nuphar lutea polysepala & Nuphar luteum polysepalum*.)
Also **Cow-lily, Indian Pond-lily.** *Plate 18.*

> 1–3 feet tall, sprouting from a perennial rhizome at the bottom of a pond. Leaf blades float on top of the water, shaped like an elongated heart at the end of a long petiole. Flowers a deep, rich yellow, 2–4 inches across, 7–9 yellow petal-like sepals. Shallow ponds below 8000 ft.

These bright pots of gold float on the surface of small, shallow, quiet ponds like the one on the side of the trail on your way up to Cathedral Lake. *Nuphar* is the Arabic name for pond lily, *luteum* references the yellow color and *polysepala* means "many-sepaled"—important because those yellow sepals are what we perceive as petals from a distance. (The petals themselves look more like stamens.)

The only other pond lily in our area is the non-native **White Waterlily** (*Nymphaea odorata*) which was somehow introduced to both Lake Lucille and Lake Margery. It can be beautiful and fragrant, but is also listed as a Noxious Weed due to its ability to clog waterways.

Large-flowered Brickellbush (*Brickellia grandiflora; Asteraceae*)
Plate 18.

> 1–3 feet tall, sprouting from a perennial woody caudex. Leaves usually op-

posite, triangular, serrated. petiole short to none. Flowers a light greenish or whitish yellow, heads about 1/2 in. across, 1 in. long; no petal-like ray flowers. Rocky open forests below 8500 ft.

Not a showy flower, but very common around the southern shore of Fallen Leaf Lake and in the rocky areas bordering Glen Alpine Creek. In Camp, it is abundant in the rocky area between the boat dock and the staff cabins. John Brickell was a botanist who did most of his work in Georgia.

Canada Goldenrod (*Solidago canadensis elongata; Asteraceae*) *Plate 19.*

2–4 feet tall, perennial. Leaves lanceolate, 3–veined, margins toothed, 2–6 in. long, longest at mid-stem. Flowers yellow, many heads clustered in a dense panicle. Open woods and meadow edges below 8000 ft.

A late-blooming, showy and well-known species, many who suffer from pollen allergies curse this genus (despite the fact it means "make-well" in Greek). We probably also have **California Goldenrod** (*Solidago californica*), which has fuzzy leaves which are largest at the bottom as opposed to in the mid-way up the stem and **Northern Goldenrod** (*Solidago multiradiata*), which is smaller (6–18 in. tall), has fewer but larger heads in flat-topped clusters, and is found ABOVE 8500 feet. We could also possibly see the non-native **Late Goldenrod** (*Solidago altissima altissima*), especially along roads at lower elevations.

Rabbitbrush (*Chrysothamnus nauseosus; Asteraceae*).
Also **Rubber Rabbitbrush.** *Plate 19.*

2–3 feet tall, perennial. Leaves lanceolate, keeled, 1–3 in. long. Leaves and stem green to white-hairy (tomentose). Flowers yellow, many heads. Dry rocky slopes, up to the summits of our tallest peaks.

This shrubby species is an eye-catching late-bloomer that can be seen from great distances. A good place to see it is on the dry, rocky slopes just north of the Jumping Rocks, above the SW shore of Fallen Leaf Lake, where I took this photograph. It is also present near the summit of Mt. Tallac. The genus is well named—Greek for "gold-flower"—as is the specific epithet which references its nausea-inducing rubbery odor (just crush some leaves and smell).

Heartleaf Arnica (*Arnica cordifolia; Asteraceae*) *Plate 19.*

4–12 in. Leaves and stem covered in white hairs. Leaves opposite, ovate, 1–4 in. long, 2–3 pairs along stem plus a basal rosette. Flower a composite (sunflower-type) head, 1–3 flowers per plant. Each head with usually 6–11 petal-like ray flowers 1/2–1 in. long, narrow, pointed, sometimes notched. Intergrades with Sierra Arnica (*A. nevadensis*). Coniferous forests and meadows, 6500–10,000 ft.

These delicate little sunflowers dot small clearings along the trail up to Angora Lakes. *Arnica* is Latin for "lambskin," a reference to their soft, hairy leaves. An early bloomer, the Sierra Arnica often goes to seed as early as the first week of July.

Arrowleaf Groundsel (*Senecio triangularis; Asteraceae*). Also **Ragwort** or **Butterweed**. *Plate 19.*

> 1–4 ft. Leaves 2–5 in. long, elongated triangular to arrowhead-shaped, margins serrate. Flowers yellow, sunflower-like heads appx. 1 in. across, usually with 8 petal-like ray flowers, bunched in a roughly flat-topped cyme at the top of the plant. Moist places in open forests, 3200–10,000 ft.

Camp's Witch's Pond usually hosts a nice collection of these plants near its southern shore. The genus name, *Senecio*, means "old man," from the white parachute-like appendage (pappus) on the seeds.

Arrow-leaved Balsam-root (*Balsamorhiza sagittata; Asteraceae*) *Plate 19.*

> 1–2 ft. Leaves basal, arrowhead-shaped, 8–20 in. long. Flowers yellow, in composite heads (sunflower-like), 2–4 in. wide, 1–3 heads per stem. Dry open forests, 4500–8500 ft.

Commonly mistaken for the better-known **Wooly Mule's Ear**, (*Wyethia mollis*) also found in our area (*Plate 18*), the Arrow-leaved Balsam-root is distinguished by its namesake leaves. Balsam-root gets its name from the sticky sap in its roots (from *balsamon*, Greek for "a gummy resin"). Look for these at the sunny opening at the top of the Nature Trail at Camp.

6. White Flowers

2 PETALS

Mugwort (*Artemesia douglasiana; Asteraceae*) *Plate 20.*
> Erect stems 1–6 ft. tall. Leaves 1–6 inches long, small leaves simple, narrowly elliptic; large leaves deeply incised with up to five pointed lobes, white-tomentose (hairy) above, more so below. Pungent aroma when rubbed. Flowers on a terminal spike of spikelets, many tiny (1/4 in.) nodding green bells enclosing little yellow heads, some filaments barely protruding. Open or shady areas, esp. near drainages, below 7200 ft.

Mugwort and its close relatives, such as Wormwood (*A. absinthium*), have long held important places in herbal medicine. The distinctive, pungent aroma is rumored to aid in remembering one's dreams. When pounded into a poultice, the juicy preparation can help to dissolve the rash-inducing oils of Poison Oak (which fortunately keeps below 5000 feet). As the name implies, Wormwood was used to expel parasites of the intestines.

Mugwort is widespread and sprouts in patches from perennial underground rhizomes, especially near Camp's Witch's Pond.

Enchanter's Nightshade (*Circaea alpina pacifica; Onagraceae*)
Plate 20.

>2–16 in. tall. Leaves opposite, 1–4 in. long, ovate to cordate, mildly serrate. Flowers in a branched panicle; each flower tiny (1/8 in.), white, 2 lobed petals held erect, 2 sepals reflexed, 2 stamens. Fruit a hooked-hairy (Velcro-like) knob. Moist, shady forest floors below 9000 ft.

Although not a true nightshade (Solanaceae), European relatives of this species were supposedly used by the Greek enchantress Circe (hence the genus name) to turn men into swine. These plants can be found in wet shady spots along the road just NW of Camp's Old Lodge and near Witch's Pond.

3 PETALS

Leichtlin's Mariposa Lily (*Calochortus leichtlinii; Liliaceae*). Also **Mariposa Tulip.** *Plate 20.*

>2–12 in. tall. Leaves linear, basal, 4–6 in. long, withering before flowering. Flower with 3 white petals, 1/2–2 in. long, each having a yellow base topped by a dark purple triangular spot; 6 saggitate anthers. Dry, gravelly clearings in montane forests or chaparral. 4300–10,000 ft.

This well-known member of the Lily Family gets its common name from the Spanish word for "butterfly," a reference to its well-marked petals. The genus name is Greek for "beautiful grass," because of its skinny, grass-like leaves. Mariposa Lilies are commonly found among the balsam-root and sagebrush at the highest point along Camp's Nature Trail, just off Stanford Hill road. Their bulbs are eaten by bears, skunks, raccoons and humans. Therefore, they persist most abundantly in rocky areas that making digging difficult. (Please do not dig for them unless you are near starvation.)

Another mariposa lily, the **Sierra Star Tulip** (*Calochortus minimus*), Plate 20, can be found in forest clearings in our region. It has pure white, more delicate-looking petals, light purple stamens and is about half the size of Leichtlin's.

4 PETALS

Rock Cress (*Arabis holboellii; Brassicaceae*) *Plate 20.*

>Erect stem, 1/2–2 ft. Leaves mostly in a basal rosette, oblanceolate. Flowers white to light purple or pink, four petals. Petals close around pollinated pistil as it grows into an erect, skinny pod 1–4 in. long. Dry rocky slopes and pine forests, 5000–10,000 ft.

Arabis is a fairly large, diverse genus. For this reason, the species listed here is only one possibility. Species with reflexed or hanging seedpods are likely to be *A. rectissima rectissima* or *A. repanda repanda*. The common name "rock cress" is used to refer to any member of this genus so it is accurate as long as you do not get into the Latin.

5 PETALS

Spreading Phlox (*Phlox diffusa; Polemoniaceae*) *Plate 20.*

> 2–8 in. tall, perennial evergreen. Leaves needle-like, < 1 in. long. Flowers white to purple-tinged, 5 petals, < 1 in. across. Dry rocky areas above 4000 ft.

Like some other species of white flowers, phlox petals turn purplish after being pollinated. It is assumed this makes them less attractive to pollinators which therefore concentrate their time on those flowers that still need their services. There are a couple other species in our area that could be confused with Spreading Phlox: **Granite Gilia** (*Leptodactylon pungens*) which has spiny leaves and vase or funnel-shaped flowers; and **Cushion Phlox** (*Phlox condensata*) which grows in an even denser, cushion-like hemisphere.

Thimbleberry (*Rubus parviflorus; Rosaceae*) *Plate 20.*

> 1–6 ft. tall. Leaves palmately 3–5 lobed, soft-fuzzy, 2–10 in. wide. No prickles or thorns. Flower white, 5 petals, many stamens, about 2 in. across. Fruit a small, red raspberry. Moist woods in partial shade below 8200 ft.

Quite possibly the tastiest "berry" around, Thimbleberries are also the hardest to gather because of their tendency to fall apart when picked. This may be why they never show up at the grocery store. The difficulty of transportation makes this delicate delicacy all the more special to have as a mid-hike snack. (Thimbleberries are prolific near Witch's Pond, along sections of Camp's Nature Trail and across the road from Camp's boat dock shed.)

Mousetail Ivesia (*Ivesia santolinoides; Rosaceae*) *Plate 21.*

> 1/2–2 ft. tall. Basal leaves resemble grayish (tinged green or pink) furry mousetails, 2–5 in. long. Flowers in an open cyme, each tiny (1/4 in.), with five rounded white petals and 15 yellow stamens. Bare granitic sand and rock crevices, 8500–10,000 ft.

A peculiar member of the Rose Family, Mousetail Ivesia is a true alpine recluse, only found on high, windswept ridges. The saddle between Island and Tyler Lakes has a decent-sized population.

Vari-leaved Phacelia (*Phacelia heterophylla virgata; Hydrophyllaceae*) *Plate 21.*

> 1/2–4 ft. tall. Leaves ovate to lanceolate, 1–5 in. long, larger leaves with basal portion variously dissected to form 5–9 lobes. Flowers grouped into 1-sided coils; 5 white petals, stamens extremely exserted (2X petal length). Dry slopes, flats and roadsides. 400–9800 ft.

These plants grow in Camp in front of "the row" of staff cabins opposite the boat dock. Take care in handling as the stiff hairs which cover the plant may irritate the skin. A number of other similar members of this genus can be found in our region as well.

Hot Rock Penstemon (*Penstemon deustus pedicellatus; Scrophulariaceae*).
Also **Scabland Penstemon.** *Plate 21.*

> 2–16 in. tall. Leaves 1/4–2 in. long, lanceolate, often folded along midvein, margins smooth to serrate or dentate. Flowers about 1/2 in. long, trumpet-shaped, white with purple throat lines, three large lower lobes and two smaller upper ones. Open rocky areas, 1700–10,000 ft.

This small, white-flowered penstemon grows in clumps between rocks at the north end of Camp's Nature Trail and other rocky habitats throughout Desolation Wilderness.

White-veined Wintergreen (*Pyrola picta; Ericaceae*).
Also **White-veined Shin-leaf.** *Plate 21.*

> Single straight stem, 4–15 in. high. Flowers usually white (rarely green or pink), five-petaled, with conspicuously bent pistil extending beyond petals. Flowers hang alternately from small pedicels along top half of stem. Leaves only at base of plant, ovate, leathery, dark green with white outlining main veins. Forest duff, 1200–8000 ft.

Instead of moist bogs, this wintergreen inhabits forest floors. True to its name, it has white veination on its leaves and keeps the small basal rosette of leaves year-round. Flowering stalk similar to Pink Pyrola except its flowers are white. A good place to look for this one is along the Angora Trail in early summer. The alternate common name, Shin-leaf, references its medicinal use as a poultice for bruises—often on the shins after hiking.

One-sided Wintergreen (*Orthilia secunda; Ericaceae*).
Previously *Pyrola secuda; Pyrolaceae*. *Plate 21.*

> 2–8 in. tall. Leaves near base of stem, ovate, margins sometimes finely round-toothed, 1/2–3 in. long. Flowers creamy white to greenish, 5-petaled but usually not fully opened, styles exserted, held in an arching, one-sided raceme (becoming erect in fruit). Dry, shady forests. 3200–10,000 ft.

One-sided Wintergreens are aptly named and easily identified. These diminutive plants can be found hiding under larger, shade-providing plants along the road to Lily Lake. The scientific name of this species has been recently changed (see above), making it the only representative of its genus in California. In addition, *Ericaceae* (the Heath Family, including manzanitas and rhododendrons) has now absorbed what used to be *Py-*

rolaceae (the Wintergreen Family) and *Monotropaceae* (the Indian Pipe Family, including saprophytes like Snow Plant and Pine Drops).

California Grass-of-Parnassus (*Parnassia californica; Saxifragaceae*). Previously *Parnassia palustris californica*. Plate 21.

> 6–18 in. tall. Leaves basal, 2–5 in. long, ovate, tapered at base, often semi-folded lengthwise. Flowers on solitary stems with one small leaf-like bract more than half-way up the stalk. Flowers with 5 rounded white petals, smooth-margined. Wet slopes, banks and meadows below 10,000 ft.

This beautifully delicate flower is an exhilarating find in Desolation Wilderness. The genus was first described on Mount Parnassus in Greece. The best way to view these flowers is to hike up the "waterfall" (more accurately a gentle granite slope covered with running water) which runs from Fontanillis Lake and into Upper Velma Lake.

Naked Buckwheat (*Eriogonum nudum; Polygonaceae*) Plate 21.

> Erect branching stem, 1/2–4 ft. Leaves in a basal rosette only, obovate, spoon-shaped, 1/2–4 in. long. Flowers tiny, white, often tinged red, clustered in dense groups at points where the stem branches. Dry open places below 10,000 ft.

This plant earns its name because it has no leaves to cloth its erect stem, leaving it "naked." Rumor has it that the reddish tinge which appears on some plants is actually a blush due to embarrassment. Although much taller than its yellow congeneric, the Sulfur Flower, Naked Buckwheat is often missed because its thin stem and tiny flower bunches are often lost against the background of their dry, rocky habitats. Found in dry clearings along Camp's Nature Trail and roadsides.

Alpine Knotweed (*Polygonum phytolaccifolium; Polygonaceae*) Plate 21.

> 2–6 ft. Leaves 4–8 in. long, wavy, ovate to lanceolate, base rounded, tip acutely tapered. Flowers white, 1/4–1/2 in. across, 5–petaled, clustered in cymes. Wet rocky streamsides and meadows, 5000–9200 ft.

A fairly large buckwheat, Alpine Knotweed can resemble a gangly sorrel (*Rumex* spp.) when not in flower. This plant grows along the tributaries of Glen Alpine Creek and other waterways.

Cow Parsnip (*Heracleum lanatum; Apiaceae*) Plate 22.

> Thick, hairy stalk 3–9 ft. tall. Leaves palmately ternate, coarsely dissected with serrate margins, 8–20 in. across. Flowers tiny, white, clustered in fairly dense compound umbels. Moist places, shaded or open. Below 8500 ft.

The genus name compares this plant's large stature to that of the legendary Hercules and with good reason. *Lanatum* means "wooly," after its hairy stems and leaves. This substantial plant gets its common name from the fact that it is a favored browse plant for many animals (including cattle) and its parsnip-like smell. Peeled (to remove a mild toxin) stems of this Celery Family species are edible, but not suggested. (Cow Parsnip is often confused with its deadly European cousin, **Poison Hemlock**, *Conium maculatum,* which rarely occurs above 3000 feet and is usually in disturbed areas.) Cow Parsnip is the only *Heracleum* species native to North America. **Brewer's Angelica** (*Angelica brewerii*), *Plate 22,* has twice-pinnate, 2–4 in. serrate leaflets which are *smooth*.

Ranger's Buttons (*Sphenosciadium capitellatum; Apiaceae*). Also **Swamp White Heads.** *Plate 22.*

> 1–5 ft. tall. Leaves pinnate, 4–20 in. long, celery-like leaf sheaths enlarged along stem. Flowers in 4–18 dense, white spheres supported by white-hairy stems 1–4 in. long. Wet meadows and streamsides, 3000–10,000 ft.

The compact clusters of flowers on this plant really do look like large white buttons. Like many Celery Family members, it is toxic to livestock. One place Ranger's Buttons can be found is above Horsetail Falls between Pitt and Ropi Lakes.

Parish's Yampah (*Perideridia parishii latifolia; Apiaceae*) *Plate 22.*

> Thin stem, 1/2–3 ft. Leaves narrowly ternate, leaflets lanceolate to linear. Flowers tiny, white, in small, flat-topped umbels. Moist meadows and open coniferous forests, 6000–10,000 ft.

The root of this delicate, thin member of the Parsley/Carrot/Celery Family was an important food source for Native Americans.

Macloskey's Violet (*Viola macloskeyi; Violaceae*) *Plate 22.*

> 1–6 in. high. Leaves basal, blades round to roundly heart-shaped, 1/2–3 in. across. Flowers held singly on an erect, candy-cane-shaped stalks. Flowers with 5 white petals: top pair reflexed, side pair thrust forward, single lower lip; bottom 3 petals purple-veined. Wet, shady places. 3200–9000 ft.

With a little imagination, the geometry of the petals makes it appear as if this flower is holding out its arms to receive a hug. Macloskey's Violets hide at the bases of larger shade-providing plants. They are especially abundant in the alder thicket just east of Camp's Witch's Pond.

White Heather, see p. 54, *Plate 14*, White or Alpine Heather, with Red Heather.

6 "PETALS" or "TEPALS" (petals & sepals which look the same)

White-flowered Bog-Orchid (*Plantanthera leucostachys; Orchidaceae*). Previously *Habenaria dilatata leucostachys*. Also **Rein-orchid, Sierra Crane Orchid** or **Scentbottle**. *Plate 22*.

> Single stem, 1/2–3 ft. tall. Leaves at base and along stem, elongated and triangular, without stalks, 2–10 in. long, 1/4–1 in. wide at base. Flowers white, in a dense spike, orchid-shaped with long, curved spur below. Wet places below 10,000 ft.

These beautiful, exotic-looking white orchids shoot up from moist, marshy areas and are especially prolific along the streams on Stanford Hill. The **Green-flowered Bog-Orchid**, *P. sparsifolia*, (similar, but with green flowers) is also found in our area and has been seen along the road to Lily Lake.

Death Camas (*Zigadenus venenosus venenosus; Liliaceae*) *Plate 22*.

> 1/2–3 ft. tall. Leaves lanceolate to linear (grass-like), 4–16 in. long. Flowers in a raceme-like cluster at the top of the stem, flower-stems ascending, about 1/2 in. long. Flowers have 6 white "petals" with yellow-green glands at their bases, are less than 1/2 in. across, 6 erect stamens about as long as the petals. **POISONOUS**. Moist meadows and rocky slopes below 8500 ft.

One can probably deduce that this plant is *not* on any "edible" list. Death Camas is so named because its bulbs resemble those of the food plant *Camassia quamash* (Camas Lily) but contain deadly alkaloids. Many Native American tribes used Camas Lily bulbs extensively as a food source and actively weeded out this look-alike killer from their harvesting areas.

(Fat) False Solomon's Seal (*Smilacina racemosa; Liliaceae*) *Plate 23*.

> 1–3 ft. Leaves roundly ovate, alternating along stalk. Flowers in dense, fuzzy panicle, individual flowers hard to distinguish. Each flower white with 6 tiny (1/8 in.) "petals," exceeded by 6 longer stamens. Fruit a round green berry (1/4–1/2 in.), maturing to reddish with purple dots. Moist woodlands, below 6600 ft.

(See following paragraph describing both False Solomon's Seals.)

Star (Slim) False Solomon's Seal (*Smilacina stellata; Liliaceae*) *Plate 23*.

> 1–3 ft. Leaves narrowly lanceolate, alternating along stalk. Flowers in a loose raceme, individual flowers each with their own 1/2 in. stalk, well separated from each other. Each flower white with 6 "petals," 1/4–1/2 in. long, stamens only about half the length of "petals." Fruit green, vertically striped with purple, maturing reddish-spotted to black. Moist woodlands below 8000 ft.

These two species are the only *Smilacina*s in California and are readily distinguished by their leaves (implied by their common names), flowers and flowering structures. They are both wonderfully fragrant.

The infamously misleading parts and names that lead to confusion follow:
- *S. racemosa* is actually paniculate, *S. stellata* is racemose in their flowering pattern.
- *Smilacina* means "little *Smilax*" but they do not resemble *Smilax* species.
- These plants do not even look like Solomon's Seal to begin with.

The berries have been reported by some as "insipid and diarrhea-inducing" while others say they are "distinctive and delicious." If you decide to sample them, make sure you have access to a toilet and doctor—just in case.

California Corn Lily (*Veratrum californicum californicum*; Liliaceae) Plate 23.

> 3–6 ft. tall. Leaves corn-like, parallel-veined, ovate, 8–16 in. long. Flowers in a densely clustered panicle, each with 6 green–based white "petals." Wet meadows and streamsides, 3300–10,000 ft.

Another plant with toxic alkaloids, California Corn Lilies have been the "last supper" of many now-dead cattle. Corn Lily is so named because it distantly resembles a corn plant, especially before it flowers.

Washington Lily (*Lilium washingtonianum washingtonianum*; Liliaceae) Plate 23.

> 2–8 ft. tall. Leaves in 1–9 whorls, 1–5 in. long, oblanceolate, margins sometimes wavy. Flowers large (3–5 in. long), white lilies with 6 "petals," 6 stamens and an upturned style. Open coniferous forests, 4000–7200 ft.

This is arguably the largest and most impressive flower which naturally occurs around Fallen Leaf Lake. A gorgeous, four-foot tall specimen has grown under the Jeffery Pines south of Glen Alpine Creek, about a hundred yards west of the fire station. It's strong perfume and large, white blossoms indicate that it is pollinated by nocturnal moths.

MANY "PETALS"

Yarrow (*Achillea millefolium*; Asteraceae). Also **Milfoil**. Plate 23.

> Erect stem, 1/2–5 ft. Leaves finely 3–pinnate, appearing almost fuzzy. Flowers composite, 3–8 white or yellow rounded petal-like ray flowers in flat-topped clusters. Widespread below 10,000 ft.

Due to recent findings, all previous species of this genus in California have been lumped into this single species. This makes identifying Yarrow down to its species quite a snap. (Do keep in mind, however, that Golden- or Yellow-Yarrow is *Eriophyllum confertiflorum*, not even in the same genus as "Yarrow" proper and is therefore unaffected by this change.)

This genus honors Achilles of ancient Greek mythology because of its healing properties. Look for tiny crab spiders on the flowers waiting to ambush unwary pollinators.

White Hawkweed (*Hieracium albiflorum; Asteraceae*). Also **Shaggy Hawkweed.** *Plate 23.*

> Erect stems 1–4 ft. tall. Basal leaves shaggy-hairy, oblanceolate, 3–6 in. long. Flowers in tiny (<1/2 in.) composite heads composed solely of white petal-like ray flowers (like a dandelion) with toothed tips. Dry, open forests below 9800 ft.

This native plant may look like a typical weed at first glance, but closer inspection reveals its delightful inner character: Delicate heads of white ligulate flowers interspersed with tiny yellow stamens tower above basal leaves covered in long, shaggy peachfuzz…a lovable weed indeed. One of these perennials lives across the road from Camp's boat dock.

Alpine Pussy-toes (*Antennaria media; Asteraceae*). Previously *Antennaria alpina media.* Also **Alpine Everlasting.** *Plate 23.*

> 2–6 in. tall. Leaves basal and along stem, linear to spoon-shaped, 1/4–1 in. long, densely wooly. Flower heads elongated, creamy white, papery, appx. 2–7 clustered at the end of each stem. Alpine snow basins, meadows and rocky areas. 5900–10,000 ft.

A creamy-white version of Pink Pussy-toes found at higher elevations in our area.

White Pond-Lily, see p. 65, *Plate 18,* Yellow Pond-Lily.

7. Green (or non-showy) Flowers

0 PETALS (or petals inconspicuous)

Meadow-Rue (*Thalictrum fendleri fendleri; Ranunculaceae*) *Plate 24.*

> 2–5 ft. tall. Dioecious (individual plants either "male" or "female"). Leaves compoundly 1–4-ternate. Each leaflet generally 3–lobed, margins smooth or serrate, 1/2–1 in. long. Staminate flowers with 15–28 pendulous stamens: filaments purplish, anthers yellow. Pistillate flowers in clusters of 7–20 acuminate capsules about 1/4 in. long with ±3 ribs. Moist, shady to open woods. 3000–10,000 ft.

This member of the Buttercup Family is common in moist shady forests. Of interest is the fact that this species is *dioecious*. This means that each individual plant of this species bears either staminate (pollen-producing) or pistillate (ovary-holding) "flowers," but not both. This feature assures that self-pollination cannot take place. Since it is wind-pollinated, neither "flower" is especially showy.

Stinging Nettle (*Urtica dioica holosericea; Urticaceae*). Also **Hoary Nettle.** *Plate 24.*

> Single ribbed stem, 2–6 ft. tall, covered with tiny stinging hairs. Leaves opposite, 2–6 in. long, lanceolate to ovate, margins serrate. Flowers small, inconspicuous, greenish-yellow, in axillary panicles 1/2–3 in. long. Various marginal habitats, generally sunny and moist areas below 8000 ft.

The genus name, *Urtica*, means "to burn" and refers to the feeling which follows a brush with this plant. The tiny, rigid "hairs" along its stem are nature's miniature version of hypodermic needles. The hollow core of each stinging hair is filled with formic acid, the same chemical present in ant and bee venom. When human skin contacts these sharp, brittle hairs they are driven into the skin and broken off, effectively injecting their irritant into our bodies. Because it is only a shallow injection, Stinging Nettles rarely cause more than a temporary burning, itching rash. Cortisone cream, Calamine lotion and cold salt-water compresses help alleviate these temporary symptoms which usually disappear on their own within a matter of minutes or hours.

Stinging Nettles, however, are not all bad: the young shoots can be steamed and eaten like spinach (take care in harvesting); the fibrous stalks have been used to make twine, cloth and paper during war-time shortages; Native Americans twisted and wove the stems into nets for birds and fish; nettle teas are used medicinally; and Native American warriors used the stinging stems to keep them awake during all-night vigils (a natural substitute for caffeine pills).

Watch out for nettles around Camp on the road up to Witch's Pond (bordering the alder thicket) and around Lakeview Cabin (opposite the kitchen's loading dock).

5 PETALS

Brewer's Bishop's Cap (*Mitella breweri; Saxifragaceae*). Also **Mitrewort.** *Plate 24.*

> Flower stalk 4–12 in. high. Leaves basal, blades 1–4 in. across, roughly circular, shallowly 7–11 lobed, roundly toothed. Flowers tiny, greenish, 5-petaled, petals finely 5–9 pinnately divided, stamens alternate petals. Moist slopes, 5000–9,000 ft.

This is the most commonly described mitrewort of the Sierra Nevada. *M. pentandra*, **Five-point Bishop's Cap** (with stamens opposite the petals) is also present, but is much rarer. Because of their small stature, tiny greenish blooms and swampy habitat preferences, people rarely see these delicate little members of the Saxifrage Family. The lacy blooms of these plants can be viewed in the moist area just above Camp's water storage pool. Fruits resemble tiny bishop hats.

Dwarf Lousewort (*Pedicularis semibarbata; Scrophulariaceae*)
Also **Pinewoods** or **Bearded Lousewort.** *Plate 24.*

> 1–6 in. high. Flowers not obvious or showy. Short spikes of club-shaped to hooded, dull yellow, green, or purple flowers often grow under leaves. Leaves in basal rosettes, lanceolate and highly divided (11–25 pinnate segments), lobed to toothed, 3–10 in. long. Coniferous woodlands (esp. Red Fir), 5000–10,000 ft.

Members of this genus (and many others in this family, i.e. *Castilleja*) are infamous for being parasites on the roots of the trees they grow under. Although they are green and produce their own sugars, they are just too "lazy" (or "smart") to get their own water.

Each species of lousewort has a slightly different flower shape that fits the anatomy of only a very few (often just one) species of bumble bee. This is just one more example of how plants have evolved to use their valuable pollen most efficiently.

Pedicularis is Latin for lice, a name that originated from an old myth that implicates this plant in the infestation of lice on any animal that consumes it (or rids the animal of lice, depending on which story you hear). Lousewort and *Pedicularis* are still suitable names, however, if one likens this plant's parasitic effect on trees to that of lice on animals.

These plants are likely to be encountered in Mokelumne Wilderness, on the Red Fir forest sections of the trail to Winnemucca Lake and other open forests in our region.

6 PETALS

Green-flowered Bog-Orchid (*Platanthera sparsiflora; Orchidaceae*)
Plate 24.

Our only green orchid. See **White-flowered Bog-Orchid,** page 73, for information.

MISTLETOES

Western Dwarf Mistletoe (*Arceuthobium campylopodum; Viscaceae*)
Plate 24.

This is our most common mistletoe, found on pines and firs (mostly Jeffrey Pine but also reportedly found on White Fir). It has yellowish stems with greenish-blue berries and is only 2–6 inches long (hence "dwarf").

The fruits of this genus explode as a way of dispersing their sticky seeds.

In California, there are about a dozen species of dwarf mistletoes, each usually specializing on a single host species of tree, although often not entirely restricted to that species. Other possible species in our area include: ***A. abietinum*** (on firs), ***A. americanum*** (on Lodgepole Pine), ***A. californicum*** (on Sugar Pine), ***A. tsugense ssp. mertensianae*** (on Mountain Hemlocks). Dwarf mistletoes are often responsible for inducing abnormal hyper-branching in its host that results in "witch's brooms."

The often larger, greener sister genus, also has two species in our area: ***Phoradendron juniperinum*** (on Western Junipers) and ***Phoradendron libocedri*** (on Incense-cedars). This genus prefers to employ birds to consume its whitish fruits and the birds then defecate its sticky seeds directly onto tree branches. Species of this genus are often collected for Christmas decorations in North America (mostly from oaks) although the traditional European mistletoe is in the genus *Viscum*—revered for retaining its green leaves (a symbol of life and fecundity) throughout the winter. The crushed berries (and the scat produced by birds after eating the berries) are so sticky that they were smeared on branches to trap small birds (birdlime). The European genus is the root of viscous or viscid, meaning "sticky." *Phoradendron* translates as "tree thief." The common name is derived from Old Anglo-Saxon roots: "Mistel" meant dung and "tan" meant twig—after the observation that this plant sprouts where birds defecate on branches.

Mistletoes mostly tap into the xylem (which transports water and minerals) of the plant. This is presumably because they have their own chlorophyll and can simply use the tree as a long straw and perch. This can leave the phloem of the tree (which transports the sugars and amino acids formed through photosynthesis) largely untouched.

EDIBLE AND MEDICINAL PLANTS

By Rebecca Chaplin

NOTE: *This chapter is meant to be informational only, like the rest of this book. The consumption of wild plants, especially those known to have medicinal properties, is dangerous for many reasons. Possibly lethal mistakes can be made in species identification, the part of the plant, the correct location or time of harvest, the method of preparation and the dosage. In addition, individual reactions or allergies are hard to predict.*
PLEASE DO NOT EXPERIMENT!

Few of us stop to think about where our food and medicines come from, other than the supermarket. Even if we are so worldly as to consider the process of farming, we rarely think about the ancestors of the few common plants we have now domesticated, or about their thousands of wild relatives that indigenous peoples survived on for millennia. The local Native American tribe, the Washoe, lived in our area without a salad bar, dinner buffet line or first aid closets. Even in a place so far from lush as to be called "Desolation" Wilderness, there are resources all around you if you look closely. In this chapter, I list some of our more common plant species with nutritional and medicinal properties. Hopefully after having read this, you'll be able to teach others about the plants you pass by while on a hike, or share an anecdote with a friend who happens to be standing near a plant of interest. Knowing the secrets of what the plants around them have to offer (other than aesthetics) may help people feel more connected to their environment.

Arnica (*Arnica cordifolia* and other Arnica species) *Plate 19.*

Found: On the slopes of Angora Peak and in the flower beds around Camp. The medicinal properties of this herb are still only beginning to be understood. The herb is not usually recommended for internal use because it can irritate the stomach and may result in vomiting and diarrhea, though the Native Americans did drink concoctions of various arnica species as a narcotic. Arnica can be used externally as a salve or tincture to heal wounds, bruises, arthritis and skin irritations. Only very dilute solutions of the tincture should be used, as the herb can cause blistering and inflammation. Native Americans used arnica as an ointment for stiffened, cramped muscles and on sprains. Cancer research has been focused on arnica species in recent year due to their properties of stimulating immune function and healthy cell division.

Columbine *(Aquilegia formosa)* Plate 16.

Found: up the Tamarack Trail and other shady wet places.

Columbine flowers taken with wine promote perspiration and the seeds with wine are said to speed the delivery of a child. A lotion made from the fresh root and rubbed on the affected area can relieve rheumatic aches and pains.

Corn Lily *(Veratrum californicum)* Plate 23.

Found: wet seeps such as at the top of Stanford Hill Rd.

This plant is highly toxic and potentially fatal, the highest concentration of toxins being in the roots. The Washoe administered the crushed roots of the Corn Lily to pregnant women to induce miscarriage and to other women as a contraceptive when food was scarce and the tribe couldn't take on the responsibility of any more members. As far as I know, no research has been conducted to determine the source of the Corn Lily's abortifacient properties, but cattle-ranchers will remove the plant immediately from the pastures because it has been known to cause birth defects and miscarriages in cows.

Dandelion *(Taraxacum officinale)*

Found: roadsides, i.e.; at the top of Camp's Nature Trail.

The French named the dandelion "dente de lion," which means "tooth of the lion," referring to the distinctively jagged shape of the leaves. The ancient Greeks considered this plant a cure-all, as indicated by its genus name: "taraxos" means disorder and "akos" means remedy. In fact, this weed is one of the most useful plants around. Instead of spraying dandelions with chemicals in your yard, you might consider gathering them instead (but make sure nobody else has sprayed them first!). The young leaves can be gathered and eaten raw. They're high in vitamin A and C and iron and add a spicy flavor to your salad. They also speed up your metabolism and stimulate weight loss. The flowers can be eaten in bud (they taste best fried) and have similar nutritional properties. The milk from the hollow stem can be applied to pimples, canker sores, ulcers, eczema and sores. The roots have been used in amazingly diverse ways, ranging from a coffee substitute (after roasting and boiling) to remedies for ailments such as yeast infections, digestive problems, kidney and liver disorders and hepatitis.

Death Camas *(Zigadenus venenosus) Plate 22.*

Found: top of Stanford Hill Rd.

While the flower of this plant would never be confused with the Camas Lily (*Camassia quamash*, found in the meadow at the north end of the lake), when the flowers have withered away these two species are difficult to tell apart because their bulbs are nearly identical. This presented quite a dilemma for the Washoe, since the Camas Lily bulbs were an important food source for them and Death Camas bulbs are, as you might have guessed, fatal. The Washoe had to keep track of which plants grew where while they still were distinguishable and remember which places to avoid when they would dig up the bulbs in the autumn.

Horsetail *(Equisetum arvense) Plate 8.*

Found: top of Stanford Hill Rd.

Horsetails are among the most primitive vascular plants still on the earth. These plants were here when the dinosaurs were and back then some grew as tall as trees. Young horsetail can be boiled in tea as a good source of calcium and silica. Older horsetails should not be ingested, as they accumulate toxins. However, the silica these plants sequester make them excellent natural scrubbing agents; indeed, the first settlers to this area called them "scrub rush" for that reason. You can also burn several horsetails and use the ash to make a good ointment for severe burns.

Juniper (*Juniperus occidentalis* or *Juniperus communis*) *Plate 3.*

Found: near the entrance of Camp, along Stanford Hill Rd.

Though usually in fruit during the summer, junipers are dioecious, meaning there are separate "male" plants and "female" plants, so some trees will never bear fruit. The distinctive blue berries, best known as the main ingredient in gin, have a variety of medicinal uses. The berries can be eaten or steeped as tea to counteract digestive problems and gastrointestinal infection. The oil can be used in a hot vapor bath; inhaling the steam is said to cure respiratory infections, colds, asthma, bronchitis, etc. The pure oil should not be rubbed on the skin as it can be very irritating and cause blisters.

Manzanita *(Arctostaphylos patula) Plate 4.*

Found: the road coming into Camp and at the start of the Nature Trail. *Plate 4.*

The berries on this shrub look nice but are too bitter and sour to eat, or at least to enjoy eating. They apparently make a nice jelly, though and the Native Americans made cider out of them, which is what led the Spaniards to name the plant "manzanita" or "little apple." The leaves and bark can be boiled to make a poultice for sunburn or poison oak irritation (fortunately, poison oak does not grow above about 5,000 feet at out latitude).

Mariposa Lily *(Calochortus leichtlinii) Plate 20.*

Found: rocky or gravelly soils such as the side of the road near Glen Alpine's Lower Falls.

The bulb of the Mariposa Lily can be boiled like a potato or dried and ground into a powder to make porridge. Bulbs were often gathered and stored by Native Americans for when food was scarce. The flower buds are edible raw and can be added to salads. A tea of the leaves and flowers was used to ease pain from rheumatic swellings and childbirth.

Miner's Pepper *(Lepidium densiflorum)*

Found: roadsides, such as near Camp's boat dock and loading dock.

Chew one of the tiny seed pods of this plant and you'll notice an impressively spicy flavor. Early pioneers did in fact use this plant to spice up their food, which is how it got its name.

Monkshood *(Aconitum columbianum) Plate 10.*

Found: wet areas such as at the top of Stanford Hill Rd.

This species is toxic and can be fatal. In medieval times, it was called wolfsbane, since arrowheads were dipped in juices from the plant to kill wolves. It is also, however, a traditional medicine for the external relief of pain. Monkshood provides the drug aconite, which is used in analgesics.

Pine *(Pinus species) Plate 2.*

Found: throughout.

We have three different species of pine around Camp: the Sugar Pine (*Pinus lambertiana*), one of which is above the road right after the entrance of Camp and can be easily recognized by its long, pendulous cones; the Lodgepole Pine (*Pinus contorta*), which have relatively short needles and small (approximately 2 inch long) cones; and the Jeffrey Pine (*Pinus jeffreyi*), with big fat cones and a faint vanilla or butterscotch smell emanating from the bark. (The Jeffrey Pine is easily confused with the Ponderosa Pine, *Pinus ponderosa*, but I haven't seen any Ponderosas right around Camp and their cones are distinctively prickly, unlike the Jeffrey cones.) In general, most edible and medicinal uses of a pine can be applied to any species, though some lend themselves better to certain uses. One of the main uses of pines by Native Americans was to collect the cones and eat the seeds or "nuts". Pine nuts are a great source of protein and high in fat and thus were very important to the Washoe during times of food scarcity. Cones were collected on the tree (before they had opened and dispersed their seed) using sticks or rocks to knock them off the branches. They were placed under the coals of a fire because the heat would cause the scales to split and then the seeds could be removed. Other uses of pine included chewing the sap (especially of the Sugar Pine, which has the sweetest sap) to treat sore throats and colds, applying the resin to heal wounds and making tea from the needles as a source of vitamin C (five times as much as lemons!). In a survival situation, the cambium layer just behind the bark can be stripped and eaten. It's high in carbohydrates. Understand, however, that stripping the cambium around the whole perimeter of the trunk will kill the tree. (Granted, if it's a real survival situation, that's probably the least of your worries.)

Sierra Onion, Swamp Onion *(Allium campanulatum, A. validum)* Plate 15.

> Found: rocky soils at the top of Camp's Nature Trail (Sierra Onion); halfway up the Nature Trail from Witches Pond, around the part where streams run down the hillside (Swamp Onion).

Onions in general have many nutritional and medicinal properties and most species of wild onions (including both of these) can be consumed in the same manner and offer the same benefits of our domesticated onions. All parts of the plant are edible: root (bulb), stem and flower. The onion was domesticated at least 5,000 years ago and was reputed in ancient Mesopotamia to cure virtually anything. The Egyptians even went so far as to deem the onion an object of worship. They believed onions symbolized eternity, with their circle-within-a-circle structure. The onion's more well-established properties include thinning the blood, lowering overall cholesterol, raising the "good" (HDL) type of cholesterol, preventing blood clots and atherosclerosis, fighting asthma, chronic bronchitis, hay fever and diabetes and acting as an anti-inflammatory, antibiotic, antiviral agent. Many people also believe onion to have diverse anti-cancer powers. So forget your apple a day—have an onion a day!

Sierra Stonecrop *(Sedum obtusatum)* Plate 18.

> Found: rocky areas such as Camp's Nature Trail, near the treehouse.

Stonecrop is a succulent, using a type of metabolism called CAM. This special metabolism allows succulents to conserve water by opening their stomates at night to take in CO_2 when it's cool and they won't lose as much water in the process. Most plants can't do this because they haven't figured out how to store CO_2. Like other succulents (including the well-known Aloe Vera), the flesh of the stonecrop has soothing properties for cuts and burns. Rubbing the flesh of a leaf on the skin relieves itching and irritation.

Stinging Nettle *(Urtica dioica)   Plate 24.*

Found: right outside Lakeview.

Don't touch! Very unpleasant sensations and rashes result from contact with the bristly hairs of the nettle plant, which act like a tiny hypodermic needles, injecting an irritant substance under the skin. (*Urtica* is from the latin "uro," which means burning.) However, those brave enough to harvest this plant or smart enough to wear protective clothing will enjoy a very nutritious food source once the plant is boiled to remove all the treacherous hairs. The leaves are high in vitamin A and C (especially important in a place like the Sierras where no citrus grows) and magnesium and iron. A tincture made of the seeds can raise thyroid activity and may be used to treat thyroid-related obesity. Finally, boiled leaves applied topically will stop bleeding almost immediately and pulped leaves make a fantastic compress to bring cooling relief from inflammation (ironically, even perhaps the inflammation resulting from gathering those raw leaves in the first place).

Thimbleberry *(Rubus parviflorus)   Plate 20.*

Found: common at our lower elevations near water, such as next to Camp's Witches Pond.

A very tasty snack for bears and people alike, these berries ripen around August and you should sample one if you get a chance. These berries are high in vitamin A. Young shoots can also be eaten, boiled or fresh. Root and bark were boiled by some Native American tribes and made into soap. Possibly the most interesting use of this plant was rubbing the leaves on the faces of young Native Americans to prevent pimples.

Yampah *(Perideridia parishii)   Plate 22.*

Found: top of Stanford Hill Rd., the meadow on the north end of Fallen Leaf Lake and throughout Desolation.

This plant is in the carrot family and, like many carrots, it has a large main taproot. The root of Yampah was in fact one of the staple foods of the Washoe Indians. It can be stored for long periods, eaten raw or boiled and has a sweet nutty taste that has earned Yampah the reputation of the best-tasting wild root in the mountains. The seed was used as a seasoning (similar to caraway) and the young leaves can be eaten raw or cooked.

The root acts as a diuretic and a mild laxative, can be applied as a wash to sores and wounds or as a poultice to reduce swelling and the juice of the slowly chewed root is said to treat sore throats and coughs.

Yarrow *(Achillea millefolium) Plate 23.*

Found: dry rocky soils throughout.

Crush Yarrow's leaves and you can smell its medicine. It can be applied topically to treat wounds and toothaches (chew the leaves), or ingested (usually in tea) to treat colds, cramps and fevers. It was also apparently used for smallpox, typhoid fever, measles, malaria and in chickenpox to relieve itching. Unlike aspirin, which has similar pain-relieving qualities, yarrow has the bonus of being an effective blood clotting agent. It's also rumored to be a good insect repellent. Its generic name (Achillea) stems from ancient myths surrounding this plant: the Greek hero Achilles was taught by the centaur Chiron to use Yarrow to heal wounded soldiers during the Trojan War.

Willow *(Salix lucida* and other Salix species) *Pages 13-14.*

Found: around lakes and creeks.

The active ingredient in aspirin, Salicylic acid (named after the willow genus) comes from the willow. Native Americans often used willow bark to splint breaks, as they recognized that using this type of bark tended to reduce inflammation better than others. (FYI: Salicylic acid is also the active ingredient in most acne medications; it is unknown whether adolescent Native Americans scrubbed with willow bark.)

I've focused on only a few, more common species of edible and medicinal plants in our immediate vicinity. There are entire books (see Bibliography) detailing many more throughout the Sierras and even they barely scratch the surface of the knowledge that would have been carried by every Washoe. The importance of preserving these wild plants and the indigenous botanical knowledge of their uses goes far beyond saving your life if you happen to be stranded in the wilderness for a few days. In fact, modern-day health depends on wild sources of food and medicine, though we may not realize it.

As we grow more and more homogenous in our farming habits, we make ourselves more and more vulnerable to pathogen outbreaks and maintaining wild plant diversity is essential to our food security. The eventual solution to the Irish potato famine was to return to the origin of the wild potato, in the Andes, to find a potato species that was resistant to the fungus that could be crossed with our domesticated varieties. Crop scientists are now attempting a similar strategy with a fungus that plagues bananas. Meanwhile, pharmaceutical developers are engaged in an arms race with bacteria and viruses, as resistant strains seem to emerge as fast as the newest drug can be concocted. Most synthetic drugs synthesized are modeled after compounds found in plants. We never know what wild plant (or insect, or some other animal) may hold the cure for the next epidemic.

Biodiversity offers us a huge genetic library from which we can improve our crops and medicines or even develop new ones. As we modify more and more habitat to fit our various land-use needs, we drive many species to extinction and start to reduce our genetic library and what is essentially our safety net against unknown future calamities. The problem is that most of us are so unaware of our dependence on wild species that we don't understand the danger in severing our connection to them. The types of edible and medicinal services provided by the plants just around Fallen Leaf should give you an idea of the wealth of resources nature has to offer that is so often overlooked by modern society.

—Rebecca Chaplin

AMPHIBIANS
CLASS *Amphibia*

ORDER *Caudata*, salamanders

Family *Ambystomatidae*, mole salamanders

Ambystoma macrodactylum sigillatum — Long-toed Salamander (Southern)

Family *Plethodontidae*, lungless salamanders

Hydromantes platycephalus — Mount Lyell Salamander

ORDER *Anura*, frogs & toads

Family *Hylidae*, tree & chorus frogs

Pseudacris (Hyla) regilla — Pacific Chorus Frog (Treefrog)

Family *Ranidae*, true frogs

Rana muscosa — Mountain Yellow-legged Frog

Rana catesbeiana — Bullfrog*

Family *Bufonidae*, true toads

Bufo boreas halophilus — Western Toad (California)

*introduced species

AMPHIBIANS
Class *Amphibia*

This Class translates as "both lives," referring to the ability to live both in water and on land. This awe-inspiring trait has enthralled humans of many cultures for thousands of years. Proof is found in drawings from ancient civilizations in places as diverse as China, Egypt and the Roman Empire. Their transformation from aquatic larvae to terrestrial adults still seems to stir some ancient wonder, pride and great sense of accomplishment in us. Maybe we respond to them so strongly because of a long-dormant memory from our own beginnings, or perhaps it is just their ability to achieve what seems impossible. Regardless of why, amphibians fascinate us.

However, most of these wonderful creatures are declining world-wide. Ironically, the life histories and adaptations that served them so well for so long have now become serious liabilities. Freshwater habitats are being degraded, polluted, invaded or eliminated. Their thin, breathable skin and shell-less eggs provide little protection against the many factors that now threaten their very existence.

Factors contributing to the decline of our amphibians:

- Habitat loss (the converting, draining, isolating and paving of wetlands)
- Introduced species (especially predatory trout, other fish and bullfrogs)
- Ozone depletion (increases in ultraviolet radiation, especially at high elevations)
- Climate change (drought, loss of glaciers and snowfields, extreme weather events)
- Pollution (including airborne pesticides and other chemicals from the Central Valley)
- Livestock grazing (erosion, siltation, loss of riparian vegetation and nutrient loading)
- Pathogenic fungi and parasites (which can thrive in artificially modified systems)
- Bacterial (i.e. "red-leg") and viral diseases

Eradicating introduced trout and bullfrogs could have an incredibly positive effect on all our native amphibian populations. Get your fishing license and start doing your part!

SALAMANDERS, Order *Caudata*

MOLE SALAMANDERS, Family *Ambystomatidae*

(Southern) Long-toed Salamander
Ambystoma macrodactylum sigillatum (Baird, 1849). *Plate 25.*

    4–6 inches

The Long-toed Salamander is very widespread and inhabits a great diversity of habitats—from sagebrush steppe to wet western valleys and at almost every elevation. This is due in no small part to their ability to disperse over half a mile and quickly colonize new or temporary ponds (moving mostly at night).

The Long-toed is most easily identified by the irregular, broken yellow stripe along the back of its dark gray body, which can look like ancient runes written in gold leaf—and earns our subspecies its name. (Only in rare melanistic individuals is the yellow stripe entirely absent.) The entire three-part name roughly translates as "decorated large-toed blunt-mouth," a fitting description (the very long fourth toes on the hind feet are diagnostic of this species). Upon close inspection, the dark body is sprinkled with what looks like a very light dusting of powdered sugar-tiny bluish-white stipples. They earn their common family name, Mole Salamanders, by spending much of the year in the burrows of small mammals.

The eggs of the Long-toed Salamander are attached to submerged wood or vegetation, singly or in clusters of up to a hundred. They have thick jelly layers that make the eggs large (over half an inch) and appear widely-spaced when clumped. Young larvae look like tadpoles at first, but retain long, external gills and quickly sprout all four legs. At high elevations (over 7,000 feet), it may take two summers before metamorphosis.

In 1999, surveys in Desolation Wilderness indicated that these salamanders may be much more widespread in our area than previously thought—albeit primarily in small, fishless ponds and lakes.

LUNGLESS SALAMANDERS, Family *Plethodontidae*

Mount Lyell Salamander
Hydromantes platycephalus (Camp, 1916). *Plate 25.*

    3–5 inches

This "flat-headed water prophet" seems to relish playing the part of mountain hermit. Found in the cracks between slabs of granitic rock at high elevations, the Mount Lyell Salamander is well-camouflaged with dark gray and black blotches. Females lay 6–14 eggs (probably in deep, moist cracks) which hatch into fully-formed young (no larval stage).

Living at elevations of up to 12,000 feet, the Mount Lyell Salamander is nocturnal and active even at sub-freezing temperatures. It can easily amble across snowfields and will not emerge at temperatures above 52 degrees. Its flattened body is ideal for exploring the deep cracks created by exfoliating granodiorite and exploiting a niche (literally!) few other predators can access. This salamander can also climb wet, vertical rock faces with the aid of its webbed hind feet, sticky secretions and almost prehensile tail. And all without lungs: exchanging gases directly through its skin instead.

However, the most truly awe-inspiring and unique trait of this genus is its tongue—the longest and just about fastest of any salamander. Anchored to its pelvis, a muscular sheath surrounds a long, tapered tongue "bone" (actually seven cartilaginous segments joined by flexible joints) on each side of its body. When these muscles contract, the tongue bones zip forward like pinched watermelon seeds, come together in the mouth and propel the tongue out to half the body's length (about 2 inches) in mere milliseconds. The end of the tongue is flattened into a mushroom-like process that helps expand the sticky surface area for capturing prey. This ability may help *Hydromantes* acquire prey items without having to move quickly, which might otherwise expose them to falling off the often vertical surfaces where they forage. (To see this tongue in action, check out Professor Stephen M. Deban's excellent site at http://autodax.net/hydro-movie.html)

This genus has only three species in North America—all narrow Californian endemics. Members of this genus are also found in the Alps of Italy and France—the only other members of this entire family found outside North America. As Gary Nafis states so well, "Why *Hydromantes* is found only in Europe and California is an amazing biogeographical mystery." Nafis took the photograph on plate 25 at Smith Lake, just west of Mt. Price in our Crystal Range, where over 30 individuals have been collected from 1980 to 2002.

This genus played an important role in the career of Charles Lewis Camp (1893–1975). While earning his bachelor's degree from UC Berkeley, he was the first to find *Hydromantes* in North America. The first pair of these salamanders were caught in his trap line meant for small mammals on Mt. Lyell in Yosemite. This was also when he discovered the Mountain Yellow-legged Frog and Yosemite Toad. Camp received advanced degrees at Columbia and went on to have a very distinguished and diverse career with his final post being the chair of the paleontology department at Cal.

As a Species of Special Concern (both state and federal), this salamander should not be harassed, but do let the Forest Service know if you find any on this side of the Crystal Range—it would be a new species for the Tahoe Basin. (Also, there is circumstantial evidence that the secretions of this salamander can cause temporary blindness—up to three days—yet another good reason not to pick one up.)

FROGS & TOADS, Order *Anura*

TREE FROGS or CHORUS FROGS, Family *Hylidae*

Pacific Chorus Frog (Treefrog)
Pseudacris (Hyla) regilla (Baird & Girard, 1852). *Plate 25.*

1–2 inches

The smallest and most widespread frog in the West, this is the species most likely to be encountered (and heard) in our area. It has a year-round dry croak and more musical mating call employed in the spring. This spring vocalization is amplified by the male's throat sac—which can inflate to an incredible size—and by the dozens to hundreds of frogs that can be calling from a single location. The Pacific Chorus Frog can be shades of green, brown, gray or mottled, but the black "Lone Ranger" stripe that runs through its eyes is always there. (To help camouflage themselves, individual frogs can darken or lighten the tone of their background color, but cannot completely change colors.) Enlarged toe pads are also a good diagnostic feature.

A waxy secretion that helps retard water loss enables this species to roam relatively far from streams and ponds. Or, as they do at the Flanders cabin (above the Lower Falls of Glen Alpine Creek), they might just like to live in your shower. Always friendly-looking, they are a cheery sight to wake up to (if you are expecting them)!

Eggs are laid in clusters about two inches across containing roughly 20–50 eggs and are attached to submerged vegetation. The clusters have the appearance of being tightly packed with eggs due to the relatively thin jelly layer (less thick than the diameter of the egg, about 1.5 mm.) surrounding each one. Color of embryo is tan above and creamy gold below. Tadpoles are generally light in color, often with gold flecks and have a round whitish belly. When viewed from above, tadpole eyes are dark and protrude slightly out to the sides. Collections have been made near Fallen Leaf and Grass Lakes.

Debate as to the correct genus has been on-going since 1986, but *Pseudacris* has been accepted by many since 1997. It means "false Cricket Frog" (with the Cricket Frog genus being named after the Latin term for locust, *acris*). That being said, many people still use the common name of "Pacific Treefrog," since it is well-known and common names have never been required to have a direct relationship to the scientific name. However, a study has shown that a single male does act as "chorus master" and induces surrounding males to begin calling—a good reason to change the name. Others refuse to change at all and still use *Hyla* (meaning "of the woods"), even though they are often found in grasslands. (Also, according to Greek mythology, *Hylas* was one of Jason's Argonauts who was pulled into a spring by a naiad while trying to replace an oar for Heracles.) Not sure why it is "regal," but it can squat very well with its nose in the air.

TRUE FROGS, Family *Ranidae*

Mountain (Sierra) Yellow-legged Frog
Rana muscosa (sierrae?) (Camp, 1917). *Plate 25.*

2–3 inches

This beautiful frog of glacial tarns and alpine lakes has recently disappeared from nearly its entire former range in the Sierras. In Desolation Wilderness, there were strong populations in many of our highest southwestern lakes until the late 1980's. Many specimens were collected from Heather Lake (1900), Lake of the Woods (1945 & 1966), Hemlock Lake (unknown date), Grouse Lake (1974), Tamarack Lake (1975) and Smith Lake (1974 & 1975).

As an example, Pyramid Peak Lake (immediately northwest of the peak, at an elevation just shy of 9,000 feet) used to be packed with these frogs, with one every two feet of shoreline up until 1988. In 1995, there were only two adults, four tadpoles and two egg masses found. By 1999, the only apparently viable population in the Tahoe Basin was documented in Hell Hole Meadow, but it also appears to be declining.

The very nature of their small, isolated populations predispose Mountain

Yellow-legged Frogs to local extirpations (caused by a number of naturally-fluctuating factors). Natural re-colonization becomes more and more difficult as existing populations become further isolated from each other due to introduced trout, damaged habitats, drought, pollution and previously unknown pathogens. In addition, because of the almost 32-degree water in most glacial tarns, it can take two, three or possibly even four years before tadpoles are big enough to metamorphose into adults—further exposing the larvae to many threats over multiple years. Finally, their high-elevation homes make Mountain Yellow-legged Frogs especially vulnerable to the potentially damaging effects of increased ultraviolet radiation.

Only two specific agents have been documented as directly killing large numbers of these frogs: the "red-leg" disease caused by the bacterium *Aeromonas hydrophila* and a Chytrid fungus (*Batrachochytrium dendrobatidis*) that damages the mouthparts of tadpoles and the skin of adult frogs. Both of these have always been present in the environment, but only recently have become pathogenic. Hypotheses as to why center on subtle changes in water chemistry and temperature as well as more virulent strains incidentally introduced via fish stocking.

Please keep an eye out for surviving populations—if you find one in our area, notify the Forest Service! The Mountain Yellow-legged Frog is currently listed as Threatened under the Endangered Species Act, Sensitive by the USDA Forest Service and Species of Special Concern by California. Not that anyone should handle these critically imperiled frogs, but if you do happen to catch one by mistake, they apparently emit a garlic-like odor. The lichen-like patterning on the back earns this species the name *muscosa* (meaning "mossy"…or lichen-y).

Bullfrog
Rana catesbeiana (Shaw, 1802). *Plate 25.*

3 ½–8 inches

Around 1900, restaurateurs introduced this frog to the West from the Eastern U. S. in hopes of providing a local source of meaty legs for their business. The conspicuous, large ear drum (tympanum) is diagnostic, as is the large size. Vocalizations include a loud, low-pitched, cow-like "moo" (hence the common name) and a frightened, beepy squeak given as they jump into the water to avoid predators. The scientific name honors Mark Catesby, an English naturalist who did extensive work in the Southeastern U. S. in the early 1700's.

With ravenous appetites, Bullfrogs take heavy tolls on anything that moves and can fit in its mouth—including baby ducks, snakes and each other. These frogs evolved with predatory fish and easily out-compete our native frogs where fish have been introduced. In addition, they can lay up to 20,000 eggs at a time—ten to one hundred times as many as our native frogs. With a California fishing license in hand, you can take as many of these as you can catch—and please do! Not common in our watershed, but Bullfrogs have been increasingly detected above their previous elevational limit here: 6,000 feet.

Note: The **Northern Leopard Frog**, Rana pipiens, *(the stereotypical biology class frog) was historically present near the south shore of Lake Tahoe but it is unclear whether this population represented a failed introduction or a native extirpation. Collections were made near Fallen Leaf Lake in 1919 and in lower Taylor Creek in 1965. If you find a spotted frog with conspicuous cream-colored dorsolateral folds, notify the Forest Service!*

TRUE TOADS, Family *Bufonidae*

Western Toad (California)
Bufo boreas halophilus (Baird & Girard, 1852). Plate 25.

2–5 inches

Love them, warts and all! Toads are cool—literally: they usually remain underground during the day and are most active at night. However, in the late summer and early fall, the recently metamorphosed young can swarm the edges of ponds and lakes during the day. Hundreds of them can create moving carpets of charcoal-colored, inch-long "toadlets." In our area, look for these toads near small ponds and lakes—ideally ringed with some vegetation and with deep soils nearby—below about 8,000 feet.

Toad tadpoles are similarly gregarious and aggregate in large schools that cruise the shallows. In late spring, females lay about 12,000 eggs in long strings, often in parallel pairs and hatch in about a week (give or take a few days depending on the warmth of the water). The dark black tadpoles then spend the entire summer feeding and growing. Adults often have a light stripe down the middle of their back and prefer to walk rather than hop.

Some animals, such as our garter snakes, are immune to the poison secreted by the paratoid glands—located just behind their eyes—and eat toads with impunity. When captured, toads may puff up, secrete a milky poison, urinate or "twitter" (a male telling the captor he is not a female ready to be mated). Breeding vocalizations are a series of soft, high-pitched cheeps. The scientific name translates as "northern sea-loving toad," due to its range: as far north as Alaska and, our subspecies, along the Pacific Coast.

REPTILES
CLASS *Reptilia*

ORDER *Squamata*, lizards & snakes

LIZARDS

FAMILY *Phrynosomatidae*, spiny lizards

Sceloporus occidentalis occidentalis   <u>**Western Fence Lizard**</u> (NW)

Sceloporus graciosus gracilis   <u>**Sagebrush Lizard**</u> (Western)

FAMILY *Anguidae*, alligator lizards

Elgaria coerula palmeri   <u>**Northern Alligator Lizard**</u> (Sierra)

SNAKES

FAMILY *Boidae*, boas

Charina bottae   <u>**Rubber Boa**</u> (Northern)

FAMILY *Colubridae*, garter snakes, etc.

Thamnophis sirtalis fitchii   <u>**Common Garter Snake**</u> (Valley)

Thamnophis elegans elegans   <u>**W. Terrestrial Garter Snake**</u> (Mountain)

Thamnophis couchii   <u>**Sierra Garter Snake**</u> (W. Aquatic)

REPTILES: Lizards and Snakes
Class *Reptilia*, Order *Squamata*

Our area only has representatives from a single order of reptiles, *Squamata*, which includes both lizards and snakes. (We don't have any turtles: they seem to stay below about 4,000 feet.) Some people are surprised to hear that the legged and the legless reptiles belong to a single order. Sure, lizards have legs, eyelids, moveable eyes and external ear holes, but deep down inside, the two really are not that different.

Many of our reptiles bear live young (instead of laying eggs) as a way to deal with the relatively cool, short summers of our high elevations.

LIZARDS
SPINY LIZARDS, Family *Phrynosomatidae*

Western (Northwestern) Fence Lizard
Sceloporus occidentalis occidentalis (Baird & Girard, 1852). *Plate 26.*

> 6–8 inches

Good climbers, these lizards are commonly spotted on fence posts, the males doing stiff push-ups to defend territories, attract mates and earn their other common name: "blue belly." The solid blue patch on the male's throat (even if divided in half by a line of white scales) distinguishes this species from the Western Sagebrush Lizard, which has a pale, mottled blue throat. Both males and females of this genus can have blue patches on the sides of their bellies, but the male's patches are much larger and deeper in color. Fence lizards can be found as high as 9,000 feet and seem to prefer rocky areas.

Sceloporus means "leg-pore" and refers to the line of pores on the underside of the thigh that is unique to this genus. Another common name for the group, "swifts," is also very accurate—just try to catch one. Our subspecies is referred to as the Northwestern (despite the "western-western" translation). The species is called the Western Fence Lizard.

Favored spots for hibernation include rotten logs, rodent burrows and other underground chambers. Mating takes place in the spring. By early summer, females are burying clutches of 3–17 eggs in loose, moist soil that will hatch in about two months.

The most fascinating recent discovery regarding Western Fence Lizards is their role in interrupting the transmission pathway of Lyme disease. Western black-legged ticks are the main vector of Lyme disease in our area. These ticks, especially in their tiny (1/20th inch) nymphal stage, commonly feed on Western Fence Lizards—one often finds them imbedded in lizards ears, necks, armpits and other less-protected areas. (See photo, plate 26). It turns out that Western Fence Lizards have a substance in their blood that kills the spirochete bacteria (*Borrelia birgdorferi*) that is responsible for causing Lyme disease in humans. This has the effect of disinfecting every tick that feeds on a fence lizard. The result is that in regions without these lizards, about half of ticks carry Lyme disease. In areas with Western Fence Lizards present, the incidence of infection drops to between one percent and five percent of adult ticks. This leaves a person in our area with pretty good odds against contracting Lyme disease, even if they are bitten by the right species of tick.

So, next time you see a fence lizard, thank it for performing this invaluable service. (And thank Professor Robert Lane and Gary Quistad of UC Berkeley who discovered this fact in 1998 and the National Institutes of Health for funding their research.)

Sagebrush Lizard (Western)
Sceloporus graciosus gracilis (Baird & Girard, 1852). *Plate 26.*

4–6 inches

Found in brushy areas even without sagebrush, this is the smoothest-looking member of its genus—hence the name, "graceful & slender." The rear of the thighs have smooth granular scales as opposed to the prickly ones sported by the fence lizard. The mottled or speckled light blue & white throat is diagnostic on the males. All individuals in this genus can have blue patches on the sides of their bellies, but males have the largest and most deeply colored patches. The smaller size is also a good indicator of this species and also correlates to the mean prey size: *S. occidentalis* averages prey items slightly longer than 5 mm while *S. graciosus* takes prey averaging slightly less than 5 mm. In the Great Basin these lizards are lighter brown and more longitudinally striped but on the west side they are not easy to tell apart from fence lizards at first glance.

They mate in the spring and lay 2–7 eggs in the summer that hatch in the fall. Sagebrush Lizards are probably less common than the fence lizard in our watershed and are usually found below 8,000 feet.

Like many of our herps (reptiles & amphibians), this species was described by Spencer Fullerton Baird and Charles Girard in the "Catalogue of North American Reptiles" they published while working together at the Smithsonian Institution.

ALLIGATOR LIZARD, Family *Anguidae*

Northern (Sierra) Alligator Lizard
Elgaria coerulea palmeri (Stejneger, 1893/Wiegmann, 1828). *Plate 26.*

8–10 inches

Our largest lizard is definitely well-named. Not only because it is big and looks like a small alligator (especially the males, with their more broadly triangular heads), but because it will readily bite like one when captured (don't worry—they rarely draw blood). Adults are brown, checkered with black spots and lines; young have copper-colored backs. Females incubate their eggs internally and give birth to 2–12 live young in the late summer.

These lizards frequent forests and shrubby hillsides, rocky slopes, creek sides and meadows. A collection was taken from near Fallen Leaf Lake in 1919.

They wriggle like snakes through the grass when trying to escape, readily shed their tails as a distraction and will bite and defecate as a final defense—Alligator lizards are definitely not content to go quietly into the night. In addition to the regular lizard fare of insects and other arthropods, these big boys (and girls) will also eat smaller lizards and snakes.

Elgaria is supposed to sound like alligator and *coerulea* is after the dark bluish back of the type specimen. The subspecies honors Theodore Palmer (1868–1955), a Californian-born ornithologist who worked for the U.S. Biological Survey, the Smithsonian Institution and the Audubon Society. He collected this type specimen in 1891 and has many other species of various taxa named after him.

SNAKES

BOAS, Family *Boidae*

Rubber Boa (Northern)
Charina bottae (Blainville, 1835). *Plate 27.*

1–2 feet

The smooth, loose skin and equally blunt ends do make this snake appear like a thick piece of brown rubber. With two head-like ends, this snake is a real-life Pushmi-Pullyu. Small, inconspicuous eyes and the lack of enlarged chin shields aid in its convincing defensive ruse: coiled up, ready to strike—

with its tail. The blunt tip of the tail is armored with a large, solid, cap-like scale and will even simulate striking movements. This deceptive act attracts attacks to the more expendable and better-protected end of its body.

Although it can use this hoax with predators (combined with a stinky musk secretion), the head-like tail is probably most often employed to distract fiercely protective mothers while calmly gulping down their babies with its other end. If you manage to capture one, look for tiny telltale scars on the tail, as well as the unique vestigial "legs" which appear as spur-like scales on either side of the vent (most obvious on males).

The Rubber Boa is extremely docile and never bites in defense. This easygoing personality may be why it prefers to prey on the helpless nestlings of small mammals (specializing in mice & shrews). It will also eat just about any other young, defenseless animal (or egg) that will fit in its mouth. It will use the family's famous method of subduing prey—constriction—but only on the rare occasion that it attempts a meal that puts up a struggle. Ethically questionable feeding strategies aside, these snakes can be delightful companions and can be content to become living necklaces or bracelets for an hour or more.

Rubber Boas often go unnoticed due to their preference of being active at night and often in underground burrows. However, they are common around human habitations (where mice proliferate) and can be found during the day while taking shelter under logs, rocks or other cover. Females give birth to 1–8 live young (which are pinkish-brown and can resemble earthworms from a distance) between August and October. I once found an adult Rubber Boa in the rocks on the other side of the road from Camp's Boat Dock shack—no doubt living large off the mice attracted to the nearby staff cabins. Collections have been taken near Glen Alpine Creek and Osgood Bog.

Paolo Emilio Botta (1802–1870) was the physician/naturalist (as they all were back then) on the French merchant ship "*Heros.*" He collected the type specimen while they were in California and sent it to Blainville at the *Museum National d'Histoire Naturelle* in France.

GARTER SNAKES, Family *Colubridae*, Genus *Thamnophis*

The garter snake genus translates as "shrub-snake." Our three species share many common traits. They are all longitudinally striped (usually in at least shades of yellow and black) and have keeled scales (as if they had been folded in half lengthwise and still retain the ridge in the middle)— except, of course, the smooth head and belly scales.

Adults are generally 1½–3 feet long. All live near water, but the Sierra is the most aquatic, closely followed by the Common; our Mountain subspecies of the Western Terrestrial spends relatively little time directly in the water.

All three species prey on amphibians (including toxic ones that some are resistant to), amphibian larvae, fish, leeches, small mammals, reptiles and young birds. Juveniles often specialize on earthworms and slugs. Females usually bear about 5–20 live young in the late summer.

Here is a table to help with identification:

SPECIES	U.L.S.	COLOR/PATTERN
Common (Valley)	7	red flecks in the black; broad yellow stripes
W. Terrestrial (Mountain)	8	thin pale yellow stripes, well-defined on bl.
Sierra (W. Aquatic)	8	dark, more spotted than striped, bronze/bl.

U.L.S. refers to Upper Labial Scales, the number of scales along one side of the upper lip (not counting the "rostral" scale at the very tip of the snout). The main difference is actually the number that are between the eye and the nostril—either three or four (all garter snakes have four upper labial scales from below the middle of the eye back). To see this well, you either need a good pair of binoculars or the snake in hand. Since garters can be surprisingly quick, especially if warm, I'd try the binoculars first.

When handled, they may emit a smelly musk from their anal glands that can be difficult to wash off, but are otherwise relatively harmless—although some of the larger individuals will bite if provoked.

Garter snakes are famous for their large communal hibernacula (shared with other species of garter snakes and even other snakes, like Rubber Boas) and will travel significant distances to rocky, south-facing slopes for their long winter's sleep.

The names for our species are Common, Western Terrestrial and (was) Western Aquatic; our respective subspecies are Valley, Mountain and Sierra (now elevated to a full species). There is still debate as to the systematics of this group, so I listed the most commonly recognized name first and the other name in parentheses (usually the subspecies, but sometimes a former name).

Common Garter Snake (Valley)
Thamnophis sirtalis fitchii (Fox, 1951). *Plate 27.*

   1½–3 feet

Our largest and most colorful species. Rare individuals have exceeded four feet, but such size is unlikely at our elevations. Our Valley subspecies of the Common Garter Snake is our only snake that has red scales sprinkled (or grouped into larger irregular spots) throughout the wide black stripes on either side of its body. This species also has the widest, richest yellow stripe running down the center of its back and along both sides.

The Common Garter Snake is the most widespread snake in North America: a dozen subspecies range from the tip of Florida to the panhandle of Alaska. It is also our largest state's only reptile. The specific epithet, *sirtalis*, also means "garter" and is another reference to its suspender-like stripes.

Here is a behavioral cue to tell this species from the next one: if you startle a garter snake on a stream bank, a Common will dive into the water to escape (and even stay at the bottom until it is safe) while a Mountain will flee into the grass. Not fool-proof, of course, but this has been field-tested many times and some herpetologists swear by it.

Our subspecies is named after Henry Sheldon Fitch(1909–) who did his undergraduate work at University of Oregon. He then studied under Grinnell at Cal while writing his master's thesis on alligator lizards and doctoral dissertation on garter snakes. Although emeritus, he is active at the University of Kansas and was still leading field trips as recently as 2001. *[Chasing snakes: a sure way to keep you in shape and feeling young! I recommend it to everyone.]*

Western Terrestrial Garter Snake (Mountain)
Thamnophis elegans elegans (Baird & Girard, 1853). *Plate 27.*

1½–3 feet

Our Mountain subspecies of the Western Terrestrial is indeed elegant: the pale yellow stripe down the center of the back is neatly delineated from the black. This is the species most likely to be seen far from water, although they seldom stray very far from moist riparian areas. Collections have been taken from near Cathedral Lake, Lake of the Woods and Grouse Lake.

Enlarged rear teeth and mildly toxic saliva (no threat to humans) aid this species in taking slightly larger, furrier and harder to handle prey. It has been documented using its coils to hold prey while slowly chewing its weak poison into the unfortunate animal's system.

Sierra (Western Aquatic) Garter Snake
Thamnophis couchii (Kennicott, 1859). *Plate 27.*

1½–3 feet

Our most highly aquatic snake, this species is invariably found within arm's reach of water, most often along rocky streams and lake shores. Because it spends a great deal of its time foraging for fish and amphibians in cold water, it also spends a lot of time sunning itself to get warm. The Sierra is our darkest, dullest and spottiest garter snake: the stripe down its back is reduced to a broken, thin line of dark creamy-bronze and it has two rows of staggered, overlapping splotches of dark brownish-black on a creamy or bronze background which barely shows around the edges. It also sports the most acutely pointed snout and wide-eyed look.

Named after Darius Nash Couch (1822–1897) by Robert Kennicott. Couch was a West Point graduate and First Lieutenant in the US Army who led a personal expedition to northern Mexico in 1853, collecting many species for the Smithsonian.

Kennicott (1835–1866) was one of the original members of the Megatherium Club—a group of enthusiastic young naturalists overseen by Baird at the Smithsonian. Kennicott also raised awareness about the lamentable and increasing loss of native prairie in the Midwest and helped in the race to document the species before they were plowed under. At the age of 21, he was one of the founders of Chicago's first museum in 1856—the Academy of Sciences: a place where city-dwellers could reconnect with the wonder of the natural world. Although the Great Fire destroyed everything six years later, the museum received replacement specimens from all over the world continues its strong tradition today as the Notebaert Nature Museum in Lincoln Park. He suffered from poor health throughout his life, but he loved being in the field and went on many collecting expeditions for Baird, dying of a heart attack in Alaska at the age of 31.

Note: Thamnophis couchii was split into four species in 1987: T. couchii, T. atratus, T. gigas and T. hammondii.

BIRD SPECIES CHECKLIST

ANSERIFORMES
ANATIDAE
Greater White-fronted Goose
Snow Goose
Canada Goose
Tundra Swan
Wood Duck
Gadwall
American Wigeon
Mallard
Cinnamon Teal
Northern Shoveler
Northern Pintail
Green-winged Teal
Canvasback
Ring-necked Duck
Greater Scaup
Lesser Scaup
Bufflehead
Common Goldeneye
Barrow's Goldeneye
Hooded Merganser
Common Merganser
Ruddy Duck

GALLIFORMES
PHASIANIDAE
Blue Grouse

ODONTOPHORIDAE
Mountain Quail

GAVIIFORMES
GAVIIDAE
Common Loon

PODICIPEDIFORMES
PODICIPEDIDAE
Pied-billed Grebe
Horned Grebe
Red-necked Grebe
Eared Grebe
Western Grebe
Clark's Grebe

PELECANIFORMES
PELECANIDAE
American White Pelican

PHALACROCORACIDAE
Double-crested Cormorant

CICONIIFORMES
ARDEIDAE
Great Blue Heron
Great Egret
Black-crowned Night-Heron

CATHARTIDAE
Turkey Vulture

FALCONIFORMES
ACCIPITRIDAE
Osprey
Bald Eagle
Northern Harrier
Sharp-shinned Hawk
Cooper's Hawk
Northern Goshawk
Swainson's Hawk
Red-tailed hawk
Ferruginous Hawk
Rough-legged hawk
Golden Eagle

FALCONIDAE
American Kestrel
Peregrine Falcon
Prairie Falcon

GRUIFORMES
RALLIDAE
American Coot

CHARADRIIFORMES
CHARADRIIDAE
Killdeer

SCOLOPACIDAE
Spotted Sandpiper

LARIDAE
Ring-billed Gull
California Gull
Herring Gull
Caspian Tern
Forster's Tern
Black Tern

COLUMBIFORMES
COLUMBIDAE
Band-tailed Pigeon
Mourning Dove

STRIGIFORMES
STRIGIDAE
Flammulated Owl
Western Screech-Owl
Great Horned Owl
Northern Pygmy-Owl
Spotted Owl
Long-eared Owl
Northern Saw-whet Owl

CAPRIMULGIFORMES
CAPRIMULGIDAE
Common Nighthawk
Common Poorwill

APODIFORMES
APODIDAE
Black Swift
Vaux's Swift
White-throated Swift

TROCHILIDAE
Anna's Hummingbird
Calliope Hummingbird
Rufous hummingbird
Allen's Hummingbird

CORACIIFORMES
ALCEDINIDAE
Belted Kingfisher

PICIFORMES
PICIDAE
Lewis's Woodpecker
Williamson's Sapsucker
Red-naped Sapsucker
Red-breasted Sapsucker
Hairy Woodpecker
White-headed Woodpecker
Black-backed Woodpecker
Northern Flicker
Pileated Woodpecker

PASSERIFORMES
TYRANNIDAE
Olive-sided Flycatcher
Western Wood-Pewee
Willow Flycatcher
Hammond's Flycatcher
Dusky Flycatcher
Pacific-slope Flycatcher
Black Phoebe

VIREONIDAE
Cassin's Vireo
Warbling Vireo

CORVIDAE
Steller's Jay
Western Scrub-Jay
Clark's Nutcracker
American Crow
Common Raven

HIRUNDINIDAE
Tree Swallow
Violet-green Swallow
Barn Swallow
Cliff Swallow

PARIDAE
Mountain Chickadee

SITTIDAE
Red-breasted Nuthatch
White-breasted Nuthatch
Pygmy Nuthatch

TREES

White Fir p. 2
Abies concolor

Red Fir p. 3
Abies magnifica magnifica

Mountain Hemlock top and cones p. 4
Tsuga mertensiana

Douglas-fir cone p. 4
Pseudotsuga menziesii

Lodgepole Pine cone p. 5
Pinus contorta murrayana

A Nature Guide to the Southwest Tahoe Basin Plate 1

TREES

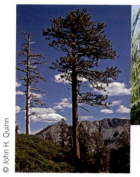

Jeffrey Pine, above, and cones at right
Pinus jeffreyi
p. 6, 82

Whitebark Pine   p. 9
Pinus albicaulis

Western White Pine cone, at top, and Sugar Pine cone, at bottom, showing typical size difference between the two species. (Camera lens cap shown for size comparison.)

Western White Pine bark   p. 8
Pinus monticola

Sugar Pine   p. 8, 82
Pinus lambertiana

Plate 2   A Nature Guide to the Southwest Tahoe Basin

TREES

Incense-cedar, detail above p. 10
Calocedrus decurrens

Western Juniper p. 11, 81
Juniperus occidentalis australis

Mountain Alder p. 15
Alnus incana tenuifolia

Mountain Maple,
seed pods in lower photo
Acer glabrum torreyi
p. 16

SHRUBS

Huckleberry Oak p. 25
Quercus vaccinifolia

Bush Chinquapin p. 25
Chrysolepis sempervirens

Tobacco Brush p. 25
Ceanothus velutinus velutinus

Mountain Whitethorn p. 26
Ceanothus cordulatus

Greenleaf Manzanita p. 27, 81
Arctostaphylos patula

Sierra Coffeeberry p. 26
Rhamnus rubra

Pinemat Manzanita p. 27
Arctostaphylos nevadensis

Plate 4 — A Nature Guide to the Southwest Tahoe Basin

SHRUBS

Mountain Sagebrush   p. 28
Artemesia tridentata vaseyana

Serviceberry,
flower above,
fruit at right
Amelanchier spp.
p. 28

Bitter Cherry,
fruit above,
flower at right
Prunus emarginata
p. 29

Western Choke-cherry
Prunus virginiana demissa
p. 29

A Nature Guide to the Southwest Tahoe Basin

SHRUBS

Mountain-Ash, fruit on left; flower on right
Sorbus spp. p. 29

Red Elderberry, flower on left, fruit below
Sambucus racemosa microbotrys p. 30

Blue Elderberry p. 30
Sambucus mexicana

Creek Dogwood p. 31
Fruit on left, flower above
Cornus sericea sericea

Plate 6   A Nature Guide to the Southwest Tahoe Basin

FERNS AND FERN ALLIES

Bracken Fern p. 37
Pteridium aquilinum pubescens

Leather Grape-Fern p. 37
Botrychium multifidum

Indian Dream p. 38
Aspidotis densa

Five-finger Fern p. 38
Adiantum aleuticum

Bridge's Cliff-brake p. 38
Pellaea bridgesii

American Parsley Fern p. 38
Cryptogramma acrostichoides

Lace Fern p. 39
Cheilanthes gracillima

FERNS

Common Horsetail p. 39, 81
Equisetum arvense

Lady Fern p. 40
Athyrium filix-femina cyclosorum

FLOWERS, BLUE-PURPLE

Alpine Speedwell p. 41
Veronica wormskjoldii

Mountain Jewelflower
Streptanthus tortuosus var. orbiculatus
p. 42

Explorer's Gentian p. 42
Gentiana calycosa

Alpine Blue Flax p. 42
Linum lewisii alpicola

Small-flowered Stickseed p. 43
Hackelia micrantha

Waterleaf Phacelia p. 43
Phacelia hydrophylloides

A Nature Guide to the Southwest Tahoe Basin — Plate 9

FLOWERS, BLUE-PURPLE

Purple Nightshade
Solanum xanti
p. 43

Showy Penstemon
Penstemon speciosus
p. 44

Rydberg's Penstemon
Penstemon rydbergii oreocharis
p. 44

Towering Larkspur
Delphinium glaucum
p. 44

Nuttall's Larkspur
Delphinium nuttallianum
p. 44

Monkshood
Aconitum columbianum
p. 45, 82

FLOWERS, BLUE-PURPLE

Mountain Pennyroyal p. 45
Monardella odoratissima pallida

Nettle-leaf Horsemint p. 45
Agastache urticifolia

Lupine p. 46
Lupinus spp.

Western Blue Flag p. 46
Iris missouriensis

Camas Lily p. 47
Camassia quamash

Western Aster p. 47
Aster occidentalis occidentalis

A Nature Guide to the Southwest Tahoe Basin

FLOWERS, PINK

Fireweed p. 47
Epilobium angustifolium circumvagum

Smooth-stemmed Fireweed p. 48
Epilobium glaberrimum glaberrimum

Rockfringe p. 48
Epilobium obcordatum

Interior Rose p. 48
Rosa woodsii ultramontana

Sierra Gooseberry: flower on left, fruit below
Ribes roezlii roezlii p. 49

Plate 12 A Nature Guide to the Southwest Tahoe Basin

FLOWERS, PINK

Sierra Currant p. 49
Ribes nevadense
Flower on left, fruit above

Sticky Currant p. 50
Ribes viscosissimum

Pink Pyrola p. 50
Pyrola asarifolia asarifolia
(with Scouring Rush)

Spreading Dogbane p. 51
Apocynum androsaemifolium

Whisker Brush p.50
Linanthus ciliatus

Pink Alumroot p. 51
Heuchera rubescens glandulosa

Elephant's Head p. 51
Pedicularis groenlandica

A Nature Guide to the Southwest Tahoe Basin · Plate 13

FLOWERS, PINK

Lewis's Monkeyflower
Mimulus lewisii
p. 52

Mountain Pride   p. 52
Penstemon newberryi newberryi

Brewer's Monkeyflower   p. 53
Mimulus breweri

Mountain Spiraea   p. 53
Spiraea densiflora

Creeping Snowberry   p. 54
Symphoricarpos mollis

Sierra Shooting Star   p. 53
Dodecatheon jeffreyi

Red Heather   p. 54
Phyllodoce breweri

Alpine Laurel   p. 54
Kalmia polifolia microphylla

FLOWERS, PINK – RED

Swamp Onion　　　　　p. 55, 83
Allium validum

Sierra Onion　　　　　p. 55, 83
Allium campanulatum

Pink Pussy-toes　　　　p. 55
Antennaria rosea rosea

Pussypaws　　　　　　p. 56
Calyptridium umbellatum

Anderson's Thistle　　　p. 56
Cirsium andersonii

Snow Plant　　　　　　p. 56
Sarcodes sanguinea

Pine Drops　　　　　　p. 57
Pterospora andromedea

A Nature Guide to the Southwest Tahoe Basin　　　　　Plate 15

FLOWERS, RED – ORANGE

California Fuchsia p. 58
Epilobium canum latifolium

Scarlet Gilia p. 58
Ipomopsis aggregata

Crimson Columbine p. 59
Aquilegia formosa

Rosy Sedum p. 59
Sedum roseum integrifolium

Applegate's Paintbrush p. 60
Castilleja applegatei

Spotted Coralroot p. 60
Corallorhiza maculata

Giant Paintbrush p. 60
Castilleja miniata miniata

Sierra Tiger Lily p. 61
Lilium parvum

Plate 16   A Nature Guide to the Southwest Tahoe Basin

FLOWERS, YELLOW

Hooker's
Evening Primrose p. 61
Oenothera elata hirsutissima

Sierra Wallflower p. 61
Erysimum capitatum perrene

Graceful Cinquefoil p. 62
Potentilla gracilis

Sticky Cinquefoil p. 62
Potentilla glandulosa

Shrubby Cinquefoil p. 61
Potentilla fruticosa

Bird's-foot Lotus p. 62
Lotus oblongifolius oblongifolius

Seep-Spring Monkeyflower
Mimulus guttatus p. 63

A Nature Guide to the Southwest Tahoe Basin Plate 17

FLOWERS, YELLOW

Plantain Leaf Buttercup p. 63
Ranunculus alismifolius

Western Sweet Cicely p. 63
Osmorhiza occidentalis

Sierra Stonecrop p. 64, 83
Sedum obtusatum obtusatum

Woolly Mullein
Verbascum thapsus
p. 64

Pine Violet
Viola pinetorum pinetorum
p. 64

Prettyface p. 65
Triteleia ixoides anilina

Yellow Pond-lily p. 65
Nuphar polysepala

Large-flowered Brickellbush p. 65
Brickellia grandiflora

Plate 18   A Nature Guide to the Southwest Tahoe Basin

FLOWERS, YELLOW

Rabbitbrush p. 66
Chrysothamnus nauseosus

Canada Goldenrod
Solidago canadensis elongata
p. 66

Arrow-leaved Balsam-root, *Balsamorhiza sagittata*, above, and Wooly Mule's Ear, *Wyethia mollis*, on right, with which Arrow-leaved Balsamroot is sometimes confused. p. 67

Heartleaf Arnica p. 66, 79
Arnica cordifolia

Arrowleaf Groundsel p. 67
Senecio triangularis

A Nature Guide to the Southwest Tahoe Basin

FLOWERS, WHITE

Mugwort p. 67
Artemesia douglasiana

Enchanter's Nightshade p. 68
Circaea alpina pacifica

Leichtlin's Mariposa Lily p. 68, 82
Calochortus leichtlinii

Sierra Star Tulip p. 68
Calochortus minimus

Spreading Phlox p. 69
Phlox diffusa

Rock Cress p. 68
Arabis holboellii

Thimbleberry p. 69, 84
Rubus parviflorus

Plate 20 A Nature Guide to the Southwest Tahoe Basin

FLOWERS, WHITE

Mousetail Ivesia
Ivesia santolinoides
p. 69

California Grass-of-Parnassus
Parnassia californica
p. 71

Hot Rock Penstemon
Penstemon deustus pedicellatus
p. 70

Vari-leaved Phacelia
Phacelia heterophylla virgata
p. 69

One-sided Wintergreen
Orthilia secunda
p. 70

Naked Buckwheat
Eriogonum nudum
p. 71

White-veined Wintergreen
Pyrola picta
p. 70

Alpine Knotweed
Polygonum phytolaccifolium
p. 71

A Nature Guide to the Southwest Tahoe Basin — Plate 21

FLOWERS, WHITE

Cow Parsnip
Heracleum lanatum
p. 71

Brewer's Angelica
Angelica brewerii
p. 72

Parish's Yampah
Perideridia parishii latifolia
p. 72, 84

Ranger's Buttons   p. 72
Sphenosciadium capitellatum

Macloskey's Violet   p. 72
Viola macloskeyi

White-flowered Bog-Orchid
Plantanthera leucostachys
p. 73

Death Camas   p. 73, 81
Zigadenus venenosus venenosus

Plate 22 A Nature Guide to the Southwest Tahoe Basin

FLOWERS, WHITE

(Fat) False Solomon's Seal p. 73
Smilacina racemosa

Star (Slim) False Solomon's Seal p. 73
Smilacina stellata

California Corn Lily p. 74
Veratrum californicum californicum

Washington Lily p. 74
Lilium washingtonianum washingtonianum

White Hawkweed p. 75
Hieracium albiflorum

Alpine Pussy-toes p. 75
Antennaria media

Yarrow p. 74, 85
Achillea millefolium

A Nature Guide to the Southwest Tahoe Basin   Plate 23

FLOWERS, GREEN

Meadow-Rue p. 75
Thalictrum fendleri fendleri

Stinging Nettle p. 46, 76, 84
Urtica dioica holosericea

Brewer's Bishop's Cap p. 76
Mitella breweri

Dwarf Lousewort p. 77
Pedicularis semibarbata

Green-flowered Bog-Orchid p. 77
Platanthera sparsiflora

Western Dwarf Mistletoe p. 77
Arceuthobium campylopodum

AMPHIBIANS

Long-toed Salamander (Southern) p. 89
Ambystoma macrodactylum sigillatum

Mount Lyell Salamander p. 89
Hydromantes platycephalus

Pacific Chorus Frog (Treefrog) p. 91
Pseudacris (Hyla) regilla, green form

Pacific Chorus Frog (Treefrog) p. 91
Pseudacris (Hyla) regilla, gray form

Mountain Yellow-legged Frog p. 92
Rana muscosa

Bullfrog p. 93
Rana catesbeiana

Western Toad p. 94
Bufo boreas halophilus

Western Toad juveniles p. 94

A Nature Guide to the Southwest Tahoe Basin

REPTILES

Western Fence Lizard   p. 96
Sceloporus occidentalis occidentalis

Western Fence Lizard, shown with ticks on its neck.

Western Fence Lizard, ♂ ventral view   p. 96

Sagebrush Lizard, ♂ ventral view   p. 97
Sceloporus graciosus gracilis

Sagebrush Lizard, ♂   p. 97
Sceloporus graciosus gracilis

Sagebrush Lizard, ♀   p. 97
Sceloporus graciosus gracilis

Northern Alligator Lizard   p. 98
Elgaria coerulea palmderi

Plate 26   A Nature Guide to the Southwest Tahoe Basin

REPTILES

Rubber Boa p. 98
Charina bottae

Common Garter Snake p. 100
Thamnophis sirtalis fitchii

Western Terrestrial Garter Snake p. 101
Thamnophis elegans elegans

Sierra Garter Snake p. 101
Thamnophis couchii

Sierra Garter Snake, shown swimming

(All reptile and amphibian photos from http://www.californiaherps.com/*)*

A Nature Guide to the Southwest Tahoe Basin   Plate 27

BIRDS

Greater White-fronted Goose
Anser albifrons
p. 107

Snow Goose p.107
Chen caerulescens

Tundra Swan p.107
Cygnus columbianus

Canada Goose p.107
Branta canadensis moffitti

Gadwall, ♂ p.107
Anas strepera

Wood Duck, ♀ and ♂ p. 107
Aix sponsa

American Widgeon, ♂
Anas americana
p.107

Mallard, ♂ & ♀ p.107
Anas platyrhynchos

Plate 28 A Nature Guide to the Southwest Tahoe Basin

BIRDS

Cinnamon Teal, ♂ p.107
Anas cyanoptera

Northern Shoveler, ♂ p.107
Anas clypeata

Northern Pintail, ♀ & ♂ p.107
Anas acuta

Green-winged Teal, ♂ p.107
Anas crecca

Canvasback, ♂ p.107
Aythya valisineria

Ring-necked Duck, ♂ p.107
Aythya collaris

Greater Scaup, ♂ p.107
Aythya marila

Lesser Scaup, ♂ & ♀ p.107
Aythya affinis

A Nature Guide to the Southwest Tahoe Basin

BIRDS

Bufflehead, ♂ p.107
Bucephala albeola

Common Goldeneye, ♂ & ♀ p.107
Bucephala clangula

Barrow's Goldeneye, ♂ p.107
Bucephala islandica

Common Merganser, ♀ p.108
Mergus merganser

Ruddy Duck, ♂ p.107
Oxyura jamaicensis

Mountain Quail p.109
Oreortyx pictus

Blue Grouse ♂ p.108
Dendragapus obscurus sierrae

Blue Grouse ♀ p.108
Dendragapus obscurus sierrae

Plate 30   A Nature Guide to the Southwest Tahoe Basin

BIRDS

Common Loon　　　　　　　　　　p.110
Gavia immer

Pied-billed Grebe, w/young　　　　p.111
Podilymbus podiceps

Horned Grebe, winter plumage　　p.112
Podiceps auritus

Red-necked Grebe, winter plumage　p.112
Podiceps grisegena

Eared Grebe, breeding plumage　　p.111
Podiceps nigricollis

Western Grebe　　　　　　　　　p.112
Aechmophorus occidentalis

Clark's Grebe　　　　　　　　　　p.112
Aechmophorus clarkii

American White Pelican　　　　　p.112
Pelecanus erythrorhynchos

A Nature Guide to the Southwest Tahoe Basin　　　　Plate 31

BIRDS

Double-crested Cormorant
Phalocrocorax auritus p.113

Great Blue Heron p.113
Ardea herodias

Black-crowned Night-Heron
Nycticorax nycticorax p.114

Great Egret p.114
Ardea alba

Snowy Egret p.114
Egretta thula

Turkey Vulture p.115
Cathartes aura

Osprey p.116
Pandion haliaetus

Bald Eagle p.116
Haliaeetus leucocephalus

Northern Harrier, ♂ p.116
Circus cyaneus

Plate 32   A Nature Guide to the Southwest Tahoe Basin

BIRDS

Sharp-shinned Hawk
Accipiter striatus
p.117

Red-tailed Hawk, immature   p.118
Buteo jamaicensis

Golden Eagle   p.118
Aquila chrysaetos

American Kestrel, ♀   p.119
Falco sparverius

American Coot   p.119
Fulica americana

Killdeer   p.120
Charadrius vociferus

Spotted Sandpiper   p.120
Actitis macularius

Ring-billed Gull   p.121
Larus delawarensis

California Gull   p.121
Larus californicus

A Nature Guide to the Southwest Tahoe Basin

BIRDS

Caspian Tern p.121
Sterna caspia

Forster's Tern
Sterna forsteri
p.121

Band-tailed Pigeon p.122
Patgioenas fasciata

Mourning Dove p.123
Zenaida macroura

Western Screech-owl p.123
Megascops kennicottii

Great Horned Owl p.124
Bubo virginianus

Northern Pygmy-Owl p.124
Glaucidium gnoma

Spotted Owl
Strix occidentalis
p.123

Northern Saw-whet Owl
Aegolius acadicus
p.123

Plate 34 — A Nature Guide to the Southwest Tahoe Basin

BIRDS

Common Nighthawk p.124
Chordeiles minor hesperis

Common Poorwill p.125
Phalaenoptilus nuttallii

Calliope Hummingbird, ♂ p.126
Stellula calliope

Anna's Hummingbird, ♂ p.126
Calypte anna

Rufous Hummingbird, ♂ p.127
Selasphorus rufus

Belted Kingfisher, ♂ p.127
Ceryle alcyon

Lewis's Woodpecker
Melanerpes lewis
p.128

Williamson's Sapsucker, ♂
Sphyrapicus thyroideus thyroideus
p.129

A Nature Guide to the Southwest Tahoe Basin Plate 35

BIRDS

Red-breasted Sapsucker   p.130
Sphyrapicus ruber daggetti

Hairy Woodpecker, ♀   p.130
Picoides villosus

White-headed Woodpecker   p.131
Picoides albolarvatus albolarvatus

Black-backed Woodpecker, ♀
Picoides arcticus
p.131

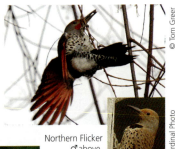

Northern Flicker
♂ above,
♀ on right
Colaptes auratus collaris
p.132

Western Wood-Pewee
Contopus sordidulus veliei
p.133

Pileated Woodpecker, ♂
Dryocopus pileatus   p.132

Willow Flycatcher
Empidonax traillii
p.134

Plate 36   A Nature Guide to the Southwest Tahoe Basin

BIRDS

Hammond's Flycatcher   p.135
Empidonax hammondii

Pacific-slope Flycatcher   p.135
Empidonax difficilis

Black Phoebe   p.136
Sayornis nigricans

Cassin's Vireo   p.1363
Vireo cassinii

Warbling Vireo   p.137
Vireo gilvus

Steller's Jay
Cyanocitta stelleri frontalis
p.138

Western Scrub-Jay   p.137
Aphelocoma californica

Clark's Nutcracker   p.137
Nucifraga columbiana

A Nature Guide to the Southwest Tahoe Basin   Plate 37

BIRDS

American Crow p.139
Corvus brachyrhynchos

Common Raven
Corvus corax
p.139

Tree Swallow
Tachycineta bicolor
p.140

Barn Swallow p.140
Hirundo rustica

Cliff Swallow p.141
Petrochelidon pyrrhonata

Mountain Chickadee p.141
Poecile gambeli abbreviatus

White-breasted
Nuthatch
*Sitta carolinensis
aculeata*
p.142

Red-breasted Nuthatch, ♂ p.142
Sitta canadensis

Plate 38 A Nature Guide to the Southwest Tahoe Basin

BIRDS

Pygmy Nuthatch p.143
Sitta pygmaea

Brown Creeper p.143
Certhia americana

Rock Wren p.144
Salpinctes obsoletus

House Wren
Troglodytes aedon parkmanii
p.144

Canyon Wren p.144
Catherpes mexicanus

American Dipper, immature
Cinclus mexicanus
p.145

Marsh Wren p.145
Cistothorus palustris

Golden-crowned Kinglet, ♂ p.145
Regulus satrapa

Ruby-crowned Kinglet, ♂ p.146
Regulus calendula cineraceus

A Nature Guide to the Southwest Tahoe Basin — Plate 39

BIRDS

Mountain Bluebird, ♂ p.147
Sialia currucoides

Western Bluebird, ♂ p.147
Sialia mexicana

Townsend's Solitaire p.147
Myadestes townsendi townsendi

Hermit Thrush p.148
Catharus guttatus

American Robin, ♂ p.148
Turdus migratorius propinquus

Varied Thrush, ♂ p.149
Ixoreus naevius

American Pipit
Anthus rubescens
p.149

Orange-crowned
Warbler, ♂
*Vermivora celata
lutescens*
p.150

Plate 40 — A Nature Guide to the Southwest Tahoe Basin

BIRDS

Nashville Warbler, ♂ p.150
Vermivora ruficapilla

Yellow Warbler, ♂ p.151
Dendroica petechia

Yellow-rumped Warbler, ♀
Dendroica coronata auduboni
p.151

Black-throated Gray Warbler, ♀ p.152
Dendroica nigrescens

Townsend's Warbler, ♀ p.152
Dendroica townsendi

Hermit Warbler, ♂ p.152
Dendroica occidentalis

MacGillivray's Warbler, ♂ p.153
Oporornis tolmiei tolmiei

Wilson's Warbler, ♂
Wilsonia pusilla chryseola
p.153

A Nature Guide to the Southwest Tahoe Basin

BIRDS

Western Tanager, ♂ p.154
Piranga ludoviciana

Green-tailed Towhee p.154
Pipilo chlorurus

Spotted Towhee, ♂
Pipilo maculatus
p.155

Brewer's Sparrow
Spizella breweri
p.156

Song Sparrow p.157
Melospiza melodia

Lincoln's Sparrow p.157
Melospiza lincolnii alticola

White-crowned
Sparrow
*Zonotrichia
leucophrys
oriantha*
p.158

Golden-crowned Sparrow, immature p.158
Zonotrichia atricapilla

Plate 42   A Nature Guide to the Southwest Tahoe Basin

BIRDS

Dark-eyed Junco, ♀ p.159
Junco hyemalis

Black-headed Grosbeak, ♂
Pheucticus melanocephalus
p.159

Lazuli Bunting, ♂ p.160
Passerina amoena

Red-winged Blackbird, ♂
Agelaius phoeniceus nevadensis
p.161

Western Meadowlark p.161
Sturnella neglecta

Yellow-headed Blackbird, ♂
Xanthocephalus xanthocephalus
p.161

Brewer's Blackbird, ♂
Euphagus cyanocephalus
p.162

Brown-headed Cowbirds, ♂ p.162
Molothrus ater

A Nature Guide to the Southwest Tahoe Basin

BIRDS

Purple Finch, ♂ p.165
Carpodacus purpureus

Cassin's Finch, ♂ p.165
Carpodacus cassinii

Red Crossbill, immature, ♂ p.166
Loxia curvirostra

Pine Siskin p.166
Carduelis pinus

Evening Grosbeak, ♂ p.167
Coccothraustes vespertinus brooksi

MAMMALS

Pika p.175
Ochotona princeps muiri

Sierra Nevada Snowshoe Hare p.176
Lepus americanus tahoensis

Nuttall's Cottontail (Mountain)
Sylvilagus nuttallii
p.177

(Sierra Nevada) Mountain Beaver (Boomer)
Aplodontia rufa californica p.178

Yellow-bellied Marmot p.180
Marmota flaviventris flaviventris

Belding's Ground Squirrel
Spermophilus beldingi
p.180

Golden-mantled Ground Squirrel p.181
Spermophilus lateralis chrysodeirus

California (Beechey) Ground Squirrel p.181
Spermophilus beecheyi sierrae

A Nature Guide to the Southwest Tahoe Basin

MAMMALS

Lodgepole Chipmunk　　　　　　　p.183
Tamias speciosus frater

Long-eared Chipmunk　　　　　　p.183
Tamias quadrimaculatus

Douglas's Squirrel (Chickaree)　　p.184
Tamiasciurus douglasii

Mountain Pocket Gopher　　　　p.186
Thomomys monticola

Deer Mouse　　　　　　　　　　p.187
Peromyscus maniculatus gambelii

Montane Vole　　　　　　　　　p.189
Microtus montanus

Northern Flying Squirrel
Glaucomys sabrinus lascivus
p.185

Porcupine
Erethizon dorsatum
p.190

Plate 46　　　　　　　　　A Nature Guide to the Southwest Tahoe Basin

MAMMALS

Coyote p.191
Canis latrans

Sierra Nevada Black Bear p.192
Ursus americanus californiensis

Long-tailed Weasel p.196
Mustela frenata nevadensis

Badger
Taxidea taxus
p.196

Striped Skunk
Mephitis mephitis
p.197

Bobcat
Lynx rufus
p.198

Mountain Lion p.198
Puma concolor

Mule Deer
Odocoileus hemionus
p.199

A Nature Guide to the Southwest Tahoe Basin

Middle Velma Lake

Looking northwest from near Lake Lucille, down the Glen Alpine Valley, towards Fallen Leaf Lake

CERTHIIDAE
Brown Creeper

TROGLODYTIDAE
Rock Wren
Canyon Wren
House Wren
Winter Wren
Marsh Wren

CINCLIDAE
American Dipper

REGULIDAE
Golden-crowned Kinglet
Ruby-crowned Kinglet

TURDIDAE
Western Bluebird
Mountain Bluebird
Townsend's Solitaire
Hermit Thrush
American Robin
Varied Thrush

MOTACILLIDAE
American Pipit

PARULIDAE
Orange-crowned Warbler
Nashville Warbler
Yellow Warbler
Yellow-rumped Warbler
Black-throated Gray Warbler
Townsend's Warbler
Hermit Warbler
MacGillivray's Warbler
Wilson's Warbler

THRAUPIDAE
Western Tanager

EMBERIZIDAE
Green-tailed Towhee
Spotted Towhee
Chipping Sparrow
Brewer's Sparrow
Fox Sparrow
Song Sparrow
Lincoln's Sparrow
White-crowned Sparrow
Golden-crowned Sparrow
Dark-eyed Junco

CARDINALIDAE
Black-headed Grosbeak
Lazuli Bunting

ICTERIDAE
Red-winged Blackbird
Western Meadowlark
Yellow-headed Blackbird
Brewer's Blackbird
Brown-headed Cowbird

FRINGILLIDAE
Gray-crowned Rosy-Finch
Black Rosy-Finch
Pine Grosbeak
Purple Finch
Cassin's Finch
Red Crossbill
Pine Siskin
Evening Grosbeak

BIRDS

This segment, like the rest of this guide, is meant to supplement, not replace, the excellent identification guides already available. This section may help in identification, but that is not its primary purpose. The paragraphs contain interesting facts not found in most field guides, as well as information specific to our area. Very rare and accidental species are generally not covered. If you see a species not on this list, please report it to the author and the Forest Service.

Bird Names and Order of Lists

The American Ornithologists' Union (AOU) has taken the initiative to establish a Check-list of "correct" common names for North American birds. This list (currently in its 7th Edition, 46th Supplement) makes sure that each capitalized common name corresponds to one and only one scientific name and each scientific name corresponds to one and only one capitalized common name. In so doing, the AOU has enabled the many non-Latin, non-Greek and non-Science speakers of the world to communicate exactly which avian species they are referring to without having to learn another language. This improves communication between scientists and hobbyists, makes for more accurate record keeping, allows accurate lists to be made with just common names and greatly increases the value of amateur observations.

This list is roughly organized from what is thought to be the "least evolved" to the "most evolved." The order appears arbitrary and illogical to the beginning birder, but is standard and is used (with minor variations) in just about every field guide and pamphlet, so it pays to get used to it. Readers unfamiliar with this order may find it easier to use the index when searching for a particular species or group. (Note: although the AOU checklist now begins with Geese, most field guides currently available begin with Loons.)

GEESE and DUCKS, Family *Anatidae*

In the summer, Fallen Leaf Lake almost always has an attending flock of Canada Geese, some Mallards and a handful of Common Mergansers.

The Canada Goose and Mallard are "dabblers"—those that feed by filtering plant and animal food out of the water. Their feet are positioned at the midpoint of their body so they can tip their heads down to the bottom while their rump points to the sky.

Non-breeding rare-but-regular species include: **Tundra Swan, Greater White-fronted Goose, Snow Goose, Gadwall, Green-winged Teal, Cinnamon Teal, American Wigeon, Northern Pintail, Northern Shoveler, Wood Duck, Ruddy Duck, Canvasback, Ring-necked Duck, Lesser & Greater Scaup, Common Goldeneye, Bufflehead** and **Hooded Merganser**. Many of these species used to breed on Rowland's Marsh before Tahoe Keys was developed and some still breed in what is left of the marsh. **Barrow's Goldeneye** was recorded nesting in a snag (they are cavity-nesters) on Upper Velma Lake from 1911 through 1914, but was never common and probably continues to breed on remote alpine lakes. *(Plates 28–30)*

Canada Goose, *Branta canadensis moffitti. Plate 28*

Canada Geese are common on the shores of Fallen Leaf and Lake Tahoe throughout the summer. They have become relatively tame and even dependent upon humans because of the irresistible urge people feel to feed them. Take care not to upset them—tame or not, a full-grown goose can break a person's leg with a single beat of its wing.

At least a few confirmed records of breeding are known from our immediate area, including successful nests at Lily Lake and the cliff behind the staff cabins at Camp. Rowlands Marsh used to support a fair-sized breeding population. Rubicon Point and the island in Emerald Bay have also hosted nesting "honkers" in the past.

Mallard, *Anas platyrhynchos. Plate 28*

The mallard is one of the most common and easily recognized bird species in the northern hemisphere. It is also the wild precursor to Old MacDonald's domestic whites. This duck's *platyrhynchos* (broad nose) gives away its "dabbling" feeding habits.

On Fallen Leaf, this duck (like the Canada Goose) will practically eat a potato chip out of your mouth. When people say, "Let's go feed the ducks," the Mallard is usually the one who ends up with a stomach full of stale bread crusts.

Because the Mallard is widespread, adaptable, handsome, approachable and tasty, it is often used as a symbol for outdoor-oriented organizations. Many hunting groups have contributed even further to its success by purchasing habitat, influencing legislation and supplementing wild populations with farm-raised birds.

Common Merganser, *Mergus merganser. Plate 30*

The most "hip" bird on Fallen Leaf Lake, the female merganser sports a stylish reddish-brown punk haircut: the feathers at the back of her head stick straight out to create one of Nature's best bed-heads. The male, on the other hand, looks very dapper and almost "preppy" in his smooth, iridescent green hood. He can be told apart from the male Mallard by his skinny reddish beak and white breast.

The genus, *Mergus*, means "diver" and the specific epithet, *merganser*, "diving-goose." Mergansers tool along the surface of the lake like a confused submarine, intermittently periscoping the depths below them. When a juicy crayfish or fingerling trout is spotted, the chase begins. The rear-positioned legs help propel the bird after its prey while the serrated, tweezer-like bill ensures its victim will not escape.

Female mergansers can have eight to twelve fledglings following them around or riding on their back as early as May or as late as July. Males are rarely seen between June and October. The family size sometimes decreases by half over the summer. Broods larger than a baker's dozen are created when "egg-dumping" (intra-specific brood parasitism) occurs or the young of another female are orphaned.

Beginning in fall, large groups of mergansers (up to 75) can be found on Fallen Leaf Lake near the Jumping Rocks. Seeing one of these flocks floating together in tight formation, it is clear why they are called as "rafts" by ornithologists. (Note: a vagrant **Hooded Merganser** did show up on Fallen Leaf for a few days late one winter, but such sightings are very rare.)

GROUSE and QUAIL, Family *Phasianidae*

This group of chicken-like game birds includes wild turkeys and pheasants, but only grouse and quail inhabit our high elevations. They spend most of their time on the ground, but are capable of strong (but brief) flight.

Blue Grouse, *Dendragapus obscurus sierrae* (of the Pacific, Sooty or *fuliginosus* group). *Plate 30*

The eerie hoots emitted by breeding males of this species are so low-pitched that they are almost felt more than they are heard—sounding a lot like someone blowing over the mouth of a gallon jug. Inflatable neck sacs help amplify these sounds the same way a frog's expanded throat pouch does. The male's fanned, light-edged tail and yellow neck sacs are usually only visible when actively courting a female.

Although the hoots are usually given from a branch 20-40 feet up in the deep forest, a great deal of summer foraging occurs on the ground in the open areas above 8,000 feet. Sightings have been common throughout Desolation Wilderness, especially near Mt. Tallac, Lake Aloha, Dick's Lake and Tyler Lake. Series of about six hoots can carry over a quarter mile in early spring, mostly on forested slopes (i.e. of Angora Peak).

Our grouse have a highly unusual migratory pattern: instead of moving down-slope or south, they actually migrate *up-slope*—on foot—for the winter. Since grouse are well-insulated and eat conifer buds and young cones during the winter, they may as well spend it in a relatively predator-free environment. Desolation Wilderness's deep snowpack (often exceeding 10 ft.) offers further protection and no reason at all for them to leave the forest canopy, where they remain until spring.

Taking advantage of its excellent camouflage, freezing is the Blue Grouse's first line of defense. If you happen to spot one, freeze yourself: with patience, a whole family often materializes out of the rocks around you. If you don't see them before you almost step on one, their explosive, loud, flapping bursts into the air can be incredibly startling.

Dendragapus means "tree-loving." Both the specific epithet and subspecies refer to its dark, gray-black coloring.

In 1931, our local subspecies was referred to as the Sierra Grouse, *Dendragapus fuliginosus sierrae*, but was quickly re-lumped with the interior Dusky Grouse within a few years. However, a 2004 study published in *Molecular Ecology* by G. F. Barrowclough, *et al.* (Volume 13, Issue 7, p. 1911-1922) makes a more convincing argument to elevate the two "groups" to full species status. This study effectively tells the story of how grouse re-colonized the West after our most recent Ice Age through phylogeographical and coalescent analyses of mitochondrial DNA evidence. The report also helps explain why there are differences between the two groups in morphology, vocalizations and courtship behavior.

Mountain Quail, *Oreortyx pictus. Plate 30*

Slightly larger than its lowland cousin, this quail has two long, straight, thin head plumes instead of a stubby nodding one. Mountain Quail keep to slopes covered with manzanita and ceanothus shrubs, making them more often heard than seen. The males' hoarse *quee-ark* mating calls can be heard echoing over the Glen Alpine Valley in the early spring.

Like many mountain birds, the quail undertakes a vertical migration instead of the more well-known latitudinal (north-south) migration: moving up slope for the summer and down again in the fall. The difference is that these birds make the twenty-mile migration largely on foot—and very small feet, at that. Name appropriately translates as "painted mountain-quail."

LOONS, Family *Gaviidae*

Because they were traditionally thought of as being "least evolved," loons were historically given the distinction of being the first family treated in almost any bird guide. Their heavy skeletal structure and thick bills are reminiscent of prehistoric sea birds. These properties assist them in diving after fish to depths down to three hundred feet.

Although their heavy build enables them to dive deeply, it also necessitates a long runway and low angle during take-off. This periodically strands loons on small, forest-lined lakes while they wait for a day windy enough to get airborne again.

Common Loon, *Gavia immer. Plate 31*

Common Loons probably bred in our area historically but now only rest on Sierra Nevada lakes during both spring and fall migrations. Thick bills and dark plumage help in identifying these rare birds. No other species of loon is known to regularly migrate overland in western North America.

Like most living organisms, loons do not waste time when they are on their way to breed and rarely stay longer than twelve hours in the spring. April is the best month to spot these impatient individuals—often already in full breeding plumage. If you are a light sleeper or an early riser, you may just hear one of their strange, transfixing yodels.

On the way back from their Canadian breeding grounds, however, they are likely to stay on our lakes for a few days or even longer. October and November are both likely months to see this fall visitant in its *immer* (sooty) winter plumage.

GREBES, Family *Podicipedidae*

Instead of webbed feet, grebes have lobed toes. The lobes automatically collapse during forward motion to reduce drag and flare out during the backward thrust to provide more area. The extreme rear position of their legs (*podiceps* means "rump-feet" in Latin) helps to make grebes among the best pursuers of fish in the avian world. Unfortunately, this rear positioning also rules out walking gracefully: a grebe on land can be likened to a fish out of water—or a small, feathered seal.

Grebes can regulate their otherwise cork-like buoyancy by exhaling and compressing their feathers to squeeze out trapped air. If a predator is spotted nearby, grebes can quickly and quietly sink straight down without attracting attention.

Pied-billed Grebe, *Podilymbus podiceps. Plate 31*

This thick-billed grebe is usually seen on Fallen Leaf Lake in the late summer and early fall. Winter sightings are less common, though not unheard of. Pied-billed Grebes used to breed (and possibly lived year-round) at Rowlands Marsh. The Pied-billed Grebe's chunky silhouette, drab brown color and thick bill help to distinguish it from other grebes that also pass through our area.

The common name refers to the black splotch that appears mid-bill during the breeding season. It comes from the Old English, pie, something jumbled, mixed, or splotched—i.e. chicken pot pie, or, when referring to an irregular color pattern, especially black and white—i.e. a piebald horse. Young birds are also camouflaged with black and white stripes.

The genus roughly translates as "rump-diver," which is also a contraction of two other grebe genera. The specific epithet is borrowed from the previous genus, emphasizing the similarity. The total scientific name can therefore be ridiculously translated as "grebe-grebe grebe." Clarence Lesson obviously did not want to break any new ground when he described this species.

Eared Grebe, *Podiceps nigricollis. Plate 31*

Another spring and fall visitor, the Eared Grebe appears to be a cross between our other two grebes. It has black and white coloring similar to the Western or Clark's Grebe, but it is very close to the Pied-billed Grebe in size. The specific epithet means "black-necked," a striking trait in their breeding plumage (in contrast, the similar Horned Grebe has a chestnut-colored neck).

The golden plumes that fan out behind the eyes to form the namesake "ears" are only there for the breeding season. Because breeding no longer occurs nearby (due to the elimination of Rowlands Marsh), full-fledged "eared" sightings are unlikely at Fallen Leaf. Summer and fall are feasting times for Eared Grebes: gathering by the hundreds of thousands, they feed on the abundant brine shrimp of Mono Lake. Some winter there as well, but most fly either west to the coast or south across the border.

Any small, black and white grebe seen in the summer is most likely an

Eared Grebe. (**Horned** [Plate 31] and **Red-necked Grebes** [Plate 31] are less common visitors, but Horned Grebes have been documented on Fallen Leaf during migration, especially in the early spring.)

Western Grebe, Aechmophorus occidentalis. Plate 31
Clark's Grebe, Aechmophorus clarkii. Plate 31

These two species were considered one and the same prior to 1985. Due to this historical fact, don't be too hard on yourself if you can't tell which one you are looking at. The fact that these grebes only make brief stops on Fallen Leaf Lake in the spring and fall means summer visitors probably will not have to worry about identifying either species.

Black surrounds the eye of the Western Grebe while white surrounds the eye of Clark's Grebe. The color of the Western Grebe's bill is also a light, almost greenish-yellow while the Clark's Grebe's bill is a deeper, more orangish, yellow. Hybrids (of course!) are also possible. Genus means "spear-bearer," for their long, sharp bills.

Clark's Grebe was named after the naturalist J.H. Clark, *not* after Captain William Clark, like our nutcracker. He collected the type specimen in Mexico (on Laguna de Santa Maria, SW of El Paso, Texas) while surveying for the Pacific Railroad sometime prior to 1858 (when the description was published).

PELICANS, Family *Pelecanidae*

Although the two North American pelicans appear to be almost identical in structure, they employ entirely different feeding strategies. The Brown Pelican (only present along the coast) dives for fish from a height. In contrast, the White Pelican paddles across the surface of calm water (often in groups) with the tip of its bill dipped in the water, lunging at fish as they go by.

American White Pelican, Pelecanus erythrorhynchos. Plate 31

Pelicans are sometimes spotted high in the sky in the spring and fall on their way between their wintering grounds and inland breeding lakes.

Historically, hundreds of White Pelicans would make brief stopovers at the mouth of the Upper Truckee River, but few, if any, stop near the Tahoe Keys housing development which now covers the site.

When flying at high elevations, pelicans can be mistaken for Snow Geese because of their similar black & white coloring. Check for the pelicans' longer wings as well as large orange bills and feet. Pelicans also soar more often on set wings while geese flap most of the time.

CORMORANTS, Family *Phalacrocoracidae*

Cormorants are well-designed for pursuing fish underwater. Webbed feet are positioned at the rear of the body for jet-like propulsion, wing feathers are "wettable" (which decreases buoyancy) and the hooked bill grips slippery fish with confidence. The wettable wing feathers necessitate intermittent drying, performed by assuming the commonly seen spreadwing posture. The family and genus name means "bald crow" because European cormorants have white heads in the breeding season.

Double-crested Cormorant, *Phalocrocorax auritus. Plate 32*

A rare visitor to high Sierra Nevada lakes, this species is largely confined to the coasts, estuaries and foothill reservoirs. Most remain there to breed, but a small percentage migrate farther inland to low-altitude reservoirs and lakes. It is probably some of these inland breeders that we see on Fallen Leaf in the late summer and fall, "refueling" during their autumn migration back to the coast. Groups of Double-crested Cormorants have been spotted at the northwest end of the lake, especially near Lucky Baldwin's.

The name "Double-crested" and *auritus*, "eared," refer to the tufts of feathers that curve back from the heads of breeding adults. Our western birds have white tufts while eastern birds sport less conspicuous black tufts. Since these birds are not known to breed on Fallen Leaf Lake or anywhere close by, they are unlikely to be seen in their namesake breeding plumage.

HERONS and EGRETS, Family *Ardeidae*

The distinction between herons and egrets is by no means a clear one. Delving into scientific binomial nomenclature for answers only confirms this: the Great Blue Heron and the Great Egret have recently been lumped into the same genus, *Ardea* (Latin for heron); likewise, the Little Blue Heron and the Snowy Egret both belong to the same genus, *Egretta*. Egrets and herons stalk small animal prey on land or in shallow water.

Great Blue Heron, *Ardea herodias. Plate 32*

The largest member of its family, the Great Blue Heron (or simply "GBH") breeds around Lake Tahoe and also wanders up-slope from lower elevations after the breeding season. An individual was spotted perched pre-

© Barbara Gleason

cariously on a snag just north of Camp's happy fishing ground, Witch's Pond. However, they are not commonly seen in our watershed.

Although usually pictured in marshy areas hunting for fish and amphibians, Great Blues also hunt small mammals in open fields. (My friend Jed recounts an amazingly close observation set on the grassy margin of Stanford's Lake Lagunita that ends with audible pocket gopher squeals emitting from a descending bulge in the heron's throat.)

Great Egret, *Ardea alba. Plate 32*

An unusual vagrant, this large white bird only shows up over Fallen Leaf on rare occasions—often during windy or stormy spells in late summer or during migration. The smaller, yellow-footed, black-billed version, the **Snowy Egret,** *plate 32*, is equally rare.

Black-crowned Night-Heron, *Nycticorax nycticorax. Plate 32*

This nocturnal summer visitor is more often heard than seen. The best bet at hearing (or seeing) this bird is to lie down on a south Lake Tahoe beach (preferably near a marsh) at dusk. Stare straight up into the sky and watch the stars flicker into place. With patience, you may just hear the low, glottal, *GUAC* of the heron looking for its favorite dip. Others argue it is actually shouting, *WOK*, and simply yearning for a good fish stir-fry. With luck, you might even witness this "bird of prey" uncloak and materialize directly overhead. The scientific name means "night-crow."

RAPTORS

From the Latin, *rapere* (to seize), this word is a shorter substitute for "birds of prey." Eagles, hawks and owls all belong to this informal group of feathered carnivores. Our vultures are also sometimes included in this non-taxonomic grouping despite their lack of grasping talons and their preference for deceased prey.

AMERICAN VULTURES, Family *Cathartidae*

This family is separate from old-world vultures because of differences in the two groups' evolutionary pasts. The best available evidence traces the new-world vultures back to a lineage common to present day storks, which is why they are now classified in the Order *Ciconiiformes*. Old world vultures, in contrast, evolved from the same ancestral stock as hawks.

This is one of the more famous examples of convergent evolution. This happens when two originally dissimilar species change over thousands of generations to become similar (i.e. with respect to external appearances). This usually happens because they share a habitat, prey item, or life strategy that favors a certain kind of structure. The most obvious example that both Old World and New World vultures share is the bald head—because it is relatively easy to keep clean while plunging in and out of rotting carcasses.

Turkey Vulture, *Cathartes aura. Plate 32*

In the early part of this century, when cattle grazed Desolation Wilderness, Turkey Vultures were commonly sighted above Gilmore Lake. Now vultures rarely wander up this high and are much more common in the foothills and central valley. The few recent sightings were made northwest of Tahoe late in the summer.

Cathartes is from the same root as cathartic and there is debate as to which connotation Linnaeus was hoping to evoke: "purifying," for their role in transforming dead, rotting flesh into their own healthy, living muscle, or "purgative," for their repulsive (to humans) food preferences and appearance. *Aura* is derived from a Native American name, *auroura*, originally used in what is now Mexico.

EAGLES AND HAWKS, Family *Accipitridae*

There are only two eagles that commonly live in North America and both can be seen in the Glen Alpine Watershed.

Accipiters (Latin for "to take after") are woodland hawks equipped with short, blunt wings for powerful acceleration and long, thin tails for maximum maneuverability through thick forests. Birds make up most of their diet, but rodents are also taken. Accipiters, along with the Great Horned Owl, are infamously territorial around their nests and will violently attack any intruders—even humans.

Buteos, thanks to the highly successful Red-tailed Hawk, are the most commonly seen of all North American hawks. All are heavily built, with broad wings and often banded tails. Ferruginous and Rough-legged Hawks are only rare winter visitors.

The Osprey, or "fish hawk," is in a group of its own.

Osprey, *Pandion haliaetus. Plate 32*

The only obvious nesting of a raptor species on Fallen Leaf Lake while I worked at Camp was an Osprey on the northeast shore (the Taggart's property) and there is usually a nesting pair somewhere on the lake each year. Favorite Osprey hunting grounds include the inlet of Glen Alpine Creek, the eastern shoreline and the sheltered area near the outlet of Taylor Creek. Another nest was sighted near the entrance to Emerald Bay (SW Lake Tahoe).

Ospreys have highly evolved, specialized structures to help in the capture of fish. Ratcheted tendons are thought to have evolved in bird feet to make perching easier, so birds do not have to actively grip a twig all night long. Ospreys have enhanced this ratcheting system to help in the gripping of fish. Spiny scales on the underside of the feet also help grip their slippery prey. Lastly, one of the three forward-pointing toes has reversed to aid the rear toe in opposing the front two in order to provide maximum gripping power. Unfortunately, there are times when these specialized features are a hindrance: in extremely rare circumstances, the bird can latch onto more than it can handle and end up being drowned by an extremely large fish.

Osprey wings are longer and more angled than hawk's, looking like large gull wings. The call of an Osprey is also reminiscent of a gull, but more powerful and persistent, often rising in pitch. Usually given while circling over water, some liken it to a pool shark calling for his stick: *Cue! Cue! Cue!*

The genus is an inaccurate reference to Greek mythology (Tereus, Pandion's son-in-law, was the one transformed into a hawk) and *haliaetus* is the correct spelling of "sea-eagle" (the Bald Eagle's genus has an extra e).

Bald Eagle, *Haliaeetus leucocephalus. Plate 32*

Most abundant during the fall runs of Kokanee salmon, these white-headed "sea-eagles" have a hankering for fish flesh. Chances of seeing them during the summer are slim, but there was one at Emerald Bay in 1994 and they are probably around in low numbers every year.

Bald Eagles can catch fish, waterfowl and small mammals, but also eat carrion whenever possible. Scientific name translates as "white-headed sea-eagle."

Northern Harrier, *Circus cyaneus. Plate 32*

Sometimes seen in the late summer and fall, these long-tailed, white-rumped birds used to be called Marsh Hawks (although they will hunt over almost any grassy area—wet or dry). Their broad owl-like facial disks help them locate prey by sound alone—a key advantage in tall grass. Males are blue-gray above (hence *cyaneus*) and white below (with black on the wing tips, trailing edge and tip of tail); females brown above and streaked below; juveniles are a rich brown above and sport a solid rusty-cinnamon wash below.

Sharp-shinned Hawk, *Accipiter striatus. Plate 33*

These birds are most commonly encountered near bird feeders where their preferred prey—small birds—congregate regularly. The "mini" of the accipiters, this version is only slightly larger than a robin, has a relatively small head (forward-thrust wing tips often exceed the head) and a tail that appears like it was cut straight across at the end. Large female Sharpies can be about the same size as small male Cooper's.

Cooper's Hawk, *Accipiter cooperii*

Well-forested areas are the best places to look: Lucky Baldwin's, Lake Margery, Granite Chief Wilderness, etc. Listen for a high-pitched, harsh and persistent, *KI-KI-KI-KI-KI*... Songbird feathers sprinkled on the forest floor are also a good indication that you may be near an accipiter's favorite plucking perch. Cooper's has a proportionately larger head and longer, rounder tail than Sharpie.

This hawk was named after William C. Cooper (1798-1864) who described the Evening Grosbeak, studied everything from conchs to birds and helped to found the New York Lyceum of Natural History. (Dr. James C. Cooper, a famous California ornithologist, was his son.)

Northern Goshawk, *Accipiter gentilis*

© Barbara Gleason

Our largest, grayest accipiters are most commonly seen in the red fir forests on the way up to Cathedral Lake—probably because the slope, updrafts and distance between patches of trees provide opportunities for seeing them in the open. Goshawks can also be seen in Granite Chief Wilderness. Look for an accipiter outline about the size of a Red-tailed Hawk. These powerful shadows of the forest specialize in golden-mantled ground squirrels as well as larger birds.

Swainson's Hawk, *Buteo swainsoni*

With only a single personal record from Mokelumne Wilderness, the Swainson's Hawk is unlikely to be seen away from open grasslands except during migration. This large hawk has the unusual habit of eating an inordinate number of insects, especially large grasshoppers, while wintering in Argentina. Swainson's Hawks migrate over ten thousand miles each way between North and South America. Lizards and many small mammals are also taken, primarily during the breeding season in North America.

Keep an eye out for this narrow-winged version of the red-tail when driving through the central valley. They often perch on rocks or fence posts, waiting to pounce on whatever crawls by.

Charles Lucien Bonaparte (Napoleon's nephew) named this hawk in honor of William Swainson (1789–1855). The name is fitting since Swainson was a very well-traveled naturalist who visited South America, along with many other continents. He was an extremely versatile naturalist who studied many different taxa—from mollusks to birds. He eventually settled in New Zealand where he became their attorney general. A warbler and our thrush are also named after this admirable academic.

Red-tailed Hawk, *Buteo jamaicensis*. Plate 33

First described in Jamaica, this species ranges over our entire continent. Although not very common in the high Sierra, one is sure to see at least a few every summer.

Red-tailed Hawks are often seen perched near highways, waiting to swoop down upon unwary rodents. Immature "red-tails" actually have brown and white-banded tails and can be confused with the more highly migratory Swainson's Hawk.

Ferruginous Hawk, *Buteo regalis*

A rare migrant, named for its rusty color and regal look. Illustration at right.

© Charlie Quinn

Golden Eagle, *Aquila chrysaetos*
Plate 33

Golden Eagles are regularly but uncommonly seen careening over both Desolation and Mokelumne Wildernesses. In the early 1900s they were reported to nest on the cliffs of the Glen Alpine Valley and may continue to do so. The largest raptor in North America (save for the virtually extinct California Condor), this eagle inspires awe even from a distance. Compared to the Bald Eagle, this species has a relatively smaller head and longer tail. Juvenile birds have large, conspicuous white patches in each wing and at the base of the tail. *Aquila* is the Latin word for eagle and *chrysaetos* is Greek for "golden-eagle," after the gold-colored feathers on the back of its head and neck.

Although the Golden Eagle will eat carrion, it does so far less often than our balding national symbol. A flexible hunter, it dive-bombs for waterfowl and floats low over hills to pounce on unsuspecting mammals. In lean winters it may even take foxes, coyotes, or small deer.

FALCONS, Family *Falconidae*

© Barbara Gleason

Falcons are built for speed, with long, narrow, pointed wings. It is not mere coincidence that fighter planes mimic the structure and mechanics of falcon wings, folding in at higher speeds to decrease drag. Most falcons use their natural propensity for speed to capture other birds in mid-flight.

Currently only one species is regularly seen in the vicinity, but **Peregrine Falcons** could return in the near future due to restoration efforts and the banning of egg-shell thinning pesticides. **Prairie Falcons** and **Merlins** are also occasionally sighted in the late summer and fall.

American Kestrel, *Falco sparverius. Plate 33*

One of the most beautiful, colorful and often seen of our raptors, the kestrel is also the smallest. It will take any small animal from insects and lizards to mice and small birds (hence its former name, Sparrow Hawk).

It is most commonly seen perched on telephone wires over open fields. When perches are unavailable, the American Kestrel circles or, more stereotypically, hovers thirty feet above its target before plunging straight down.

Unlike other raptors, males can be easily distinguished from females because of their bluish-gray wings. Although they do breed in the Tahoe Basin, my only record for the area is a late-summer sighting in the meadows southeast of Lake Tahoe.

COOT, Family *Rallidae*

Although technically a rail, coots have developed lobed toes like a grebe (Plate 33) and feeding habits similar to those of a diving duck.

American Coot, *Fulica americana. Plate 33*

A small number of coots visit Tahoe and the surrounding lakes for the winter. They are likely to be seen any time between October and April, with a few arriving earlier and leaving later as well. They have been observed to form mixed rafts with overwintering ducks. "Ivory-billed Mudpecker" is a popular alternative name.

PLOVER, Family *Charadriidae*

Killdeer, *Charadrius vociferus. Plate 33*

These widespread plovers inhabit many open environs. They can be seen on beaches, golf courses, meadows and riparian flood plains. Their distinctive namesake call is most often heard at dusk and at night, when few other birds are calling: a high pitched, *DEE-dee-dee-dee* or, *Ki-dee, dee-dee-dee*.

Relying on camouflage, these birds lay their speckled eggs in shallow depressions, usually in gravel. If this strategy fails, the adult performs its famous distraction display—faking a broken wing—to lure predators away from the nest. If you happen to see one flopping around and dragging a wing, watch your step—you might just be too close to its eggs.

SANDPIPER, Family *Scolopacidae*

Spotted Sandpiper, *Actitis macularius. Plate 33*

© Barbara Gleason

A sandpiper in the mountains? Exactly. Since no other sandpiper exploits Sierra Nevada streams, the competition is pleasantly lacking.

These birds can be seen on both the Glen Alpine and Taylor creeks, teetering on stones while bobbing their tails up and down. Their bright orange bills, spotted (hence *macularia*) breasts and low, stiff flight are also helpful in identification.

Spotted Sandpipers are unusual in that females compete for males and males incubate and raise the young. This strategy frees up the female to lay as many as five clutches of four eggs each, each clutch incubated by a different male. This polyandrous (multiple-male) system probably evolved to take maximum advantage of the abundant-but-brief flush of insects available in high-altitude and high-latitude springs.

GULLS and TERNS, Family *Laridae*

The "sea" gulls we see in the Sierra Nevada are (ironically) inland breeders, only wintering along the coasts.

Looking like highly angular gulls, terns fly erratically over water in search of small fish. The few individuals that sporadically appear over Fallen

Leaf are most likely migrating to and from breeding areas in northwestern Nevada. Currently, Forster's and Black Terns are the only species that even rarely nest in the Tahoe Basin.

Ring-billed Gull, *Larus delawarensis. Plate 33*

Ring-billeds are abundant in some areas around Lake Tahoe, but are not very numerous on Fallen Leaf. More flocks pass through our area in the fall, especially during the month of October. Ring-billed Gulls are similar in appearance to California Gulls, but are a bit smaller and have pale eyes. (This species also winters on the Delaware River, where it was first collected.)

California Gull, *Larus californicus. Plate 33*

Our most common summer gull, along with Ring-billeds. Adults have dark eyes and dull greenish-yellow legs.

Mono Lake's Negit Island used to be the second largest breeding colony of California Gulls on Earth. Unfortunately, Los Angeles was allowed to divert too much of its watershed and exposed the island to mammalian predation in 1979. Recent legislation and agreements will hopefully reverse this problem.

Herring Gull, *Larus argentatus*

A rare migrant, Herring Gulls are unlikely to be seen during the summer months. Adult Herring Gulls are larger than California Gulls, have yellow eyes and pink legs. First-winter Herring Gulls are easily confused with first-winter California Gulls. The *argentatus* in the name means "silvery."

Caspian Tern, *Sterna caspia. Plate 34*

The Caspian Tern has a low croak to match its heavily built body. This species has a shorter tail, larger bill and a more angular forehead than the smaller Forster's Tern. Black legs are another distinguishing trait. A very wide-ranging species: the first scientific specimen was collected on the Caspian Sea.

Forster's Tern, *Sterna forsteri. Plate 34*

This light-weight bird can be blown around like a butterfly on windy days. Its long, swallow-like, forked tail may be the best way to tell it apart from the larger Caspian Tern. Forster's Tern also has a higher voice, smaller bill, rounder head and red feet. Forster's Tern used to breed at Rowlands Marsh.

Black Tern, *Chlidonias niger*

Common historic breeder at Rowlands Marsh where it was dependent on the emergent marsh habitat, but this unique tern is now rarely encountered near Tahoe. It resembles a huge swallow in form, flight and behavior and the genus is a misspelled version of the Greek word for swallow, *chelidonias*.

© Barbara Gleason

PIGEONS and DOVES, Family *Columbidae*

The common names "pigeon" and "dove" are applied without any strict rules. In general, the large, stocky ones are pigeons while the small, slight birds are referred to as doves. Our European city pigeon's official name was recently changed from Rock Dove to **Rock Pigeon**—look for them around South Lake Tahoe and Stateline.

These birds are among the few which actually produce a kind of "milk" for their young. A soup of sloughed esophageal skin cells specialized for this purpose is collected in the crop. "Crop milk" is higher in protein and fat than either human or bovine milk. This concentrated food is a necessity for the rapid growth of young that would otherwise have to subsist on low-fat and low-protein plant materials.

Columbids need to drink water daily to facilitate the digestion of their dry, grainy diet and will often seek out mineral springs.

Band-tailed Pigeon, *Patgioenas fasciata. Plate 34*

This native woodland pigeon is noticeably larger than its common European cousin, the Rock Pigeon. Although these two species are similar in appearance, they rarely share the same habitat. Rock Pigeons are abundant in urban areas throughout the world; the Band-tailed Pigeon keeps to the forests of the Americas. Band-tailed Pigeons winter as far south as Nicaragua, but have resident populations in the mountains of California and Mexico.

Laying only one egg a year, the band-tailed is slow to recover from population reductions. Market hunting quickly took a large toll because these birds will return to the same mineral springs every day. Fearing a repeat of the Passenger Pigeon's demise, federal legislation banned hunting of this pigeon in 1916. Having slowly recovered from near-extinction, a hunting season has been reinstated, albeit very limited.

These stocky pigeons can be seen wheeling over the tree tops of the Glen Alpine valley in search of ripening berries and fruit like those of the Mountain-ash. Their *coo* or hoot is much lower than the city pigeon's and has two parts, the second being even lower in pitch than the first. The Tamarack Trail is usually a good place to see them. The genus changed from *Columba* to *Patgioenas* in 2003.

Mourning Dove, *Zenaida macroura. Plate 34*

This slim dove gets its name not for the time of sunrise, but for its plaintive, mournful coos: *whoo-oo-whoo-whoo-whoo.*

Widespread and successful, the Mourning Dove is the most abundant dove in North America. Not surprisingly, it is also the most widely hunted and harvested game bird of our continent. It is found in a variety of habitats from urban to pristine wilderness, but almost always feeds in open areas with a nearby water source. The meadows at the north end of Fallen Leaf are often visited by these seed-searching doves in the summer.

The wings of Mourning Doves produce a distinctive "wing-whir" which is most apparent when they first spring into flight. Some ornithologists have theorized that this sound may serve as a type of alarm call, alerting other birds in the flock that a reason for flight is near.

TYPICAL OWLS, Family *Strigidae*

Only 60 percent of owls are strictly nocturnal, but they remain a secretive and elusive group nonetheless. Because Barn Owls (Family *Tytonidae*) are unlikely in our habitat, *Strigidae* will be the only owl family dealt with here. (The two owl families are separated based upon structural differences.)

Owls have the broadest skulls of all the birds. This structure gives them the best three-dimensional sight as well as a built-in parabolic microphone. This sound-collecting ability is further enhanced by the facial ruff of feathers. Since the cone-like eyes are fixed within their sockets, the head moves for them—up to 270 degrees. The "horns" or "ears" seen on many owls are actually just showy feathers, sometimes used in displays.

Because few have been recorded, the following is a wish-list of other species that could be in our area: **Great Gray Owl, Long-eared Owl, Spotted Owl,** *Plate 34,* **Western Screech-Owl,** *Plate 34,* **Flammulated Owl** and **Northern Saw-whet Owl,** *Plate 34.* Best of luck!

Great Horned Owl, *Bubo virginianus. Plate 34*

The most widespread owl of North America, the Great Horned Owl has even adapted to suburban environments. It lives as a year-round resident all across the continent from Mexico to Alaska. In the northern reaches of its range, the owls often have to defrost cached prey by "incubating" it.

This owl has a distinctive low-pitched pattern of three to eight hoots which often sounds like, *Who's a-wake? Me too!* Beware of nesting adults—they will violently defend their young. This owl may be the reason we do not see many others—they do not take kindly to competition and will readily prey upon other owls.

Northern Pygmy-Owl, *Glaucidium gnoma. Plate 34*

A well-named species, the Northern Pygmy-Owl is rarely over seven inches long. This owl is diurnal and preys upon unwary birds (sometimes larger than itself), darting through forests and plucking them from their perches. A noisy gathering of songbirds often leads to the discovery of a small owl like this one.

Call is a repeated, but well-spaced (unlike the Northern Saw-whet Owl), hoot or whistle, often doubled.

NIGHTJARS, Family *Caprimulgidae*

These birds are well camouflaged to wait out the day like a bump on a log and well equipped to spend the night as an airborne insect vacuum machine. Ultra-wide mouths make sure they do not miss any juicy morsels; stiff bristles at the gape of the mouth protect their eyes from high-speed impacts with insect parts.

Our two species divide up the night sky in what is referred to as resource partitioning. This theory argues that species which share similar resources (in this case, nocturnal flying insects) will evolve to exploit distinctly different parts of that resource. Poorwills take up low patrol while the nighthawk skims above the tree tops. This result (according to theory) is due to the selective pressure against individuals of both species which competed against each other at middle elevations. Resources are also partitioned temporally, in this case with swallows taking the day shift.

Common Nighthawk, *Chordeiles minor hesperis. Plate 35*

Chordeiles means "evening dance" in Latin and that is precisely what these birds do. High above the tree tops in the twilight of dusk, these aerial acrobats flit around on their slender white-barred wings swallowing unseen insects. Viewed from the comfort of one's sleeping bag, this is one of the few opening acts that could properly precede the unveiling of so many heavenly bodies.

Soft, nasal, *peent, beer,* or *beep* calls often punctuate their antics. The hollow *boom* or *whoof* (described as "a terrific raspy, farting noise" by Daniel Mathews and a "bovine bellow" by Edward Abbey) of courting males is usually only heard in the spring. This sound is made by vibrating primary wing feathers when the male pulls out of a steep dive at the last possible second. This sound, when combined with its erratic, crepuscular, insect-eating behavior has earned it the nickname of "bullbat" in the Southwest.

Marshy areas bordered by deep forest are excellent spots to look for these birds—Upper Velma Lake especially. Nearby rocky areas are also essential for well-camouflaged ground nesting.

Common Poorwill, *Phalaenoptilus nuttallii* (Plate 35)

Often heard during late night boat trips on the lake, this nocturnal bird lives on the slopes of Cathedral Peak and other warm, rocky mountainsides. Like its eastern cousin the Whip-poor-will, the poorwill gets its name from its repeated call, *poor-will*, or sometimes, *poor-will-ip*.

The Hopi call this bird "holchko" (sleeping one) for good reason. Although many individuals of this species migrate, those in the southwest U.S. often go into torpor for the winter months. Torpor is a state in which very little energy is expended: body temperature drops to near-ambient levels (as low as 41 degrees Fahrenheit) and both heart rate and breathing slow down considerably. This allows poorwills to use as little as three percent of the oxygen they consume in an active state and allows them the luxury of only needing 10 grams of fat to make it through the winter. Some argue that poorwills go into such a deep and extended torpor over the winter months that they are the only birds that truly hibernate. (Scientists have been able to pick them up, handle them, weigh them, and replace them without the bird ever waking up!) Others argue that since they can rouse themselves for a snack during the winter, it is not true hibernation.

Like hummingbirds and some other animals, poorwills also go into a daily torpor (only lowering body temperature to a more moderate 65 degrees) to conserve their limited energy reserves. They can also go into torpor to wait out temporary adverse conditions (i.e. lack of prey).

SWIFTS, Family *Apodidae*

Swifts have yet to be recorded, but are definitely possible. Likely species include: **Black Swift, Vaux's Swift** (shown at right) and **White-throated Swift**.

HUMMINGBIRDS, Family *Trochilidae*

These birds, like their mammalian counterparts, the shrews, are at the lower limit of body size for a warm-blooded animal. Nevertheless, some hummingbirds have lived over 12 years in the wild, whereas shrews are lucky to live 12 months. Hummingbirds have the highest metabolism of any animal (100 times that of an elephant), may consume half their body weight in sugar each day (imagine putting 80 pounds of sugar on your morning bowl of cereal) and pass over three-quarters of its body weight in water every day (the equivalent of 120 pints for an adult human). They are also significant pollinators of many plants in the Americas.

After filling their crop with nectar, a hummingbird will often perch on a good lookout branch (to keep an eye out for territorial intruders and predators) and conserve energy while they digest their liquid gold. It usually takes about four minutes to empty half of it and then they start collecting again.

Hummingbirds also take a significant number of insects to meet their protein and fat needs, especially for their young during the breeding season.

Anna's Hummingbird, *Calypte anna*. Plate 35

Normally more of a coastal bird, there have been reports of Anna's Hummingbirds around Fallen Leaf, especially at feeders. These high-elevation sightings are most likely a result of post-breeding birds following the blooming flowers and abundant insects which accompany "Spring" on her annual up-slope odyssey.

Anna's is the only hummingbird that resides year-round north of southern California—in fact, all the way up to Vancouver, British Columbia. Taking advantage of the warm maritime influence all along the west coast of the U.S., its range just barely overflows on either end into Canada and Mexico. Exotic plantings and artificial nectar sources that provide year-round nutrition have allowed the number of permanent residents to increase.

Calliope Hummingbird, *Stellula calliope*. Plate 35

Stellula translates as "starlet," and calliope (kah-lie-oh-pee) strictly translates as "beautiful singing" (after the name of the Muse of Epic Poetry). Although "starlet" is quite fitting for the smallest North American bird and the male does have a high *see-ree* song, this "beautiful singer" is rarely heard singing.

A high-country breeder, this species is a sought-after gem for many lowland birders' lists. Unfortunately, the male Calliopes leave shortly after copulating and female hummers of any species are fairly difficult to identify. This makes for a very small "easy identification window" in early spring. During the summer, the best bet is to catch migrating males on their way back from breeding farther north.

Rufous Hummingbird, *Selasphorus rufus. Plate 35*

Selasphorus, the "light-carrying" genus of hummingbirds, is infamous for the similarity of its species. Distinguishing **Rufous** from **Allen's Hummingbird**, *S. sasin*, is often done by looking at a map. Unfortunately, this does not work for our area: the Rufous breeds north of the Sierras and the Allen's breeds on the coast. Nevertheless, both pass through our area. However, Rufous is by far the most common visitor.

The Allen's is described as migrating "earlier" and having a more extensively green back and crown than the Rufous. With springtime varying slightly every year and hummingbirds zipping by at speeds close to Warp Nine, neither of these seem to help much. For your mental health, it may be better to just call any rusty-colored hummer a *Selasphorus* and leave it at that.

KINGFISHERS, Family *Alcedinidae*

For almost all intents and purposes, temperate North America (from the Mexican border north), only has one, albeit widespread, kingfisher species.

Belted Kingfisher, *Ceryle alcyon. Plate 35*

This is one of the few avian species in which the female is more colorful than the male. Appropriately, the *Alcyon* of Greek Mythology so grieved her drowned husband, *Ceryx*, that the gods turned them both into kingfishers. Her broad, rusty belly band makes it easy to distinguish the sexes, even in the field.

Both parents help dig a nesting burrow in a river bank, usually 5–10 feet deep. Parents drop dead fish into water below fledglings to teach them necessary fishing skills. After ten days of intensive training, young are able to catch their own and get chased off their parents' territories.

Kingfishers are most commonly seen in the sheltered area of Fallen Leaf Lake just above Taylor Creek. The mouth of Glen Alpine Creek and Lily Lake are also good spots. The Belted Kingfisher's loud, mechanical rattle is often heard before one can even see the water.

WOODPECKERS, Family *Picidae*

Famous for their method of extracting juicy larvae and insects from infested trees, woodpeckers can be thought of as arboreal surgeons. They perform their service of removing parasites in exchange for a small penthouse apartment in the dead core of a tree. Many other weaker-billed cavity-nesting birds depend on old woodpecker holes for nesting sites.

Most woodpeckers have two pairs of opposing toes with strongly curved claws. Their unusually stiff tail feathers also press against the tree to act as a brace, resulting in a very stable base—and it has to be. This tripod holds nature's most effective jackhammer. Without such a secure hold on the tree, the bird could never get enough leverage to make more than a dent.

In addition to their sharp vocal calls, woodpeckers also communicate using characteristic drumming patterns. Much to the annoyance of home owners, these birds will sometimes hammer on walls, drainpipes and even aluminum trash cans because of their great resonant qualities.

Woodpecker skulls have to be unbelievably strong and dense to protect the brain from constant concussions. In addition, their brains are tightly confined in their skull so as to prevent them from moving within, and sustaining concussions or whip-lash injuries. Some have tongues that are made extra-extendable by a hyoid apparatus (composed of bones and muscles) which can wrap all the way around the back and top of their skulls to attach at the base of the upper mandible (bill).

Lewis's Woodpecker, *Melanerpes lewis. Plate 35*

An irregular visitor and migrant, this species was introduced to western science by Lewis & Clark during their Voyage of Discovery. Like the Acorn Woodpecker in the same genus, Lewis's also stores acorns, but in a different way. Lewis's Woodpecker shells the acorns first and uses only natural crevices for storage. It also defends its cache individually instead of colonially. Lewis's Woodpecker eats a fair share of nuts, seeds and berries during the fall and winter, but the majority of its summer diet is of the six-legged variety.

Lewis's Woodpeckers are most likely to be seen in migration between their wintering grounds west of the Sierra Nevada and their breeding grounds east of the crest. Late summer and early fall is the best time to catch them on their way back. Jed Mitchell and I saw a pair in the trees around Lake Lucille on September 6, 1994. Please report any breeding pairs.

Keep an eye out for their atypical flight: instead of deeply undulating like other 'peckers, these birds have a more direct, crow-like flight. Because of their unusual flight and coloring, Lewis's Woodpecker could be mistaken for a very fat robin, a rose-breasted crow or mutant pigeon. In yet another departure from stereotypical woodpecker behavior, this bird is often spotted hawking insects from a tree top perch like a flycatcher.

SAPSUCKERS

Sapsuckers are a subset of woodpeckers belonging to the genus *Sphyrapicus*, meaning "hammer woodpeckers." Their tongues are shorter than most woodpeckers and have a unique structure: the barbs are modified into delicate hairs that soak up sap through capillary action—like a honey dipper. These birds drill holes or remove sections of cambium in order to feed on the sap that oozes out. Ants and other insects often get stuck in the sap, creating natural candy-coated protein supplements.

Many other animals (from hummingbirds and warblers to hornets and squirrels) "rob" sap from the wells of these industrious suckers. Secondary cavity nesters, such as Tree Swallows, depend on old sapsucker or woodpecker holes for raising families. Paul Ehrlich and Gretchen Daily (with Stanford's Center for Conservation Biology) did an amazing study at Rocky Mountain Biological Laboratory which implicated the Red-naped Sapsucker as part of a "keystone species complex." This four-species complex combined to support the existence of well over 40 other species, some even directly dependent on the complex for their survival. Sapsuckers prefer fungally-softened heartwood for their cavities.

All North American sapsuckers have white rumps, white wing patches and a varying amount of yellow on their belly. They are generally quiet and secretive, but can be quite approachable while busy drilling wells.

Williamson's Sapsucker, *Sphyrapicus thyroideus thyroideus. Plate 35*

A classic subalpine breeder, the Williamson's Sapsucker is a rare treat for the avid backpacker.

My only sighting is of an individual male between Fontanillis and Dick's Lakes. It was hammering on a series of drill holes that formed a two-foot long vertical crevice about eight feet up on a White Pine (although the literature claims a preference for Lodgepole Pine or Red Fir). There were also a number of series of horizontal holes about an inch apart lower and to the left of this crevice. Unorganized sap wells like these are almost a trademark of Williamson's. This large-diameter White Pine had distinctly checked bark and was on the east side of the trail about a hundred yards before the "T" intersection where one must choose to go to either Dick's Lake or Dick's Pass.

Listen for the Williamson's Sapsucker's drumming next time you are near Fontanillis Lake: a rapid drum roll followed by three to five shorter bursts, as if a jack hammer was running out of pressure.

Keep in mind that the female Williamson's looks more like a brown-headed Gila Woodpecker or small flicker than its mate. In fact, male and female specimens were initially classified as separate species until they were later found breeding together! This led to retaining the common name of the males collected by the surgeon on the Pacific Railroad Survey (named in 1857 in honor of Robert Stockton Williamson, the Army officer in charge) and the scientific name given to the females collected and named by John Cassin (see Cassin's Vireo) in 1851 (due to the principle of priority).

Red-naped Sapsucker, *Syphyrapicus nuchalis*

A very rare visitor and not recorded on any other Tahoe Basin list. I know only of a single sighting of this species, thanks to Jed Mitchell's 1994 Thanksgiving visit to Fallen Leaf. (Probably a late migrant on its way south from breeding grounds farther north.)

This species hybridizes with the Red-Breasted along the eastern slope of the Sierras and north into south-central Oregon. Since hybrids have been observed to be less successful (reproductively) than either species, they remain separate species. *Nuchalis* is Latin for "nape."

Red-breasted Sapsucker, *Sphyrapicus ruber daggetti* (southern subspecies) *Plate 36*

More at home near the elevations of Fallen Leaf Lake than the previous species, the Red-breasted Sapsucker is our most commonly seen sapsucker. Although its trademark is a series of neat, horizontal drill-holes, the Red-breasted Sapsucker also makes long, rectangular wells on small willows and alders in the summer. Probably because of their prolific sap production, this species prefers broad-leaved trees that grow near water.

At least one individual has worked the shrubby willows on the far side of Cathedral Lake. A juvenile Red-breasted Sapsucker has also tended wells on alders between Camp's flagpole and Fallen Leaf Lake in the past.

Hairy Woodpecker, *Picoides villosus. Plate 36*

Possibly the most common and stereotypical of our woodpeckers, the Hairy Woodpecker is named for its soft, furry appearance. Its sharp, metallic *pink*! or *chink*! and drawn-out rattle (or whinny) are heard in our forested areas year-round.

Its smaller cousin, the **Downy Woodpecker** (also named for its fuzzy appearance) has not yet been sighted in the area, but is a likely visitor in the late summer. The Downy is significantly smaller, its beak is tiny (less than half the length of is head) and its white outer tail feathers have black spots on the outer edges.

In 1994, a Hairy's nest was found six feet up in a living willow near Lucky Baldwin's.

White-headed Woodpecker, *Picoides albolarvatus albolarvatus*
Plate 36

A regular breeder on Stanford Sierra Camp property, this species has nested six to ten feet up in living Scouler Willows for at least the last three years. They nested in the tree against the southeast side of the lodge in 1992, in the tree directly behind the Aspen staff cabin in 1993 and in the tree just northwest of the rowing dock in 1994. It is likely that all three nests have been made by the same couple or at least members of the same family. The incessant peeping of the young has made many people wonder how it escapes predation. Keep your ears out for future broods!

White-headeds hammer more softly and less often than other Piciformes. It is very probable that this behavior is related to the fact that their skull is also softer and less dense than other woodpeckers'. Instead of drilling all the time, they often pry up bark to find hidden insects as well as feed on pine nuts. Only males have a red stripe across the back of their heads. Young chicks may also have a reddish spot on the top of their head, regardless of sex. Rather than "white-larva," *albolarvatus* translates as "white-masked."

Black-backed Woodpecker, *Picoides arcticus*. Plate 36

© Charles Quinn

Having a solid black back, a yellow crown and no red whatsoever make the males and immatures of this species fairly easy to identify. Mature females lack the yellow crown patch. Fortunately, its look-alike cousin, the **American Three-toed Woodpecker**, usually sticks to the Rockies and Cascades. Incidentally, the Black-backed also has only three toes.

This bird's coloring serves it well in its favorite feeding ground—a recently burned forest (trees that have been weakened by fire are often packed with hundreds of fat, juicy, wood-eating beetle grubs). It has been estimated that an individual of this species consumes more than 13,500 of these luscious larvae in a single year (Ehrlich, Dobkin, & Wheye, p. 354).

Due to the Black-backed's habitat preference, some Fallen Leaf residents may be thankful we have not seen many around the lake. This woodpecker is most commonly seen in our area on the scattered big Jeffrey Pines along the Mid-Tallac Trail. Most of the population breeds in northern Canada, hence *arcticus*.

Northern Flicker, *Colaptes auratus collaris. Plate 36*

Our race of the flicker is called "Red-shafted" because of its rusty-colored or salmon-red wing lining. Native Sierra Nevada tribes regularly used these beautiful feathers for decorating ceremonial costumes.

The "Red-shafted" form predominates west of the Rocky Mountains, the "Yellow-shafted" east of the Rockies. The two forms hybridize in western Canada, the Great Plains and other areas of overlap, thereby denying them full species status. The Gilded Flicker—now its own, full species due to recent genetic tests—lives in the southwest.

It is no mistake that the flicker is both the brownest and the most terrestrial woodpecker in North America. Because it often feeds on ground-dwelling carpenter ants, termites and seeds, it needs good camouflage. Males have a red "moustache" that angles down below the eye from the base of the beak.

The flicker's call is loud and clear. In fact, some people even think its sharp, descending call sounds like *CLEAR*! Its other, repetitious calls have been likened to *ka-ka-ka-ka* and *flicka-flicka-flicka-flicka*.

Pileated Woodpecker, *Dryocopus pileatus. Plate 36*

The second-largest* living North American woodpecker, the Pileated requires large territories of mature forest to share with its mate year-round.

The Pileated Woodpecker usually shows up around Fallen Leaf on extended bouts of winter foraging. Its tell-tale rectangular holes, however, remain to tell of its presence for many years. Some of these excavation sites can be seen on the large trees at Stanford Sierra Camp.

Listen for the Pileated's loud, *kak-kak-kak-kak-kak-kak*. This is similar to the flicker's repetitious call, but is nasal and varies a bit more in both speed and pitch. It starts and ends slower and lower, being fastest and highest in the middle.

Genus roughly translates as "tree-cleaver" or "oak-chiseler"—either accurate for these huge feathered woodworkers. *A pilleus* or *pileolus* was a red felt cap worn to signify a freed slave or other non-nobility (fishermen, artisans, shepherds) in ancient Rome. This symbol of material poverty and responsibility for the flock was taken up by the priesthood and has been transformed into the red cap worn today by Catholic Cardinals.

The even larger Ivory-billed Woodpecker was rediscovered by Gene Sparling, an Arkansas naturalist, on February 11, 2004 in Arkansas's Cache River National Wildlife Refuge after over 60 years of assumed extinction!

FLYCATCHERS, Family *Tyrannidae*

Often perched on the end of defoliated branches, these birds constantly scan for airborne, six-legged snacks. Flycatchers earn their name by darting out, snapping up an insect and returning to the same perch (a behavior also referred to as "hawking").

Being dependent on active insects for their food, flycatchers (with the exception of some southern phoebe populations) migrate south for the winter.

Olive-sided Flycatcher, *Contopus cooperi*

Infamous for its enticing song, the Olive-sided Flycatcher's *Quick, Free Beer!* vocalization has lured many a thirsty birder deep into the forest. *Quick* is an abrupt note, *Free* is noticeably higher and *Beer* descends down again. It also has a repeated, piping call note, often given in a measured *pip-pip pip-pip-pip* pattern. The bird is almost always found perched high up on the tip of a dead tree.

This flycatcher is also rather unique visually, having a kind of dark "vest" pattern on its otherwise white breast as well as a pair of white spots on its lower back. The Olive-sided is our largest flycatcher but has relatively short tarsi (*Contopus* means "small foot"). The specific epithet was changed from *borealis* to *cooperi* in 1997 because of the law of priority (it was discovered that *cooperi* was actually published first). See Cooper's Hawk for more information.

Due to a combination of its loud, distinctive vocalizations and its habit of perching on exposed branches, this is our most commonly seen flycatcher.

Western Wood-Pewee, *Contopus sordidulus veliei. Plate 36*

A fairly dark bird, the Western Wood-Pewee tends to perch at more moderate, mid-canopy heights than its larger relative. A burry, descending *bizzzz-it* or *pee-yer* is the wood-pewee's trademark. At close range a, "tee-teedle-eet," can be heard immediately preceding the down-slurred buzz.

In the early morning, they often give an alternative, more melodic song.

A nest with two young were discovered west of Lucky Baldwin's in 1994. It was situated at the end of a long horizontal branch, fairly exposed, about thirty feet up. The young would stay huddled and quiet at the bottom of the well-camouflaged nest unless a parent approached with food.

Scientific name translates as "Short-footed little dirty one"—because of its dark coloring and, like the Olive-sided, short tarsi.

EMPIDONAX Flycatchers

This genus is full of notoriously difficult to identify species. Most positive records are made on the basis of their songs and habitat rather than their appearance. The Pacific Slope Flycatcher is the only one I have been able to identify. However, the others mentioned below should also be in the area. The genus translates as "gnat king."

Willow Flycatcher, *Empidonax traillii*. Plate 36

© Charles Quinn

True to its name, this species usually nests low among willows found along streams or the margins of wet mountain meadows. Its song is a burry, "sneezy," *fitz-bew*; and its call is a rising *breet*!

Historically common, Willow Flycatchers have been hit hard by human-induced changes. Their riparian (stream-side) habitats are being destroyed by urbanization, recreation, reservoirs, exotic species and cattle grazing. Brown-headed Cowbirds now parasitize their nests so often that most of the remaining populations of Willow Flycatchers are those that have defensive behaviors, such as building new nests over top of the cowbird egg.

Dr. Thomas Stewart Traill (1781–1862) edited the eighth edition of *Encyclopedia Britannica* and was a founder of the Royal Institution and the independent Museum of Natural History in England. Audubon named this species to thank him for his support.

Until 1973, Willow & Alder Flycatchers were considered one species with two song types, called Traill's Flycatcher. They were separated after thorough field research proved their different songs prevented the two species from interbreeding.

Hammond's Flycatcher, *Empidonax hammondii. Plate 37*

More of a boreal or sub-alpine forest breeder, there are historical records of this species near the Velma Lakes. Hammond's prefers dense, shady stands of tall conifers.

Their behavior is often characterized as "nervous." Hammond's has a slight crest and the tail appears short because of the relatively long wing tips that extend over the base of the tail at rest. The three-part song starts with an abrupt, high, squeaky, *see-it*! followed by two burry notes with the last one lowest in pitch. The song is also more emphatically repeated than the Dusky's and usually from the top of the canopy.

Dr. William Alexander Hammond (1828–1900) was surgeon general of the US Army and introduced John Xantus to Spencer Baird, who sent Xantus collecting in the West. Xantus repaid Hammond by naming this bird he collected in California in his honor.

Dusky Flycatcher, *Empidonax oberholseri*

Look for a rounded head, longer bill, longer tail and shorter wing tips (usually just barely reaching the base of the tail) than Hammond's. Unfortunately, really good views are few and far between.

Contrary to their name, Duskies frequent dry, sunny shrubby areas interspersed with pines or other trees. They usually perch and nest relatively low off the ground, sometimes only 7–15 feet up. The song of the Dusky Flycatcher is usually a 3-phrase mix of clear and burry rising *sillits* with the last phrase highest in pitch.

The specific epithet honors Dr. Harry Church Olberholser (1870–1963) who worked for the US Fish & Wildlife Service in systematics and was curator of ornithology at the Cleveland Museum of Natural History.

Pacific-slope Flycatcher, *Empidonax difficilis. Plate 37*

Our most often-identified empid, the Pacific-slope used to share the name "Western" with its interior sibling species, the Cordilleran Flycatcher. The extremely high-pitched *sea-o'-wheat* song and *seet*! calls are often heard in mixed streamside forests.

This charmer has frequently been heard singing in the moist forested areas of Stanford Hill. Usually a deeper yellow-green than our other flycatchers.

Black Phoebe, *Sayornis nigricans. Plate 37*

Individuals of this species usually visit our area in September and have been seen at Witch's Pond and along the southern shore of Fallen Leaf Lake. Normally more of a lowland bird, this is probably another example of late summer up-slope drift.

It is almost always found near water and has an affinity for perching on and nesting under bridges. Its song is the namesake *fee-bee!*

VIREOS, Family *Vireonidae*

Vireos are a group of birds that few non-birders have heard of. They are often mistaken for warblers or even kinglets, but their bills are thicker and minutely hooked at the tip. Most vireos are generally drab olive-green (*Vireo* means "green" in Latin), gray, or brown, but they often have subtle washes of yellow along their sides.

Basket-like cup nests are made in the fork of a horizontal branch, often decorated with lichens held on by spider webs. Unfortunately, Brown-headed Cowbirds and riparian (stream-side) habitat destruction are taking their toll on vireo populations.

Vireos forage for insects like warblers, but are less flitty and more methodical in their searching. Our vireos live in Central America for most of the year, taking summer vacations to North America in order to breed.

Cassin's Vireo, *Vireo cassinii. Plate 37*

Until recently, this species was lumped along with the Blue-headed and Plumbeus Vireos into a single species, the **Solitary Vireo**. Cassin's is the westernmost of the three species.

Cassin's Vireos can be heard singing their well-spaced, alternating phrases from moist forested areas such as Stanford Hill. The cadence is similar to the sentences, *Where are you? . . . . . Here I am!* The first, questioning phrase is generally lower in pitch than its rising answer.

This species has incomplete eye rings that are joined by a white line above the beak, creating the appearance of glasses or spectacles. The bold wing bars and thick beak are also good identifying features.

While not rare, the Cassin's Vireo is not especially common either. With continued sightings of Brown-headed Cowbirds, one can only assume that vireos are not enjoying the reproductive rate they should be. The one saving grace for this species is that if a cowbird egg is found in its nest, it will sometimes build another layer above the first and start over again. This behavior kills the cowbird egg by depriving it of direct incubation, but costs the Solitary Vireo its first batch of eggs and postpones the date of hatching.

John Cassin (1813–1869) named nearly 200 species of birds during his life and John Xantus honored him with this name. Cassin was curator of Ornithology at the Academy of Natural Sciences in Philadelphia.

Warbling Vireo, *Vireo gilvus. Plate 37*
More common than its solitary relative, the Warbling Vireo is regularly heard belting out its song from deciduous trees growing along waterways. The distinctive, up-and-down, burry (mildly buzzy) song can be roughly matched to, *Ro-si-ta, Ro-si-ta, Ro-zeet!*

This species is fairly plain (*gilvus* translates as "dun," a gray color tending toward yellow or brown), but can be easily identified by the distinct white eyebrow stripe. Although there are many spectacled and eyebrowed vireos, we conveniently only have one of each in our watershed.

Because it lacks the nest-topping defense of Cassin's Vireo, the future of the Warbling Vireo may be in jeopardy if current cowbird invasions continue.

JAYS and CROWS, Family *Corvidae*

Intelligence, harsh vocalizations and aggressive personalities tend to describe most members of this family. Omnivorous tendencies, adaptability and lack of shyness have helped many Corvids enjoy success in the face of increasing human activity. North American Corvids have multi-purpose beaks and are colored with varying shades of blue, black and/or white.

Either **Yellow-billed** or **Black-billed Magpies** will probably be seen on your way up to Tahoe (Yellow-billeds reside only in the central valley of California, Black-billeds north and east of the Sierra Nevada). Black-billed Magpies can be seen around Lake Tahoe, especially on the east side, but I have not seen them in our watershed.

Although we have many blue-colored jays in the western U. S., the proper AOU name "Blue Jay" is technically reserved for a crested white and blue species most common in the eastern half of the our continent.

Western Scrub-Jay, *Aphelocoma californica. Plate 37*

A rare visitor during the spring and late summer, the Scrub Jay normally keeps to lower-elevation oak woodlands, scrubby savannahs and suburban environments. Its lighter coloring, lack of a crest and the questioning tone of its rising *zreek?* calls distinguish it from our common forest-dwelling Steller's Jay.

Steller's Jay, *Cyanocitta stelleri frontalis.* Plate 37

Loud, raucous and obnoxious, this not-so-demure black-crested blue jay (note: not Blue Jay!) gets along famously with food-bearing humans. If you return to your meal on the deck to find your french toast missing and your butter full of holes, chances are a Steller's Jay is perched nearby, smothered in syrup and asking for more.

In more pristine settings, they subsist on pine seeds, fruits, insects and other small animals. During the nesting season they feast on the eggs and nestlings of other birds whenever possible. Our Pacific subspecies have vertical blue streaks on the dark forehead (birds in the Rockies have white streaks).

Steller's Jays are often encountered in groups, especially around good feeding areas. Their harsh, drawn out, *shaaack* and rapid-fire *shuk-shuk-shuk-shuk* calls are familiar sounds in forested areas throughout the west. Less common vocalizations include a scream surprisingly reminiscent of a Red-tailed Hawk and a whispered, musical warble. A close friend of mine likens the latter performance to a large weight-lifter (picture Arnold Schwarzenegger in his prime) attempting to sing soprano—there are creaks and breaks in its voice and somehow it just does not seem right.

Georg Wilhelm Steller (1709–1746) was a German who became the first European naturalist to explore the Alaskan shoreline. The ill-fated Danish captain Vitus Bering took him across on a Russian ship from Kamchatka in 1741. Also named in his honor: Steller's Sea Lion, Steller's Eider, Steller's Sea Eagle and Steller's Sea Cow (a now-extinct large Alaskan cousin of the manatee).

Clark's Nutcracker, *Nucifraga columbiana.* Plate 37

The harsh calls of Clark's Nutcracker can be heard echoing off the smooth, glacial bowls of the high Sierra. A view of this bird usually means you are close to timberline, although they often undertake slight down-slope migrations in the fall and winter.

Clark's Nutcracker has a very close relationship with cone crops, especially those with large seeds, such as the Whitebark Pine. The nutcracker must store between twenty and thirty thousand seeds (or "pine nuts") each fall. The pine nuts are transported in the bird's large sublingual (under-tongue)

© Charles Quinn

pouch, which can hold as many as 150 seeds. They are then hidden in small holes in areas unlikely to be covered by heavy snow pack (usually south-facing slopes). A single individual must be successful in rediscovering over one thousand of these caches in order to make it through the winter. Clark's Nutcrackers are early breeders and also rely upon their caches to feed their young until insects become more abundant. They are also adept as scavenging carrion and food scraps left behind by careless campers.

The large gray body and bold, black and white wings of Clark's Nutcracker are unmistakable. The loud calls can be confused with the Steller's Jay's, but they are even more drawn out and grating. The type specimen was collected on a tributary of the Columbia River during Lewis & Clark's "Voyage of Discovery" and is named after Captain William Clark.

American Crow, *Corvus brachyrhynchos*   (Plate 38)

Rare stragglers of this species are periodically spotted flying through the area. Crows are more common in lowlands, especially around suburban and rural communities. A tail that is cut straight across, a smaller head and bill and a higher pitched *CAW* distinguishes this smaller species from the more "wild" Common Raven.

Common Raven, *Corvus corax*   (Plate 38)

© Barbara Gleason

Many Native American tribes revered Raven and viewed him as an embodiment of great spiritual power and prophetic abilities. Raven's deep croaking calls still garner respect when they sound over the silence of Desolation Wilderness and echo off of the valley's bare rock walls.

Probably as a result of their Corvid intelligence, Ravens are often seen "at play": doing barrel rolls, careening through high winds and other aerial acrobatics. Some of these behaviors are used in courtship, but they are also performed by solitary birds—seemingly just for fun. The "Animals at Play" article in the December 1994 issue of *National Geographic* even has photos of a raven "sledding" down a snowy hillside on its back, walking up and doing it again. Ravens also seem to enjoy "playing" with carnivores such as coyotes and grizzly bears.

The Common Raven's great size (the largest member of the "songbird" order), baseball-diamond-shaped tail and deep, croaking calls help separate this species from its smaller relative, the crow. In contrast to crows, ravens are more common in mountainous and other areas relatively devoid of human settlement. They eat carrion as well as any small animal they can capture and subdue—mostly small rodents.

SWALLOWS, Family *Hirundinidae*

These birds are fast, tiny, airborne insectivores which superficially resemble swifts in both appearance and behavior. Their lineage, however, is far from common: Swifts belong to the order *Apodiformes* (which includes hummingbirds), while Swallows are technically Passerines (members of the "perching birds" order).

Swallows spend the summer months as far north as Alaska, but most winter south of the United States-Mexico border. Their mouths can open to almost a full 180 degrees—earning them the "swallow" name and then some.

Tree Swallow, *Tachycineta bicolor. Plate 38*

Unlike the typical colonial swallows which build apartment complexes out of mud, this aptly named species prefers to nest in old woodpecker holes or some other natural cavity.

"Salvage logging" and the tendency for humans to remove dead trees anywhere they find them has decreased available nesting sites. Introduced cavity-nesters such as House Sparrows and European Starlings have further heightened the competition for the few remaining nest holes. Other native species such as House Wrens and bluebirds also compete for this now-scarce resource. Nest boxes may help alleviate this situation—as long as they are not claimed by alien species.

Luckily, however, an abundance of dead trees is one thing the Fallen Leaf basin is not lacking. Tree Swallows have been seen quite regularly around our lake, especially near the outlet of Glen Alpine Creek.

In our area, Tree Swallows are much more common than **Violet-green Swallows**, which show up only occasionally. Tree Swallows have a deep, midnight-blue sheen to their dorsal feathers and, unlike Violet-greens, lack the white patches on the rump and above the eyes. Name translates as "two-colored swift-mover." Violet-greens were historically rare in our area, but have become more common since they do well in suburban developments.

Barn Swallow, *Hirundo rustica. Plate 38*

This graceful species is where the word "swallow-tailed" comes from. In fact, the Barn Swallow is the only North American swallow with a long, deeply forked tail.

Their half-bowl-shaped nests are made out of mud and commonly plastered against the walls of human-made structures (usually just under the eaves), under bridges and on overhanging cliffs.

Cliff Swallow, *Petrochelidon pyrrhonata. Plate 38*

The scientific name translates as "flame-backed rock-swallow" and the namesake rust-colored rump is diagnostic in our area. Its pale whitish forehead and stubby square tail also help distinguish it from the similarly-colored Barn Swallow.

Cliff Swallows seem to be most abundant at the north end of Lake Tahoe, but it is quite possible to see them elsewhere. They often nest under bridges, eaves and other suitably vertical surfaces. Cliffs and bridges are often plastered with their gourd-shaped mud nests.

CHICKADEES, Family *Paridae*

Having only one species of this family present in the Tahoe area is not all bad. It makes identification considerably less difficult than in the Pacific Northwest, where there can be between two and four distinct species of chickadees within a single forest.

Chickadees have an average of seven eggs per clutch, making their frantic spring behavior understandable. Once the chicks are gone, however, they do not get much of a break before they are having a hard time finding enough food for themselves. At forty degrees below freezing, a chickadee must spend twenty times more time feeding than in the summer just to make it through the night. Spending the night in woodpecker holes or other old nesting cavities helps them conserve heat. Upon waking, however, chickadees in the northern part of their range have but a few minutes to find food before they starve and freeze to death (and you think you really need that cup of coffee!).

Mountain Chickadee, *Poecile gambeli abbreviatus. Plate 38*

This little busy-body is often seen noisily flitting through trees in search of insects. In the fall and winter, Mountain Chickadees often form loose flocks with other small resident birds such as nuthatches, kinglets and creepers. The Mountain Chickadee is the only chickadee species that sports a white eyebrow stripe through its black crown.

Its raspy, namesake call is usually repeated over and over: *chicka-dee-dee-dee* or *tsick-adee-adee*. The chickadee also has a soft, musical, spring-time warble only heard at very close range. The alternative name of the Mountain Chickadee, "cheeseburger bird," is due to its territorial mating song: a pattern of three high, thin whistles. Because the first note is higher in pitch as well as longer than the following two notes, its cadence is approximated by this famous sandwich name.

Recently changed from *Parus*, the genus *Poecile* means "pied," as in black and white. William Gambel (1819–1849) collected the type specimen in California. He was the first ornithologist to spend multiple years collecting in the state, beginning in 1841 (at Thomas Nuttall's urging). He died of typhoid while attempting a winter crossing of the Sierra Nevada. A quail is also named in his honor.

NUTHATCHES, Family *Sittidae*

The Fallen Leaf Basin is blessed with all three species of Nuthatches that occur in western North America. Their original name, "nuthacks," was derived from their habit of wedging pine nuts in crevices and then hammering away at the outer shell.

Nuthatches take insect food whenever they can, but subsist mainly on conifer seeds during the winter. Pairs defend nesting territory year-round when food holds out. Nuthatches may nest in old woodpecker holes, natural cavities, or excavate their own. Pitch is sometimes smeared around the entrance, possibly to deny climbing predators and parasitic insects a smooth entry into their home.

Red-breasted Nuthatch, *Sitta canadensis. Plate 38*

The most abundant and conspicuous nuthatch in our area, this species is almost certain to be seen (or at least heard) on any given day of the year. It is most common in open forests, such as the area around Lucky Baldwin's.

The incessant, nasal, *yank-yank-yank-yank* vocalizations draw attention to the Red-breasted Nuthatch. Its voice quality is often compared to a tiny tin trumpet or the beeping sound some trucks make when backing up.

White-breasted Nuthatch, *Sitta carolinensis aculeata. Plate 38*

Commonly associated with dry, open woodlands, the White-breasted Nuthatch depends on pine nuts or acorns cached in bark crevices to get it through the winter.

This species is neither abundant nor rare, being seen frequently but not as often as the Red-breasted. Individuals seen around Tahoe are most likely from the Great Basin, but west-side birds may also be seen. The White-breasted Nuthatch's larger body size, almost invisible eye stripe, whiter belly and higher-pitched voice help tell it apart from the Red-breasted Nuthatch.

The first scientific specimen was collected in the British colonies which are today North and South Carolina.

Pygmy Nuthatch, *Sitta pygmaea. Plate 39*

The smallest and rarest of western nuthatches, the Pygmy Nuthatch has a tiny, piping voice. This species has been seen periodically on a dead snag south of Lucky Baldwin's.

Often found in loose family groups, these birds flock and roost together in cavities during the winter to conserve warmth. Breeding units often consist of not only the mother and father, but also one to three "helpers" as well. Helpers are usually siblings or unmated sons of the pair which assist in nest building, feeding and upkeep.

CREEPERS, Family *Certhiidae*

Represented by but a single species in North America, this creeper is nonetheless widespread and extremely cute.

Instead of nesting in a cavity or on a branch, the creeper prefers to nest in the crevices between slabs of loose bark and the trunk of a large coniferous tree or snag.

Brown Creeper, *Certhia americana. Plate 39*

These tiny probers systematically corkscrew up tree trunks, inspecting every nook and cranny for insects and spiders (including larvae and eggs). Once they have finished searching a tree, they fly to the base of another to begin again. They are common year-round in open forests with large conifers.

Having a mottled brown back and white belly enables Brown Creepers to remain extremely well camouflaged. Like many animals, the dark back and lighter belly provides counter-shading. Counter-shading allows the shadow created by the animal's body to be practically "canceled out" by the light-colored underside. So, while the bark-like pattern on its back hides the bird, its light belly hides its shadow as well. This is important because creepers constantly forage on large, exposed trunks without branches.

Creeper songs vary considerably geographically, but all have very high-pitched, fast and complex *seezles*. Individuals in the forests around Tahoe seem to have patterns close to that of the Yellow Warbler, although their voice quality and habitat are quite different: *see-see-see, teedle-eet-seet* or *"sweet, sweet, sweet, I'm so sweet!"*

WRENS, Family *Troglodytidae*

Energetic and tiny, wrens will often jump, jitter, flitter and scold at anything passing by. Their short cocked tails, chunky bodies and slender curved bills make for distinctive silhouettes. Members of this family have amazing songs and short, bickering call notes.

Troglodytes literally means "cave-dweller," after their habit of nesting in "caves" of wood, rock, grass, or reeds depending on the particular species.

House Wren, *Troglodytes aedon parkmanii. Plate 39*

One of Camp's most conspicuous nesters, the House Wren's exuberant song often wakes up guests staying in the hillside cabins. This song is without a doubt energetic and lengthy, described as a cascade of complex bubbly, gurgled and liquid whistled notes. The males often sing from exposed perches such as small tree tops or roof peaks, but forage in moist deciduous undergrowth.

House Wrens owe their name to their habit of nesting in and around human structures in the East. Although they usually stick to tree cavities in the West, this did not stop a pair from nesting on the north side of Juniper Cabin. House Wrens produce two and sometimes three separate broods in a single year.

Their thin curved bills are perfectly suited to probing and picking for their favorite food—insects, spiders and other teeny creepy crawlers. Their pointed beaks are also used for piercing the eggs of any nearby competition, including other nesting House Wrens. Name roughly translates as "hole-diving nightingale."

The House Wren is the most common species in our area, but others may be seen on rare occasions:

Rock Wrens *(Plate 39)* are repetitive sing-songers (*cheery-cheery-cheery, teedle-teedle-teedle, chur-chur-chur*) that are occasionally encountered in rocky areas above 8000 feet, especially near Susie Lake, Dick's Peak and Mt. Tallac.

Canyon Wrens *(Plate 39)* were rarely encountered before Orr & Moffitt published *Birds of the Lake Tahoe Basin* in 1971: only a handful were seen in the Tahoe Area, one of them at the Glen Alpine Springs resort in March of 1903. They are now listed by the Forest Service as extirpated from the Tahoe Basin (although they are still common at lower elevations). Please report any sightings.

Winter Wrens have only been recorded a handful of times between August and March, mostly in November and December. I heard one only once, in dense riparian forest between Stanford Hill and Lily Lake.

Bewick's Wrens rarely wander up this high, preferring lower elevations.

Marsh Wrens, *(Plate 39),* used to breed in Rowlands Marsh, but are now restricted to smaller patches of emergent vegetation.

DIPPER, Family *Cinclidae*

American Dipper, *Cinclus mexicanus. Plate 39*

This dark stocky "Water Ouzel" never ventures far from the rushing streams of the mountainous west.

Exploiting basically the same food resources as trout, the American Dipper is the fly-fisherman's constant companion. Their long, musical, varied, mocking-bird like song carries above even the roar of waterfalls. Dippers have a habit of bobbing and flicking their wings incessantly. Many theories have been formulated to explain this behavior, but none are very convincing. Flashing their white eyelids, however, is generally believed to serve as some kind of signal to other dippers. Dipper nests are usually wedged underneath the lip of a waterfall for cover and protection.

Strong feet and sharp claws help dippers maintain their grip even in the swiftest of currents. Dippers can even use their wings to "fly" underwater. When watercourses freeze in the winter, Dippers are forced to move to lower elevations.

KINGLETS, Family *Regulidae*

These small, plump, olive-colored birds flit through deciduous and coniferous branches in small flocks, mixing with chickadees, nuthatches and creepers during the winter months. Their delicate, thin beaks enable them to pick insects from small branches with amazing speed and dexterity.

Kinglets make almost pendulous nests that hang from conifer branches close to the trunk. The deepness of the nest allows the female to incubate while hidden from view. Their generic name, *Regulus*, (little king) is derived from their conspicuously colored crowns and own-it-all attitudes.

Golden-crowned Kinglet, *Regulus satrapa. Plate 39*

Unlike its close relative, both sexes of this species continually sport their name-sake crowns. In addition to the strip of yellow (with a reddish middle in breeding males) at the apex of its head, the Golden-crowned Kinglet also has black and white stripes along the sides of its head.

Their high, thin call notes filter down from their tree-top homes in the coniferous canopy throughout the year. In the spring, call notes are repeated in an accelerating tempo to form a song that terminates in an extremely high-pitched, almost inaudible, trill.

Martin Heinrich Carl Lichtenstein (the describer of this species) must have thought the golden crown, kinglet and "little king" references were not enough: his specific epithet, satrapa, comes from an old Persian term, khshathrapava, meaning "protector of the people." This word was used to refer to a subordinate or provisional governor in ancient Persia—in other words, it is just another name for a "little king."

Ruby-crowned Kinglet, *Regulus calendula cineraceus. Plate 39*

Both "Ruby-crowned" and *calendula* ("small glow") refer to the red patch of the males. Unfortunately, since these scarlet feathers are only displayed during courtship or defense, one rarely sees the famed ruby crown. The tear-drop shaped white area around the eyes, incomplete eye ring, wing bars and thin bill are better identifying characteristics. Look for this perky little bird flitting among streams through shrubs and small trees, frantically searching for insects and their larvae.

The vocalizations of this kinglet are also helpful due to the uniqueness of both the call notes and the song. The calls consist of simple, two-noted scolds: *jed-it, jed-it*. The song is complex: it begins with a few very high, thin notes, then jumps down in pitch to repeat some louder notes which continue to roll upwards in pitch. Once heard, this distinctive song often becomes an instant favorite.

BLUEBIRDS, SOLITAIRES and THRUSHES, Family *Turdidae*

In a family full of familiar sights and sounds, these species give pleasure through their colors and songs. Most members of this family eat both insects and fruit (especially waxy berries, which they have evolved to digest), the proportion of each depending on the season.

These groups are members of the same family, but differ markedly in many ways. Bluebirds nest in tree holes, are bright blue, have little musical prowess and usually snatch insects out of the air or pounce on them from a perch. In contrast, thrushes make cup-shaped nests, are dull brown, have melodious songs and forage mostly on the ground. Solitaires seem to be somewhere between the two.

Some things they do share, however, is the color of their pale, bluish eggs and the scalloped or spotted look of immature individuals.

Mountain Bluebird, *Sialia currucoides. Plate 40*

Like most birds, the male of this species is much more brightly colored than the female. In fact, the female may look much more brown or gray than blue. Her less conspicuous coloration reveals how important females are to the continuation of the species. Males, on the other hand, appear to be completely expendable in their attention-grabbing breeding plumage. The pure, sky-blue feathers of the male are so intense they look dyed. Bluebirds compete with many other native and introduced birds for cavities to nest in.

These handsome birds are most often seen above 7000 feet during the summer and at the meadow northeast of Fallen Leaf Lake in the fall. Mountain Bluebirds are usually seen on low, exposed perches such as a stunted tree, barbed wire fence, or large boulder. It is from these lookouts that they scan for insects, catching them mid-air or pouncing on them from above.

Our Mountain Bluebirds winter at lower altitudes where they subsist on juniper, mistletoe and other berries. Other populations go as far south as the deserts along the Mexican border.

The rusty-breasted sister species, the **Western Bluebird** *(Plate 40)* usually remains at lower elevations and is only a rare visitor to our watershed.

Townsend's Solitaire, *Myadestes townsendi townsendi. Plate 40*

At first sight, the Townsend's Solitaire defies classification. Its unremarkable, dull gray visage only confuses the beginning birder—until it breaks into flight. Then, the orange wing patches and white outer tail feathers betray the bird's true identity without question.

Its generic name, *Myadestes*, means "fly-eater" and is well-deserved during the early summer months. As autumn approaches, however, solitaires switch to eating berries. This change in diet provides for interesting elevational movements. Early summer sees these birds following the spring burst of insects up-slope. Then, during mid-summer, they again descend to 6000 feet to begin feasting on berries. They remain close to the elevations of Fallen Leaf and Tahoe until late fall and finally descend to Juniper woodlands to subsist on fruit throughout the winter.

Although seemingly silent in the spring (singing sparingly only in the early morning and evening), males repeatedly sing their lengthy warbles to establish their winter feeding territories in the fall and winter. These songs are often thirty seconds long and quite varied. They can resemble the long-winded song of the Black-headed Grosbeak, but not as predictable, much faster and more "jumbled." Soft, repeated *toot* calls may also heard and can be mistaken for the hoots of a Northern Saw-whet or Pygmy Owl, although not given in a distinct, measured series.

These birds inhabit the scattered chaparral and shrublands of rocky slopes between 6000 and 9000 feet, scanning for insects from protruding perches. The brush-covered slopes of Cathedral Peak and Horsetail Falls are choice nesting habitat, providing hard-to-reach havens for this vulnerable ground-nester. They will also nest in cavities, especially near open clear-cuts.

John Kirk Townsend (1809–1851) did extensive collecting in the Rocky Mountains and even wrote a book about his travels. Townsend sent the type specimen of this species to Audubon, who named it in his honor.

Hermit Thrush, *Catharus guttatus. Plate 40*

The name of this genus, "pure," is an appropriate reference to the unparalleled quality of their mesmerizing songs. The Hermit Thrush's song begins with a long introductory note and then spirals, flutelike, upward. This long introductory note distinguishes the Hermit's song from that of its close relative, the **Swainson's Thrush**, *C. ustulatus* (which is unlikely in our area, but could be found in denser riparian forests at lower elevations). These thrushes sing the most just before dawn. The specific epithet, *guttatus*, "drop-like," is after the shape of the spots on the breast.

Catharus thrushes are a secretive, solitary bunch and usually search for invertebrates and berries under thick brush or, at higher elevations, in open forests. One is much more likely to hear their eerie, pre-dawn serenades than actually see this bird. Their songs have been heard drifting out of the high forests at night by campers around Lake of the Woods, Jabu Lake and Gilmore Lake. Hermit is a good name for this species—my only physical sighting was made halfway up the Cathedral Lake trail in dense chaparral.

American Robin, *Turdus migratorius propinquus. Plate 40*

Named after the smaller, only distantly-related European robin because of its reddish breast, this is quite possibly the most well-known and widespread bird in North America. Because of its love for our suburban lawns, many North Americans automatically think of a robin whenever the word "bird" is mentioned.

This species is also a common breeder in our mountains and can be found hopping along moist meadows in search of invertebrate prey. Although some have argued this robin uses its hearing to locate earthworms, at least one study has concluded they use their sight alone. In fall and winter they turn to the fruits of toyon, elderberry, mistletoe, juniper and other plants. It is not unusual for some of these fruits to ferment while still on the bush, causing drunkenness in undiscerning birds.

Humans have vastly expanded the American Robin's range by planting trees across the Great Plains (for nesting) and creating moist grasslands with irrigation (for foraging).

Varied Thrush, *Ixoreus naevius. Plate 40*

A visitor to our area mostly in the fall, the Varied Thrush sports appropriate colors for that time of year—pumpkin orange and black. This species is sometimes referred to as the "Alaskan robin" or "Oregon robin", due to its northern breeding haunts.

Being a ground-feeder, the Varied Thrush relies on open forest floors and can be found sparingly around Fallen Leaf during the fall. It often forms mixed flocks with American Robins, Dark-eyed Juncos and other ground-feeders.

Although it rarely sings while in the Sierras, keep an ear out for the dissonant, vibrating and drawn-out notes of the Varied Thrush. The genus translates as "mistletoe mountain" a food and habitat commonly used, which also may be a reference to its similarity to the Mistle Thrush of Europe, which also has spots (*naeuus*) merging into a similar breast-band.

PIPIT, Family *Motacillidae*

American Pipit, *Anthus rubescens. Plate 40*

Previously called the Water Pipit, these birds do not appear physically remarkable in any way. It is precisely this lack of unique identifying features that is often most helpful in field identification. A few hard-to-see traits that may assist in a positive identification follow: white outer tail feathers (most visible in flight), a streaky breast, a buffy eyebrow stripe and an unusually long, curved claw on the rear toe. Its tail-bobbing, wagging, or swinging behavior is also good to watch for (wagtails are also in this family).

The vast majority of pipits breed far to the north on the arctic tundra. However, since high elevations have similar environmental conditions to high latitudes (long, cold winters and brief, insect-infested summers), our particular species also nests near treeline as far south as New Mexico. Listen for their namesake *pip-it, pip-it* calls on the way to Dick's Pass, especially near moist pockets of open, tundra-like meadows. This species commonly winters along the San Francisco Bay as well as other wetland, field and beach habitats.

WARBLERS, Family *Parulidae*

Sierra Nevada Warblers adorn summer forests and stream-side thickets like brilliant yellow gems. Involved in a ceaseless search for insects, warblers scour leaves and twigs at hyper speeds. Most warblers have some amount of yellow plumage, but crisp grays, blacks and whites also decorate these living jewels.

Moist thickets are often filled with these birds, especially near Witch's Pond, Lily Lake and along streams.

Orange-crowned Warbler, *Vermivora celata lutescens. Plate 40*

A late summer visitant, the Orange-crowned Warbler comes up from downslope and down from up north after breeding, to spend some time in our part of the Sierras. This "vermin-eater" has a thin pointy beak, is washed with an olive greenish-yellow and, like the Ruby-crowned Kinglet, the male hardly ever shows its namesake cap. Its song, unlikely to be heard post-breeding, is a trill that seems to "run out of steam." Because the Orange-crowned Warbler usually sticks to thick undergrowth, rarely sings while here and lacks any obvious markings, it is rarely identified in our area.

Nashville Warbler, *Vermivora ruficapilla. Plate 41*

Unfortunately, a direct translation of the Latin, "little red-capped worm-eater," was not chosen as its common name. "Nashville" (where the type specimen was collected) seems like a poor substitute, especially since the city is only a recent obstacle in the migratory path of certain eastern populations. Nashvilles, along with MacGillivray's and Wilson's, are the most commonly seen warblers at Camp.

Like its close relative, the Orange-crowned, the male Nashville Warbler has normally-hidden rusty stripe on its crown that is almost never seen in the field. Better identifying characteristics are: complete, bold, white eye rings; a yellow throat; white patches of feathers where the legs attach to the body; and black legs. Any one of the preceding traits is sufficient to distinguish the Nashville from the similarly gray-headed, olive-backed and yellow-bellied MacGillivray's Warbler.

These two birds also have similar songs, the first part being almost identical, but the second part of the Nashville's song is a faster trill: *seetle, seetle, seetle, seetle, didididi* or *sweeta, sweeta, sweeta, didididididi*.

Listen for the Nashville Warbler in moist, deciduous thickets as well as forests with shrubby undergrowth. Singing is common in May and June as high as Gilmore Lake. Like most other "vermivores," Nashville Warblers nest on the ground under dense cover.

WOOD WARBLERS, GENUS *Dendroica*

Dendroica (literally meaning "wood-home" or "tree-dweller") warblers are often referred to generically as "wood warblers." (Although the entire Family is now officially the Wood Warbler Family, most birders still reserve the name for this genus alone.) This name is based on their preference for taller trees for both feeding and nesting than most other warblers. Wood warblers also share a common song pattern that makes distinguishing individual species by ear quite a challenge.

Yellow Warbler, *Dendroica petechia*. Plate 41

The most completely yellow of our warblers, this species is well-named. Males have subtle red to chestnut-colored streaks on their breasts (*petechia* is the medical term for reddish-purple birthmarks). I have only seen these streaks well on an individual who struck a window at Camp. This species is a summer resident in alders, cottonwoods and aspens near water.

The Yellow Warbler's song is a rapid, rich and truly sweet-sounding *sweet, sweet, sweet, little more sweet!*—dropping in pitch during the "little more" part. Usually this pattern is distinctive. In our area, however, Brown Creepers employ a very similar pattern—albeit higher, thinner and a bit more raspy. Creepers are also found in drier coniferous forests as opposed to deciduous riparian zones.

Yellow-rumped Warbler, *Dendroica coronata auduboni*. Plate 41

Almost all the Yellow-rumps (more affectionately known as "butter-butts") recorded near Tahoe have been of the yellow-throated "**Audubon's**" persuasion. The white-throated "**Myrtle**" race only shows up rarely during migration to and from its much more northerly breeding grounds. Their song is a fast, high-pitched, *weetle weetle weetle weetle weet weet weet*. Call note is a distinctive, dry *wit*.

In the early part of the century, this bird was considered to be the most common summer warbler in the Tahoe basin. Whether this is still true for Tahoe as a whole is uncertain, but the Glen-Alpine watershed has not appeared to be overflowing with them during the recent past.

Yellow-rumped Warblers are less strict insectivores than other warblers. This allows them to winter much farther north (to southwestern British Columbia), subsisting on fruit, seeds and nectar. Introduced Eucalyptus trees are magnets for wintering Yellow-rumps in California, providing nectar and insects at a time when both are otherwise scarce.

Black-throated Gray Warbler, *Dendroica nigrescens. Plate 41*

Beautiful shades of gray combine with crisp black and white patterning to produce one of the handsomest of our late summer visitors. Tiny spots of brilliant yellow between the eyes and beak set off its snow-and-coal coloring with the stunning success of a hand-painted black and white photograph.

Black-throated Grays come up from their oak woodland breeding grounds as early as late July. For this reason, their *zeetle zeetle zeetle zeetle ZEEE-chay* song should not be heard much at our elevation, especially not after July. Watch for these birds in the alder thickets near Witch's Pond and Lucky Baldwin's.

Townsend's Warbler, *Dendroica townsendi. Plate 41*

Another late summer visitor, this warbler is often seen briefly on its trip back from its breeding grounds in the forests of the Pacific Northwest. Townsend's have been spotted on Stanford Hill and at Lucky Baldwin's during August and September. Spring migration occurs at lower elevations. Because Townsend's Warblers do not breed in the Sierra nor migrate through in the spring, their songs are rarely heard here.

Dark eye patches and yellow bellies separate this species from the similar Hermit Warbler. Both species winter in coastal California as well as Mexico. See Townsend's Solitaire for information on the man honored by the name.

Hermit Warbler, *Dendroica occidentalis. Plate 41*

Even more so than other wood warblers, these "hermits" breed in coniferous canopies at high elevations. It is because of this preference for foraging at the tops of our tallest trees—not their rarity—that they are seen only periodically. Keep an ear out for their almost buzzy, high-pitched *zeedle zeedle zeedle zee teet teet teet* songs. They are present from April to September, but the highest concentrations occur in August—when our breeding birds are joined by up-slope drifters as well as northern migrants.

Solid yellow sides of the head and white bellies are key traits that distinguish them from the similar Townsend's Warbler.

MacGillivray's Warbler, *Oporornis tolmiei tolmiei. Plate 41*

One of our most common warblers, MacGillivray's is often spotted relatively near the ground in moist, deciduous woods. This warbler is regularly seen or heard while walking the Nature Trail behind Camp, especially in June.

Due to its gray head, this species is regularly confused with the Nashville Warbler. Look for the MacGillivray's gray to black throat, white crescents above and below the eyes, lack of any white below (solid yellow from breast to vent) and pinkish legs. Their calls are also similar, but the MacGillivray's has a slower, lower ending that goes up and down in pitch: *tweeta, tweeta, tweeta, tweeta, mac-gill-i-vray.*

Townsend named this bird for Dr. William Fraser Tolmie (1818–1886), a Scottish physician who worked for the Hudson Bay Company out of Fort Vancouver. Audubon also described the species and named it for William MacGillivray (1796–1852)—another Scotsman—who wrote *A History of British Birds* and helped Audubon edit his work. It was later discovered that Townsend's description was published first, but Audubon's common name was already in popular use. The genus means "end of summer (or autumn) bird" since many species of this genus were more commonly seen on the East Coast during their fall migration.

Wilson's Warbler, *Wilsonia pusilla chryseola. Plate 41*

The smallest of our warblers, Wilson's warbler is also one of the more frequently seen. Along with the less commonly viewed Yellow Warbler, the Wilson's is the brightest, richest yellow of the bunch. The black patch on top of the male's head is diagnostic.

Populations of Wilson's Warblers that breed at high elevations are significantly more successful than coastal breeders. They lay more eggs per brood, fledge more young and are likely to be polygynous. Polygyny occurs when a single male breeds with more than one female. In order for this to happen, food resources must be copious and the need for defense, minimal.

Witch's Pond regularly hosts at least one pair of these warblers each summer. Wilson's Warblers are also common in wet, shrubby areas as high as the south slope of Mt. Tallac. Listen for the repeated notes which drop in pitch and become slower near the end: *che-che-che-che-che-che-che-che.*

Charles Bonaparte named this genus after Alexander Wilson (1766–1813) who was born in Scotland but came to America in his late twenties to become the "Father of American Ornithology." In the final years of his life he published a nine-volume series filled with details on habitat, range and behavior called *American Ornithology*. It is commonly said that Audubon was a great artist with a talent for ornithology but that Wilson was a great ornithologist with a talent for art. *Pusilla* means "very small"—it is not the smallest warbler, but it is the smallest of its genus.

TANAGER, Family *Thraupidae*

Western Tanager, *Piranga ludoviciana. Plate 42*

Our sole representative of this largely tropical subfamily, the Western Tanager is our most colorful summer visitor. The male's bright reddish-orange head grades into its brilliant yellow body like a well-made Tequila Sunrise (albeit upside down). The black wings (with yellow wing bars), black back and black tail frame the audacious colors to make a bold, unquestionable statement: "I am a male Western Tanager and I am ready to mate!"

The song of the Western Tanager is similar to that of the American Robin and the Black-headed Grosbeak in pattern, but its voice quality is burry or hoarse and the phrases are shorter, more abrupt and well-spaced. The clincher is its call note: a diagnostic *pritty-dik*! The mnemonic is easy: think of a handsome, conceited male named Dick who regularly bursts out to say he's pretty.

Both *tanager* and *piranga* are terms borrowed from the language of the indigenous Tupi people who live in part of the tanagers' southern wintering grounds (the upper Amazon Basin). The specific epithet, ludoviciana, is a reference to the Louisiana Purchase (the western U.S.), where it was first encountered by Lewis and Clark.

TOWHEES, SPARROWS & JUNCOS, Family *Emberizidae*

Many of these stout-billed birds forage for insects and seeds on the ground. Most nest on the ground or in low shrubs. Sparrows and juncos commonly form large winter flocks.

Green-tailed Towhee, *Pipilo chlorurus. Plate 42*

A common breeder on the dry chaparral slopes of the mountainous west, the Green-tailed Towhee winters mostly south of the border. Green-tailed Towhees are most often sighted along the mid-Tallac and Cathedral Lake Trails. Lucky birders have sometimes found these birds as far down as the avalanche track north of Camp's parking lot.

Because Green-tailed Towhees have habitat preferences, songs and long-tailed silhouettes similar to Fox Sparrows, close visual inspection is often necessary. Fortunately, both species usually sing from exposed perches above their scrubby environment. Listen for the Green-tailed's cat-like *mew* calls as well as its song: one or two wheezy whistled notes followed by complex and variable raspy trills.

Spotted Towhee, *Pipilo maculatus. Plate 42*

Rufous-sided Towhee was the good old name of this species before it was split into Eastern (black-backed) & (western) Spotted. It is not commonplace to see this lowland bird above the Ponderosa Pine belt, but Spotted Towhees have been sighted with some regularity on the chaparral slopes east of Cathedral Peak.

Listen for the explosively fast trill of a song *Tea-eeeeeeee!* and low, rising *Frank?* call notes. The only possibility for visual confusion is the Black-headed Grosbeak, which normally keeps higher up in the trees and does not "hop-scratch" in leaf litter. If you are close enough to see it, the red eye of this species is diagnostic.

SPARROWS

"Sparrow," (from the Anglo-Saxon *spearwa*, to flutter) is a non-specific term for small, brownish Emberzids. Although they take insects in the spring and summer, most have evolved stout, seed-cracking bills to deal with their winter diets. While many simply refer to them as LBB's (Little Brown Birds), they represent a variety of genera and are often very habitat-specific. Nesting females will sometimes feign injury to distract potential predators.

A number of species that have not been recorded in the Glen-Alpine Watershed can be found at lower elevations to the east and west. Some of these species may wander into our area before and during migration. Keep an eye out for these unlikely, but possible, species: **Vesper Sparrow, Savannah Sparrow, Lark Sparrow, Black-throated Sparrow, Sage Sparrow** and **Rufous-crowned Sparrow**.

Chipping Sparrow, *Spizella passerina arizonae*

Orr and Moffit (1971) describe this species in the following manner: *"Abundant summer resident . . . one of the commonest species of birds from lake [Tahoe] level to middle elevations wherever there is open forest land with sufficient sparsely covered ground on which to forage."* However, this species is not currently common in the Tahoe Basin. This may be due to the fact that there are have not been any recent clear-cuts or big fires to provide open habitat for them.

Keep an ear out for their flat, dry, mechanical, "chipping" trills. These trills are similar to those of the Dark-eyed Junco, but are less musical and do not vary in pitch.

Brewer's Sparrow, *Spizella breweri. Plate 42*

The Brewer's Sparrow is another species lacking in recent records, but recorded in what is now Desolation Wilderness by Dudley S. De Groot in the 1930s. According to his article, "Field Observations from Echo Lake, California" (*Condor*, vol. 36), a number of Brewer's Sparrows were nesting in shrubby habitats along the Echo-Desolation Valley trail.

Look for white eye rings, a tan-colored rump, pale brown ear patches with dark outlines, a light gray eyebrow, a whisker stripe and a streaky crown. (In other words, nothing very obvious!) Listen for a varied, raspy song with trills, whistles and buzzes.

Brewer's Sparrows are most common on the brushy sagebrush slopes east of lake Tahoe. Populations have been recorded on the western slope of Genoa Peak, Spooner Station, Spooner Meadow and Glenbrook (Orr and Moffit, 1971).

Cassin named this species for Thomas Mayo Brewer (1814–1880), a Boston publisher famous for his studies of bird eggs and infamous for championing the introduction of the European House Sparrow to America.

Fox Sparrow, *Passerella iliaca megarhyncha*

A secretive denizen of the shrub understory, this bird often lurks just out of sight. A glimpse of its solid gray head and back, massive beak and streaky underside, however, is more than enough to identify it. Its song is extremely rich, variable and complex, its burry quality being the best clue available.

Their strong, stout bill (largest in our "thick-billed" group of subspecies) enables the Fox Sparrow to crack the hard seeds of the ubiquitous *Ceanothus*. The ability to exploit such a plentiful resource without much competition gives the Fox Sparrow a significant edge.

Since the Fox Sparrow gets its name from a reddish-colored subspecies of the East, westerners often have a hard time figuring out what's "foxy" about these dull little ground-feeders. Most of our Fox Sparrows winter in southern California.

Song Sparrow, *Melospiza melodia. Plate 42*

An extremely variable species both aurally and morphologically, the Song Sparrow also lives throughout most of North America. Its stripy, gray-brown head and breast usually gives away its identity, but both Fox Sparrows and Green-tailed Towhees offer some physical resemblance, habitat overlap and behavioral similarities.

Song Sparrows are most often found in brushy areas near water, their long-tailed silhouettes perched on protruding branches. From these optimal lookouts, males burst forth with their complex songs. Since they usually begin with two or three notes on the same pitch and then drift into buzzes, chirps and trills, their pattern has been likened to: *Maids! Maids! Maids! Put on your tea---- kettle-ettle-ettle!* (The creator of this mnemonic must have led the good life!)

The Song Sparrow is tied with the Yellow Warbler for the unfortunate distinction of being the most commonly parasitized species by the Brown-headed Cowbird. Luckily, populations of Song Sparrows do not appear to be suffering as much as some of the warblers. This may be due to the fact that Song Sparrows will often raise two or three—sometimes even four—broods during a single breeding season.

For those who are trying to see all 31 sub-species of the Song Sparrow, most of our accounts have been of the Great Basin form, *fisherella*. Lincoln's Sparrow inhabits similar habitats at higher altitudes.

Lincoln's Sparrow, *Melospiza lincolnii alticola. Plate 42*

This species shares many similarities with its congeneric, the Song Sparrow. Lincoln's Sparrow, however, is much smaller and more delicate-looking (its short tail being especially noticeable), has a buffy malar (mustache) stripe, has streaking on its chin and throat, a buffy eye ring, a tan wash across the breast and a more petite bill.

Its vocalizations are quite distinctive, the call notes in particular: a flat *shup* and a sharp, buzzy *zeee*. The Lincoln's Sparrow's song is a mixture of bubbling trills, the second trill often being explosively loud when compared with the rest of the song parts.

Although I have no recent sightings, Charles R. Keyes ("Some bird notes from the central Sierras," *Condor*, vol. 7) recorded a successful breeding pair at Susie Lake on July 2, 1903 and specimens have been collected near Fallen Leaf Lake as well as Camp Richardson. Wet shrubby areas above 6000 feet seem to be their preferred breeding habitat.

Thomas Lincoln (1812–1883) accompanied Audubon on a trip to the Labrador coast where Lincoln discovered this bird and Audubon named it for him.

White-crowned Sparrow, *Zonotrichia leucophrys oriantha. Plate 42*

The black and white striped caps of this species decorate wet, shrubby areas of the High Sierra from May to August. Their pale, apricot-colored beaks further enhance their "cute" appearance and their song tops it off. The scientific name translates as "White-eyebrowed banded-thrush."

Although variable, the song often begins with a long introductory note, is followed by another note (either higher or lower) and then proceeds into reedy, up-and-down trills and buzzes. I try to fit the song to its name: *Whiiiiiiite—crowned, Sparer-rarer-row.*

The subspecies that breeds in the Sierra (*Z. l. oriantha* or *Z. l. leucophrys*, depending on how up-to-date you wish to be) is identified by having black "lores," birder jargon for the area between the eye and beak. A smaller subspecies with white lores, *Z. l. gambelii*, visits us before and after it migrates north to breed: usually in April, September and October. If you are around in April and May, see if you can pin down the differences in their dialects. If that does not sound challenging enough, try to differentiate the subtle differences between local breeding populations (for example, Haypress Meadows vs. the Velma Lakes).

Arguably the most academically-famous of our sparrows, the White-crowned has been the subject of an amazing number and diversity of scientific studies. Luis Baptista was a talented researcher at the California Academy of Sciences (CAS) who studied the different dialects of White-crowned Sparrows, particularly those of the High Sierra. On any given day, Dr. Baptista could be blindfolded, spun around, led out a random door of the CAS building and be able to tell exactly where he is based on subtle differences in the White-crowned Sparrows' dialects. He was a fabulous lecturer, accomplished scientist, an amazing sonogram whistler and is greatly missed.

Golden-crowned Sparrow, *Zonotrichia atricapilla. Plate 42*

A fall visitor, this species winters on the west coast and breeds north of the Canadian border. The Golden-crowned Sparrow's plaintive, falling, *Oh, dear me!* song may be heard in western California, Oregon and

Washington during the spring migration. Specific epithet translates as "black-capped," despite the common name.

Dark-eyed Junco, *Junco hyemalis. Plate 43*

Formerly the Oregon junco, our form was "lumped" in 1983 with what used to be the Gray-headed, Slate-colored, Guadalupe, Pink-sided and White-winged species to form this "new" species. Reason for the change are new genetic discoveries and the ability of the races to interbreed.

One of the unifying morphological characteristics of this species is that all members have dark-colored eyes. This may seem petty from our anthropocentric (a species with variable eye color) point of view, but eye color clearly and easily distinguishes this species from its Yellow-eyed cousin who lives in the high forests of Mexico.

Juncos begin nesting as early as April in the Tahoe area. Because they get such an early start, Dark-eyed Juncos usually manage to have two broods fledged by mid-summer. Open forests and their edges are frequented by these birds year-round. In winter, they form flocks with a social hierarchy.

Juncos were indirectly named after the Latin for rush or reed (*juncus*) because the term was also applied to the similarly black-hooded Reed Bunting, *Emberiza schoeniclus*, of Europe. The specific epithet means "of winter" since the collector, Catesby, only knew them as a winter visitor (as does most of the U.S.).

GROSBEAKS & BUNTINGS, Family *Cardinalidae*

This family also includes cardinals, hence the Latin name.

Black-headed Grosbeak, *Pheucticus melanocephalus. Plate 43*

A long-winded melodious singer, the Black-headed Grosbeak's clear, lilting whistles filter down from the treetops in the spring. Both the American Robin and the Western Tanager have similar songs, but neither are as long or as clear. The Black-headed Grosbeak's call note, a sharp abrupt, *pik*, is also very different from either of the other species and is diagnostic when heard along with the song.

In the breeding season (the only time they are here), the male has the namesake black head as well as a bright orange breast that is more yellow around the edges and on the belly. The female has a brown back and head with small white spots, bars and stripes and a buffy-tan to white belly. Seen from below in flight, lemon yellow underwing coverts are obvious in both sexes and males have large white "windows" near the tip of the wings.

Black-headed Grosbeaks adhere less strictly than most birds to gender-based stereotypes: males help incubate, females will also sing (though not as predictably or as much) and the female will defend the nesting territory almost as vigorously as the male. Both sexes will usually sing within a hundred feet of their nest and sometimes even while incubating. Their twiggy nests are commonly located in thick streamside vegetation, but open forests with a abundant understory shrubs are also used.

The structure of the Black-headed Grosbeak's bill is primarily designed for its fall and winter diet of Central American seeds and fruit, but works perfectly well for capturing insects during their breeding season here. (These powerful bills can also draw blood from your hands if you are not careful while mist-netting and banding them!)

For those who are familiar with the Rose-breasted Grosbeak of eastern North America, this is the western version of the same genus. *Pheucticus* is either from a Greek word meaning "shy" (if so, the genus was named for a more secretive species, or possibly for the Rose-breasted's blush) or "painted with cosmetics" (which gets my vote); *melanocephalus* translates as "black head." The common name, grosbeak, is borrowed from the French "large-beaked" and does not have any specific meaning in scientific nomenclature. For example, the Evening Grosbeak is an unrelated member of the Finch family with an unusually large bill.

Lazuli Bunting, *Passerina amoena. Plate 43*

The only reports of this species in our area come from the brushy slope half-way up the Cathedral Lake Trail (which angles up the west side of Fallen Leaf Lake). However, keep an eye out for this species on other brushy slopes or in shrubby meadows.

Named for the blue semi-precious stone, the metallic blue sheen that is created by the physical structure of the male's feathers is indeed dazzling. The thick, angular, lead-gray bill looks as if it was made out of polished metal. The orange breast and white belly of this species can make this bunting look a bit like a Western Bluebird from a distance, but look for the diagnostic white wing bars (or buff wing bars on the drab brown females) and the thick bill. Their songs are lengthy series of paired goldfinch-like phrases. The scientific name roughly translates as "lovely little-sparrow."

MEADOWLARKS, BLACKBIRDS and COWBIRDS, Family *Icteridae*

Pointy beaks and shades of black, yellow and red mark most members of this diverse group. Orioles are also members of this group, but usually occur at lower elevations.

Red-winged Blackbird, *Agelaius phoeniceus nevadensis. Plate 43*

This species gets its common name from the male's bright red "shoulder" (actually wrist) patches. These patches are often referred to as "epaulets" (as in the shoulder decorations of military officers) and are primarily used as a display in territorial defense.

Their song is a distinctive "rusty gate hinge" sound, often described as, *konk-a-reee-o*, or *Pump-kin eat-er*. The streaky, brown and white females hardly look like a "blackbird" at all.

Red-winged Blackbirds are another species which used to flourish in Rowlands Marsh. Now they are comparatively rare, but can still be found in some of the remaining lower-elevation marshes of the Tahoe Valley.

Most of our breeding population comes up from the Great Basin and have thin yellow stripes just below their red patches. The central valley subspecies (*A. p. californicus*) have almost solid red patches and are usually absent from the Tahoe area. The name of the species means "flocking Phoenician," after the red color made from *Murex* mollusks that the Phoenicians (the Greek name for the people who lived on the coast of what is now Syria) introduced to the Greeks.

Western Meadowlark, *Sturnella neglecta. Plate 43*

As its name suggests, this species frequents grassland ecosystems throughout our half of the continent. Although relatively rare as a breeder, many Western Meadowlarks move up to our elevation in September and October. The most commonly visited meadows are those south of Lake Tahoe, especially the marshy grasslands formed where creeks meet the lake.

Yellow-headed Blackbird, *Xanthocephalus xanthocephalus. Plate 43*

This species may win booby-prizes for both the "Most Imaginative" scientific name ("yellow-headed yellow-head") and the "Most Beautiful" song (sounding like a bad recorder player being strangled mid-song), but it is a truly beautiful bird. The male's solid yellow head and large white wing patches on an otherwise black bird is striking.

These birds used to nest by the thousands in the tule reeds of historic Rowlands Marsh. Their nests are bulky structures of woven grasses attached to reeds a couple feet above the water. Yellow-heads rely upon emergent vegetation in deep (four to ten feet) water to keep their nests safe from marauding mammals. Although this nesting preference prevents them from competing with the shallower-nesting Red-winged Blackbirds, deep-water emergent vegetation is a much less common phenomenon. Today, Yellow-headed Blackbirds are restricted to a few remaining deep marshes at the southern end of Lake Tahoe.

Brewer's Blackbird, *Euphagus cyanocephalus. Plate 43*

This species has adapted to our presence and now rarely strays far from sources of human handouts or forgotten scraps. Although Brewer's Blackbirds can function outside of urban environs, it is unusual for most of us to see these birds in a more natural setting than agricultural areas. (Incidentally, this is a common bird around Tresidder Memorial Union at Stanford: the bulk of their calories coming from wayward french fries.)

The males have dark, glossy, iridescent black plumage and pale yellow eyes. The females are more of a dull brown, especially their heads and have solid black eyes. Brewer's Blackbirds can be distinguished from Brown-headed Cowbirds by their longer, slimmer bodies, thinner beaks and often urban habitat preference.

See **Brewer's Sparrow** for information on the common name. Scientific name means "good-eatin' blue-head"—I can only confirm that males do indeed have an purplish-blue sheen to the black feathers on their head.

Brown-headed Cowbird, *Molothrus ater. Plate 43*

The Brown-headed Cowbird is a brood parasite unintentionally introduced to the west through the spread of agriculture, tree-planting, deforestation and settlement. The first recorded observation for the Tahoe area was made on June 28, 1959 by Junea A. Kelly when she witnessed a junco feeding a young cowbird near D. L. Bliss State Park. Cowbirds owe their name to their habit of following large ungulate herds (previously bison) to feed on disturbed insects.

Brown-headed Cowbirds do not even think about making a nest or raising their young, but instead rely upon other dedicated avian parents. This strategy probably evolved as a way of reproducing and keeping up with a fast-moving bison herd at the same time. Females search through forest edges and riparian woodlands for the nests of unsuspecting flycatchers, vireos, warblers, finches and other comparably-sized, insect-feeding birds.

When an appropriate nest is discovered, the female cowbird lays an egg (or two) among the host's own eggs. Sometimes the cowbird will even remove a host egg—just in case the mother is counting. Having another's egg in the nest may not seem like the end of the world, but when they hatch a few days before the resident's, push the resident eggs out of the nest and out-compete all the smaller nestlings, the end result is that the hosts have exhausted themselves and their resources and wasted the breeding season rearing a competitor.

Favorite target species include Yellow Warblers and Song Sparrows, but over 200 other species have also been recorded as hosts of Brown-headed Cowbird young. Western birds are still evolving ways of dealing with cowbird parasitism. In the Sierras, Willow Flycatchers, Solitary Vireos, Warbling Vireos and Yellow Warblers have been especially hard-hit. Bell's Vireo has been nearly extirpated from California due to the deadly combination of riparian habitat destruction and the recent arrival of the Brown-headed Cowbird.

A few host species have developed methods of dealing with the cowbird's behavior. These counter-measures include ejecting the foreign egg, abandoning the nest, building another nest on top, chasing Brown-headed Cowbird adults away from nesting territories and simply not rearing the young cowbird. These measures, along with "natural causes" prevent about 50 percent of cowbird eggs from successfully fledging.

However, a female cowbird can lay up to forty eggs per season (due to the luxury of not having to raise them). Those which survive to breed can quickly compound next year's problems for their hosts.

The flip side of the situation is this: due to the severity of the selective pressure, once a defensive behavior is acquired in a population, it often spreads like wildfire. For the sake of our endemic populations that are inexperienced with this new invader, I hope this happens soon.

The genus is from the Greek *molobros*, "a parasite or greedy beggar," and *ater* is Latin for "black," after the body color of the male.

FINCHES, Family *Fringillidae*

This group is full of voracious seed-eaters with dark wings, dark tails and washes of yellow or red. Many finches also take insects in the spring to provide their growing young with sufficient protein.

Back-yard feeders will often attract large flocks in the fall and winter.

Mass southward movements in the late fall or winter, called irruptions, occur periodically when food becomes scarce farther north.

ROSY FINCH SUPERSPECIES (ex-Rosy Finch, ex-*Leucosticte arctoa*)

Rosy Finches have had more than their fair share of lumping and splitting. In 1983 the forms were lumped and recently they were split back apart.

Both of our finches have gray wedges extending up and behind the eye and black foreheads. These finches nest on alpine peaks and talus slopes, generally above timberline, up to some of our tallest peaks. They feed on seeds (primarily pussy-paw seeds at high elevations), white heather flowers, saxifrage leaves and insects. A good deal of their insect food is blown up-slope and onto glaciers or snow fields where they are incapacitated by the cold and become easy pickings.

Both the Gray-crowned Rosy Finch and the Black Rosy Finch (now two separate species) breed at and far above, timberline around Lake Tahoe. The Brown-Capped Rosy Finch, *L. australis* (now the third species) resides in the Colorado Rockies.

Gray-crowned Rosy-Finch, *Leucosticte tephrocotis dawsoni*

The Gray-crowned Rosy Finch usually sticks close to the Pacific Northwest, although they do nest in the northern Rockies and winter as far east as western South Dakota. Gray-crowneds have been recorded as nesting at the summit of Pyramid Peak and have been seen near Dicks Peak, Dicks Lake, Mt. Tallac and Lake Lucille in June and July. As a rule, the Gray-crowned Rosy Finch is more common than the Black Rosy Finch in the Sierra Nevada. Gray-crowneds are mostly a rich, rusty brown with washes of pink on their wings, rump and flanks.

Black Rosy-Finch, *Leucosticte atrata*

In general, most Black Rosy Finches winter east of the Sierras (including most of the Great Basin). They nest on a handful of small mountain ranges that surround southern Idaho. However, there are regular sightings on the peaks around the Tahoe Basin and a single Black Rosy Finch was sighted near Dick's Pass in late June by Jed Mitchell. This species lacks any brown at all and is mostly coal-black (males) or ash-gray (females and juveniles).

Pine Grosbeak, *Pinicola enucleator californicus*

Thankfully a long-winded and repetitive singer, the Pine Grosbeak is a rare recluse of our high-altitude forests and an exhilarating find. During the winter, these birds (and crossbills) have been reported to be "ridiculously" tame and approachable.

Pine Grosbeaks are colored in a manner similar to crossbills (see above), but are much larger, more extensively gray, have white wing bars, longer tails and a shorter, stubbier, only slightly hooked bill. Their reds tend towards rosy-pink (as opposed to orange in crossbills) and their yellows tend towards lemon-lime (as opposed to the gold in Goldfinches).

Look for these birds feeding on seeds at the tops of conifers as well as low down, on Mountain-Ash fruit and maple buds. The Sierra Nevada is the only mountain range they breed in for hundreds of miles around—the bulk of the population is in the Rockies and Canada. See Black-headed Grosbeak for information on common name. The scientific name translates as "pine-dwelling seed-extractor."

CARPODACUS ("FRUIT-EATING") FINCHES

The following two members of this genus are given a separate heading because they are infamously difficult to tell apart. Each has a long, rich warble and similar reddish or streaky plumage, depending on the sex. The best method of distinction I have found is listening for their call notes. Other visual cues are included below.

Despite the meaning of their generic name, both eat mostly seeds, but also consume fruit, flowers, buds and insects. Both form flocks, even during the breeding season. **House Finches**, *C. mexicanus*, have only been locally recorded in suburban South Lake Tahoe.

Purple Finch, *Carpodacus purpureus. Plate 44*

The male of this species is not really "purple"—at least not like the crayon color. Red would be a closer approximation, ranging from rose-red to a burgundy wine color.

The Purple Finch's red crown gradually streaks into brown at the back of the head and usually has pure white undertail coverts. The bill is sturdy and triangular, but not large compared to its head. The call note of the Purple Finch is a sharp *pik*! Our Pacific race is more common west and north of here, especially at mid-elevations. (There is also an eastern race and both races breed in Canada.)

Cassin's Finch, *Carpodacus cassinii. Plate 44*

The male Cassin's Finch normally has a bright crimson crown on its forehead that ends abruptly at a line of brown on the back of its head. Cassin's Finches also have very large, sturdy bills. Its breast is often less intensely red (more pink or rose-colored) than its crown and usually has fine, dark streaks on its flanks. Cassin's call note is an extended, slurred, rising phrase, being lowest in pitch during the middle syllable: "chill-eee-up!"

Baird named this finch to honor John Cassin (see Cassin's Vireo, pg. 136). This species is most common in forests east of the Sierras, in the interior West.

Red Crossbill, *Loxia curvirostra*. Plate 44

These nomadic finches range widely in search of ripening pine cones, although they will eat many other conifer seeds as well. Their crossed bills are adapted to pry open stubborn scales while their tongue deftly snakes out the seed from within.

Coloring varies with diet as well as with age and sex. Older males usually sport the deepest red, females more of a dull gold, immature males can appear rusty and juveniles show little yellow, if any at all, on their streaky breasts.

Flocks are usually near the tree tops (where most of the cones are found), being detected only by a rain of seed hulls and their *jip-jip, jip- jip-jip* call notes as flocks wheel overhead. The song of the Red Crossbill is a short, soft, squeaky-bubbly phrase followed by four to five high-pitched notes. Besides the distinctive crossed tips of the bill, look also for their short, notched tails.

Because of their erratic wanderings, it is hard to predict when and where they will show up. My only good look at them near our area came from the edge of an amazing crescent-shaped cliff in Granite Chief Wilderness in August. Because they are seed-eaters, they drink regularly and may frequent bird baths as well as natural water sources.

Pine Siskin, *Carduelis pinus*. Plate 44

I first heard about this species in August of 1994 through Dave Bunnett, who informed me they were consuming pound after pound of Tami's thistle seed (*Carduelis* is derived from a Latin word for thistle) at their new bird feeder. After a special trip over Angora ridge to visit their back deck, I began to see and hear large flocks whirling from tree to tree all the way up Glen Alpine Valley, especially in September.

These birds have broad, yellow stripes along their wings which become spots or bars when the wing is folded. Yellow is also prominently displayed at the base of their tail. These yellow areas may vary between bright lemon to almost white, depending on their diet and gender (males are yellower). Look also for the slimmer, pointier beak and overall brown streaking. These birds make numerous scratchy goldfinch-like twitterings while in flocks and have fast, jumbled songs. Their trademark call is a harsh, rising, almost vibrating, *zrrrreeeee*!

Unlike most songbirds, Pine Siskins remain in small flocks even during the breeding season, often nesting in tight colonies. Siskins will eat small seeds of all kinds as well as nectar, sap, buds and insects.

Evening Grosbeak, *Coccothraustes vespertinus brooksi. Plate 44*

A large and spectacularly colored resident of our forests, the Evening Grosbeak is often seen flying overhead in large flocks. Their static-like twittering helps to alert one to their presence.

Because of their long wings and distinctive plumage patterns, Evening Grosbeaks can be readily identified even while flying overhead. In fact, the sexes can even be easily differentiated in flight. Males have solid black tails, black heads and are solid yellow below. The males have their large white patches immediately next to their bodies on the trailing edge of their black wings. Females have white spots in their black tails, gray heads and are gray below. The females have small patches of yellow under the wing and a white patch in the middle of the black outer half of the wing.

Their large, stout beaks serve to crack seeds of all kinds, but also take insects during the breeding season and fruits in the summer. These beautiful baubles of nature adorn trees like holiday ornaments when the seeds ripen in the fall. Evening Grosbeaks are especially fond of Fallen Leaf's Mountain Maple seed crops in August and September, often allowing close approach while feeding. Our western birds have bills that average 15 percent larger than eastern birds.

See Black-headed Grosbeak (Page 160) regarding the common name. The scientific name translates as "evening seed-shatterer," with evening referring either to their activity and song in the evening, their sunset-like gradations of yellow, or a reference to its western-leaning distribution.

MAMMALS
Class *Mammalia*

ORDER *Insectivora* (shrews & moles)

FAMILY *Soricidae*, shrews

Sorex palustris navigator	water shrew
Sorex monticolus obscurus	dusky (montane) shrew
Sorex vagrans amoenus	wandering shrew
Sorex trowbridgii mariposae	Trowbridge's shrew

FAMILY *Talipidae*, moles

Scapanus latimanus	broad-footed mole

ORDER *Chiroptera* (bats)

FAMILY *Vespertilionidae*, evening bats

Myotis lucifugus carissima	little brown myotis
Myotis thysanodes	fringed myotis
Myotis californicus californicus	California myotis
Myotis evotis evotis	long-eared myotis
Myotis yumanensis	Yuma myotis
Lasionycteris noctivagans	silver-haired bat
Eptesicus fuscus bernardinus	big brown bat
Pipistrellus hesperus	Western pipistrelle

FAMILY *Molossidae*, free-tailed bats

Tadarida brasiliensis	Brazilian free-tailed bat

ORDER *Lagomorpha* (rabbits, hares & pikas)

FAMILY *Ochotonidae*, pikas

Ochotona princeps	pika

FAMILY *Leporidae*, hares & rabbits

Lepus americanus tahoensis	Sierra Nevada snowshoe hare
Silvilagus nuttallii	Nuttall's cottontail (mountain)

ORDER *Rodentia* (rodents)
SUBORDER *Sciurognathi*

FAMILY *Aplodontidae*, mountain beavers

Aplodontia rufa californica	mountain beaver (boomer)

FAMILY *Sciuridae*, squirrels
  SUBFAMILY *Sciurinae*

Marmota flaviventris flaviventris	yellow-bellied marmot
Spermophilus beldingi beldingi	Belding's ground squirrel
Spermophilus beecheyi sierrae	California (Beechey) ground squirrel
Spermophilus lateralis chrysodeirus	golden-mantled ground squirrel
Tamias speciosus frater	lodgepole chipmunk
Tamias quadrimaculatus	long-eared chipmunk
Tamias senex senex	Allen's (shadow) chipmunk
Tamias amoenus monoensis	yellow-pine chipmunk
Tamiasciurus douglasii	Douglas's squirrel (chickaree)

  SUBFAMILY *Pteromyinae*

Glaucomys sabrinus lascivus	Northern flying squirrel

FAMILY *Geomyidae*, pocket gophers

Thomomys monticola	mountain pocket gopher

FAMILY *Castoridae*, beavers

Castor canadensis	beaver*

FAMILY *Muridae*, mice & voles
  SUBFAMILY *Sigmodontinae* (New World mice & rats)

Peromyscus maniculatus gambelii	deer mouse
Peromyscus boylii	brush mouse
Neotoma cinerea	bushy-tailed woodrat

  SUBFAMILY *Arvicolinae* (voles & lemmings)

Microtus montanus	montane vole
Microtus longicaudus sierrae	long-tailed vole
Phenacomys intermedius	Western heather vole

FAMILY *Zapodidae*, jumping mice

Zapus princeps pacificus	Western jumping mouse

SUBORDER *Hystricomorpha*
  FAMILY *Erethizonidae*, porcupines

Erethizon dorsatum	porcupine

ORDER *Carnivora* (carnivores)

SUBORDER *Fissipedia*
  FAMILY *Canidae*, dogs

Canis latrans	coyote

  FAMILY *Ursidae*, bears

Ursus americanus californiensis	Sierra Nevada black bear

FAMILY *Procyonidae*, raccoons
  Procyon lotor   raccoon

FAMILY *Mustelidae*, weasels
  SUBFAMILY *Mustelinae*, weasels
    Martes pennanti (pacificus)   fisher (Pacific)
    Martes americana sierrae   marten (Sierra Nevada or Western)
    Mustela vison   mink
    Mustela frenata nevadensis   long-tailed weasel (Sierra Nevada)
    Mustela erminea muricus   short-tailed weasel (ermine)

  SUBFAMILY *Lutrinae*, otters
    Lutra canadensis   river otter

  SUBFAMILY *Taxidiinae*, badgers
    Taxidea taxus   badger

  SUBFAMILY *Mephitinae*, skunks
    Mephitis mephitis   striped skunk
    Spilogale gracilis   spotted skunk

FAMILY *Felidae*, cats
  Puma concolor   mountain lion (cougar)
  Lynx rufus   bobcat

ORDER *Artiodactyla* (even-toed ungulates)
SUBORDER *Ruminantia*
  FAMILY *Cervidae*, deer
    Odocoileus hemionus   mule deer

* *introduced species*

MAMMALS
Class *Mammalia*

SHREWS & MOLES, Order *Insectivora*

Although officially members of the "insect-eating" order of mammals, shrews and moles eat many other small animals, especially worms. (Hedgehogs are also members of this group.) Shrews are tiny mouse-like animals with long, tapering, heavily whiskered noses and many sharp, pointy, red-tipped teeth. Moles also have narrow, whiskered snouts but are much heavier-bodied and have very broad front paws with long claws. Both are active year-round and do not hibernate.

SHREWS, Family *Soricidae*

Shrews are our most primitive mammals, our most diminutive and our most hyper-active. Their size puts them near the absolute metabolic limit of how small a mammal can be and still maintain its body temperature (due to the high surface to volume ratio). Combined with a heart rate of up to 1,200 beats per minute, this large expenditure of energy requires ½-hour bursts of frenetic feeding followed by up to an hour of rest. Shrews can only go about three hours without eating and can eat as much as they weigh every 24 hours. Although active around the clock, their peak periods of activity are generally a few hours after sunset and about an hour before sunrise.

Because of this incredible and constant hunger, shrews are not the least bit picky about what they eat. Shrews have a voracious appetite, consuming insects (often as larvae), spiders, other arthropods, worms, seeds, fungi, lichens and carrion. They have also been documented killing and eating other shrews as well as other very small animals like small mice and small salamanders. Shrews are fierce loners and will attack other shrews almost on sight. All shrews are usually found near water, which they drink often.

The lifespan of a typical shrew is only about a year and a half. This may be in part because they are so high-strung that even a simple sudden stress (such as a loud clap) can induce cardiac arrest, or "Shrew Shock." Additionally, since they need to feed so often (and have very little stored energy), sudden drops in blood sugar levels can result in death.

With these facts in mind, you may now have a better understanding of how truly difficult *The Taming of the Shrew* might be. The genus, *Sorex*, is from the Latin meaning "shrew-mouse."

Water Shrew, *Sorex palustris navigator* (Richardson)
Total length: 6 inches

The water shrew is most commonly detected and identified because it is our largest shrew (with a three-inch body and a three-inch tail) and people tend to look down while they are crossing creeks or fishing along small streams. The occasional splash also attracts our attention as these shrews dive, swim or walk—on the stream bottom or even across the surface of the water—thanks to the extra stiff, dense hairs on their feet (fibrillae). With its distinctive coloring (black on top and white below), it is also one of the only shrews easily identified from a distance. (To identify most other shrews, one must look at their teeth with a hand lens.) In addition to the normal shrew fare, this species adds tadpoles, small amphibians, fish eggs, aquatic insect larvae, fish, snails, slugs and leeches to its menu. As one might expect, water shrews are commonly preyed upon by large trout, garter snakes, predatory birds and weasels (especially mink). *Palustris* appropriately translates as "of the marsh or swamp."

Dusky (Montane) Shrew, *Sorex monticolus obscurus* (Merriam)
Total length: 5 inches

The dusky shrew earns its common name and current subspecies (and prior specific epithet), *obscurus*. The current specific epithet, *monticolus*, means "mountain-dweller." Preferred habitats are moist mountain meadows bordered by coniferous forests.

Wandering (Vagrant) Shrew, *Sorex vagrans amoenus* (Baird)
Total length: 4 inches

Our smallest shrew, with a 1½–inch tail. This species is probably most common in our lower-elevation meadows.

Trowbridge's Shrew, *Sorex trowbridgii mariposae* (Baird)
Total length: 4 ½ inches

Tail is about 2 inches long and sharply bi-colored (white on the underside) and diagnostic of this species. Body is a mostly uniform color of dark gray-brown.

MOLES, Family *Talipidae*

Broad-footed Mole, *Scapanus latimanus* (Bachman)
Total length: up to 7 inches

We only have one species of mole in our region, making identification easy. Moles have inconspicuous ears and eyes: you have to practically dig through dense fur and skin to find them (probably to help keep the dirt out).

The scientific name translates as "broad-handed digger"—perfectly descriptive of this soil-swimming mammal which hardly ever ventures to the surface. Their "broad hands" not only have huge claws and fleshy palms, but are also oriented laterally for ideal leverage. A less obvious structural oddity of moles is their very narrow pelvis, which is small enough to allow them to turn around in their tunnels. This necessitates yet another unusual morphology—female reproductive organs are located behind the hips so they do not have to give birth through their unusually narrow pelvis. Finally, "Eimer's organs" (located in their narrow naked nose) enable a sensitivity to touch far greater than any other mammal.

Moles specialize in hunting earthworms by smell and sound waves (probably more "felt" than "heard"), but will eat other invertebrates as they come across them. Moles build a gallery of permanent tunnels a foot or more below the surface as well as temporary foraging tunnels just an inch or so below (which create raised linear bumps). "Mole hills" appear as symmetrical piles of clumpy soil pushed straight up from below with no exposed hole. (In contrast, gophers, mountain beavers and other fossorial mammals actually see the light of day as they push their dirt out.) Preferred habitats are moist meadows with plenty of loose soil.

BATS, Order *Chiroptera*

All our bats are nocturnal and insectivorous. Some favor the stereotypical "bat cave" for hibernation, but many of our western forest bats prefer to roost singly or in small groups in burnt-out snags or the crevices under peeling slabs of bark or rock during the summer.

Our bats capture insects either in their mouth (most often small insects) or in the "basket" created by the membrane stretched between their legs (usually larger insects), after which they transfer the prey directly to their mouth in an impressive show of mid-flight maneuvering.

Bats are not blind at all, but most nocturnal species do rely on echolocation (human sonar is a very primitive version of this) to navigate and hunt. They emit sounds that are often only one-thousandth of a second long, but—at 80,000 cycles per second—still manage to cram in an octave worth of change and switch from omnidirectional to very focused. This degree of refinement enables the bat to discern not only where an object is, but where it is going, how fast it is going, what it is made of and probably a lot of other things, too. Bats normally echolocate several times per second when flying in clear air, but will escalate to over fifty per second when they are within a meter of objects of interest (echolocation does not work very well beyond one meter anyway). To protect their sensitive ears, their ear canals vibrate shut during their extremely high-decibel vocalizations, only allowing in the echos that bounce back. Bats also use lower pitched vocalizations to communicate with each other that can be heard with the human ear.

Echolocation is a highly evolved and very effective means of locating prey, so it is only natural that insects have developed defense mechanisms. Some species of moths can "hear" the bat's echolocation and either "scramble the radar" by emitting confusing sounds of their own or simply fold their wings and drop out of the sky like a rock.

Genus *MYOTIS*—the little bats

Confirmed in our watershed:
Myotis lucifugus carissima **little brown myotis**
Myotis californicus californicus **California myotis**
Myotis evotis evotis **long-eared myotis**

Also possible: (recorded in the Tahoe Basin)
Myotis thysanodes **fringed myotis**
Myotis yumanensis **Yuma myotis**

If you see a small bat flying about just after sunset, chances are it will be a Myotis. Determining specifically which Myotis it is usually requires a bat detector (a device that translates a bat's ultrasonic vocalizations into wavelengths we can hear and decipher—roughly ten times fewer cycles per second) or a good old-fashioned mist net.

Bats of other genera:
Eptesicus fuscus bernardinus **big brown bat** (confirmed)

Also possible: (recorded in the Tahoe Basin)
Lasionycteris noctivagans **silver-haired bat**
Pipistrellus hesperus **Western pipistrelle**
Tadarida brasiliensis **Brazilian free-tailed bat**

One of my favorite bat memories is from a quick overnight I did up the Tamarack Trail. I got out of Camp a bit later than I had hoped and ended up preparing to sleep on a small ledge half-way up the trail. I had my sleeping bag cinched up so tight that only my face was exposed, but I could not escape them: a cloud of insects buzzed in a dense column above my exposed flesh. I was thinking that leaving my tent behind had been a foolish decision...until a shadow passed between me and the stars. The bat came back again and again, making repeated passes just feet above my face. Seconds later it was gone—along with the annoying insects. I actually called out, "Thanks, Bat!" Unmolested by further buzzing, I quickly fell asleep and had one of my best rests ever.

RABBITS, HARES & PIKAS,
Order *Lagomorpha*

Peg teeth: they are what make lagomorphs lagomorphs. Instead of having just two upper incisors like rodents, the members of this group have four. The tiny peg-like second pair are located directly behind the larger, rodent-like front pair. Both groups have continually growing incisors but the enamel is white on lagomorph teeth and a rich yellow on rodent teeth. Lagos is Greek for "hare" and morphe means "form."

All lagomorphs practice coprophagy (re-ingesting their soft, dark green, first-run fecal pellets) to maximize nutritional extraction from their tough, fibrous plant food. (Ruminants, on the other hand, deal with the same problem by having multiple stomachs and bringing up balls of cud to re-chew before they pass through.) This is why second-run rabbit pellets can be so incredibly hard, dry and compact.

PIKAS, Family *Ochotonidae*

Pika, *Ochotona princeps muiri* (Richardson)

6–8 inches   Plate 45.

These are small, round-eared, round-bodied, rabbit-like residents of rocky slopes, usually above 7,500 feet. The common name is derived from the Siberian Tungus people's name for it (their version of our onomatopoeic "squeak"). Their loud, sharp calls will echo across talus bowls at regular intervals for long periods but they are skilled ventriloquists and can be difficult to spot. The genus is from the Mongolian name, ochodona; princeps translates as "little chief or prince;" muiri is in honor of John Muir. In the early 1900s, specimens were collected on the east side of Pyramid Peak, Lake Lucille and many near Heather Lake. Healthy populations still exist throughout Desolation Wilderness today.

Huge amounts of hay are stockpiled for the winter, which they supplement with lichens and cushion plants they find under the snow. Their piles of grasses and forbs can be seen drying in crevices during the summer and it is common to see individuals carrying bundles of plants cross-wise in their mouths. Their jumbled rock pile homes provide an incredible maze of escape routes from predators like weasels and good cover from raptors. Three or four altricial young are born about a month before snowmelt. Gestation takes about a month and second broods can be born in the summer.

Pikas have been found to be keystone species in the high steppe of Asia: many other species not only depend on them as prey, but their burrows also provide nesting sites for birds, decrease soil erosion, increase water absorption and facilitate nutrient cycling. In areas where they have been poisoned on the Tibetan Plateau (due to perceived competition with livestock for forage), many other species have also disappeared and the long-term health of the entire ecosystem is in question. (Similar to our situation with prairie dogs in the Great Plains of North America.)

HARES & RABBITS, Family *Leporidae*

The main difference between hares and rabbits is that hares have precocial young (born fully furred, with eyes open) and rabbits have altricial young (born naked, with eyes sealed shut). Both are prolific breeders and are important herbivores and prey items for many predators.

Sierra Nevada Snowshoe Hare, *Lepus americanus tahoensis* (Orr)

14–16 inches long   Plate 45.

True to its name, this hare has a hind foot covered with stiff hairs and toes that can extend to make a single print over 3½ inches across. This enables the Snowshoe Hare to race across the top of the snow while many of its predators sink while in pursuit. Ears are about three inches long—almost as long as the length of its head. Our subspecies is only found in the Sierra Nevada range and is a State and Federal Species of Special Concern.

Although white in winter (with black on the tips of its ears) this species molts into a dark brown pelage in the spring. Molting is triggered by day length and late spring or early fall snowstorms (or a lack of snow in the winter) can turn them into obvious targets. Snowshoe hares prefer dense shrubby or forested habitats with plenty of food and cover. This species is largely crepuscular (active at dawn and dusk) and rests in a sheltered, shallow depression, or form, during much of the day.

Snowshoe Hares will grunt or growl when cornered and can let out a bone-chilling scream when captured or injured. They also make clicking noises. Most of their intraspecies communication, however, is through smell and a unique drumming of their feet—especially during courtship (á la Thumper).

Hares are able to breed year-round (with peak mating activity in early May) and can produce several litters of two to four young each. (This helps them keep up with the high rate of predation on this species.) Gestation lasts about 36–40 days and the young are almost independent at two weeks of age. Hares browse on plants and twigs of just about every species, but specialize on conifers in the winter—look for their trademark 45-degree cuts on twigs near where the snow level was.

*Note: The **White-Tailed Hare**, Lepus townsendii, is now considered extirpated (locally extinct) but was historically found near timberline in the Tahoe Basin in the summer. Other populations in California are now fragmented and in steep decline. It is the largest hare (up to 22 inches long), has ears that are much longer than the length of its head (up to six inches long) and is most active at dawn and dusk. Any BIG "jackrabbit" spotted in our watershed at high elevation is worthy of a call to the Forest Service.*

Nuttall's Cottontail (Mountain), *Sylvilagus nuttallii* (Bachman)

13–15 inches   Plate 45.

If you see a cute little grayish bunny with short ears and a tail that really does look like a cotton ball, you are probably seeing our only true rabbit (despite the translation of the genus, "hare of the woods"). Nuttall's or Mountain Cottontail occurs throughout most of the West, but not west of the Sierra Nevada or Cascade Ranges. They occur most commonly in sagebrush steppe and juniper woodlands, but also range up slope and into the eastern Tahoe Basin—and maybe as far west as our watershed.

Thomas Nuttall (1786–1859) was born in England and arrived in America as an eager 22-year-old botanist with no money and no connections. He soon found Benjamin Smith Barton, who took him on as an apprentice and sent Nuttall on collecting expeditions. Nuttall visited every state east of the Mississippi and followed Lewis & Clark's route up the Missouri just five years after their return. In the 1830s Nuttall published the first field guides to birds in the United States (Audubon's and Wilson's books were too heavy and expensive to be commonly used in the field.). He was a professor at Harvard, but considered that to be a waste of time and left in 1834 to go all the way up the Missouri to Oregon. He was the first scientist to cross North America and the first to visit California, still a Mexican territory at that time. Species first collected by Nuttall include our **Townsend's Solitaire, Green-tailed Towhee, Common Poorwill** (*Phalaenoptilus nuttalli*, named by Audubon), **Anna's Hummingbird** and many, many other species of birds, plants, reptiles, amphibians and mammals, especially in the West. Despite his many challenging adventures, Nuttall returned to Yorkshire to die of old age.

RODENTS, Order *Rodentia*

This order earns its name from what their famous ever-growing, yellow-enameled, chisel-like teeth do best: gnaw. This is the largest and most diverse group of mammals.

MOUNTAIN BEAVER, Family *Aplodontida*

(Sierra Nevada) Mountain Beaver (Boomer) *Aplodontia rufa californica* (Rafinesque)

12–14 inches   Plate 45.

Not really a beaver at all, but it does eat some bark and twigs. It has been described as a short-tailed beaver, an over-sized vole without a tail, a giant gopher, a tailless muskrat or simply a furry loaf of bread. They are entirely dark brown except for a small white dot just below their little round ears. It is debated as to whether boomers really do make a "booming" noise, along with some other more typical mammalian vocalizations. The genus translates as "simple tooth," from its unusually simple molars.

These expert diggers create extensive networks of tunnels (6–10 inches in diameter) through the deep soils in wet meadows and along creeks. These mammals are rarely seen by humans because they only make short trips away from their burrows at night. They feed on plants of all kinds, including many that are toxic or otherwise problematic to other animals. Documented foods include: alder, aspen, willow, creek dogwood, columbine, larkspur, lupine, thimbleberry, fireweed, cow parsnip, corn lily, thistle, foxglove, nettles, red fir, Douglas-fir, grasses, sedges and ferns. It could be that their "primitive" filtering system (see below) enables them to excrete the problematic chemicals more quickly and effectively than "higher" mammals. Like Pikas, they will cut and dry large piles of "hay" in the late summer and practice coprophagy (see Pika). They are often cursed by tree growers for their ability to feed on the tips of young conifers and tree bark, especially in the winter when little else is available.

The Boomer is our most primitive rodent and only remaining member of a family that dates back 50 million years, to the upper Eocene. (A great feat since the average species only exists for 1–10 million years.) However, there are some drawbacks to not updating your system for such a long time. It cannot thermoregulate very well (does not sweat or pant) and overheats easily. The only way a Boomer can deal with being too hot is to sprawl to maximize heat loss and not move until it has cooled down. Needless to say, this behavior can make them easy prey. In addition, *Aplodontia* kidneys lack Loops of Henle and cannot concentrate urine—which necessitates voiding a third of their body weight each day. As a result, Boomers like it dark, wet and cool: restricting this species to the moister forests of the Pacific Northwest.

To keep this primitive "giant gopher" company, we have one of the largest and most primitive fleas in the world, *Hystricopsylla schefferi*. Large females can approach half an inch—but don't worry—they are completely restricted to feeding on this one species of mammal.

The Mountain Beaver was introduced to western science by the Lewis & Clark Expedition. On November 17th, 1805, Sergeant Patrick Gass wrote of the first observation: "*some have robes made of muskrat skins sewed together.*" (These were most likely robes made from mountain beaver, as later discovered by Lewis.) On Thursday, November 23rd Clark writes, "*They also procure a roabe from the nativs above, which is made of the Skins of a Small animal about the Size of a Cat, which is light and dureable and highly prized by those people.*" On Friday, December 13th, Clark purchased a couple of these *swalál* from the native people he intended to make a cape out of. Finally, on Wednesday, February 26th, 1806, Lewis wrote a full description of the *Sewelel* (or Sewellel, assigning the species a common name which actually refers to the robe made of their skins). He based the description on the skins and a single observation of some of his men. (Lewis assumed the tail was always severed before making the robes.)

California Department of Fish & Game compiled a comprehensive report (Steele, 1989) that notes three Mountain Beaver specimens taken from near Fallen Leaf Lake in August of 1917. There is also a specimen at UC Berkeley's Museum of Vertebrate Zoology taken from near Echo Lake in September of 1976.

Aplodontia rufa is a State and Federal Species of Concern. The species includes seven subspecies, two being small, isolated coastal populations (*A.r.phae*, found only on Point Reyes & *A.r.nigra*, found only on Point Arena—70 miles to the north). *A.r.nigra* is a Federally listed Endangered Species.

SQUIRRELS, Family *Sciuridae*

Out of the 66 species of squirrels in North America, 65 are found west of the Mississippi River and only 11 are found east of it. In our watershed, we probably have nine species.

SUBFAMILY *Sciurinae*

Yellow-bellied Marmot, *Marmota flaviventris flaviventris* (Audubon & Bachman)

20–28 inches   Plate 45.

Marmots are our largest member of the squirrel family, weighing up to ten pounds just prior to hibernation. Half of the weight is pure fat that will be burned off by the time they emerge at the end of April. They are also called rockchucks (as opposed to their close relatives, the woodchucks) and are indeed found on rocky slopes near the top of Tallac. Their shrill alarm chirp is even louder than a Pika's and can vary depending on the perceived threat.

Marmots live in colonies and even hibernate in groups to keep warm. They have a strict social hierarchy and the dominant male defends over an acre for himself and his harem of 2–3 females. Females give birth to 3-8 young (usually every other year) and the two-year-olds are chased off to find their own breeding territories. Yellow-bellied Marmots have a bushy tail up to eight inches long and are mostly a grizzled brown above with a black and white face and orangish-yellow shoulders and underparts. *Marmota* is from the French word for this animal; *flaviventris* means yellow-bellied.

Belding's Ground Squirrel, *Spermophilus beldingi beldingi* (Merriam)

10–12 inches   Plate 45.

The "picket pins" of our high mountain meadows. In response to hikers, colonies of these squirrels will often give 6-8 shrill call notes, run to their burrow entrances and stand straight up on their hind legs for a better view of possible danger. (In so doing, they resemble the long stakes, or picket pins, used to tether horses for grazing.) Most populations combine their aestivation (summer torpor) and hibernation into one, long rest that can begin as early as August and end as late as April, often being awake for only four months out of the year.

Not-so-fondly referred to as "sage-rats" in some agricultural areas of the West, these animals have a long history of persecution that continues today. However, they continue to thrive despite our best efforts—probably because they have 6–8 young per year and are used to being prey for hawks, eagles, weasels, coyotes and badgers. Their burrows also benefit the soil and other creatures that use them. They are mostly uniform grayish with a vague reddish-brown line down the back and have a narrow, 2–3 inch, black-tipped tail. Often found above 8,000 feet in our area.

This species was "discovered" in 1888 by Lyman Belding, a man more famous for his ornithological leanings and described by Dr. Clinton Hart Merriam (1855–1942), the originator of the "life zone" theory (animal and plant distributions based on specific temperature extremes). The genus means "seed-lover," although they also consume a lot of grass and other plant material.

California (Beechey) Ground Squirrel
Spermophilus beecheyi sierrae (Richardson)

12–18 inches   Plate 45.

This ground squirrel lives at lower elevations than Belding's—mostly below 7,000 feet in our area. It is much larger, heavier-bodied and more likely to tolerate nearby human activity. These squirrels are common around Fallen Leaf Lake and regularly make their homes under cabins, docks and other structures. They have white crescents above and below their eyes, a long, bushy tail, flecks or crescents of light gray on their dark brownish-gray back and a distinctive light silvery wash extending from the back of their head down past their shoulders.

Ground squirrels will stuff their cheek pouches full of any food items they can get their hands on before retreating to the safety of their burrow. Beechey squirrels are not truly colonial, but can be found living in small groups. 5–7 young are born in the late spring and are on their own before the end of the summer.

Frederick William Beechey (1796–1856) explored Northern California as captain of HMS Blossom from 1826–1828 and was later president of the Royal Geographic Society.

Golden-mantled Ground Squirrel
Spermophilus lateralis chrysodeirus (Say)

9–11 inches   Plate 45.

Often mistaken for a chipmunk, Golden-mantled Ground Squirrels are larger, chunkier and bolder. Unlike chipmunks, these squirrels have stripes that stop at their shoulders and do not extend onto their face. Their shoulders and face are a solid rusty-gold color and earn them the nickname of "coppertops." (A nickname that also provides meaning beyond appearance: these stout squirrels are the most common source of energy for goshawks and some of our medium-sized weasels.)

Even more so than Beecheys, these squirrels can be fearless around picnic tables. They seem to magically appear when you pull out your lunch—even above 9,000 feet. However, they can carry plague-laden fleas, so hand-feeding them is discouraged. Besides, they do much better on a more natural and varied diet. Hibernation occurs from early October through mid-April in the Tahoe Basin.

Coppertops are truly omnivorous and eat just about anything—from seeds, leaves and fungi to insects, eggs and carrion. They transport food in their cheek pouches to their underground winter stores (just in case they wake up during hibernation and need to eat more to keep warm). Name translates as "side-(lined) seed-lover."

CHIPMUNKS, Genus *Tamias*

The only truly "unambiguous" (as the taxonomists put it) way to tell apart different species of chipmunks is to take a close look at their genital bones (*baculum* in males, *baubellum* in females). That is pretty hard to do in the field, even with binoculars. So I have narrowed the list to our most usual suspects and included a few easier-to-see clues below. Do not feel bad if you cannot come up with a 100-percent positive identification: even the experts allow that, "The systematics of Western chipmunks remain enigmatic."

Chipmunks do not seem to subscribe to the "Weight Gain 2000" strategy of the ground squirrels (hence their relatively dainty appearance). They store food (*Tamias* means "storer") instead of fat for the winter and may wake up every two days to two weeks to eat snacks during hibernation. This gives their little cheek pouches a good workout in the summer and makes their hyperactive behavior a bit more understandable. In addition to storing food in their burrows, chipmunks will also dig little holes (about two inches deep) to bury food in on the surface. The locations of these caches become obvious when they are exploited in the early spring and become curious little craters scattered over the forest floor. Chipmunks eat seeds, leaves, fruit, fungi, eggs (bird and amphibian) and any small animal it can catch (insects, slugs, snails, baby mice, small amphibians and young reptiles, to name a few).

Least Chipmunks (*Tamias minimus*) are present in the Tahoe Basin, but are more common in sagebrush on the east slope.

Lodgepole Chipmunk, *Tamias speciosus frater* (Merriam)

8–10 inches   Plate 46.

Some experts say the Lodgpole has the most distinct striping and deepest orange fur (*speciosus* means "showy") of our three species while others contend it is only slightly brighter than the Shadow Chipmunk described below. Although in the same general size range as the Long-eared and Shadow, this species averages a bit smaller—but still larger than the Yellow-Pine. Look for the Lodgepole Chipmunk in its namesake pine forests as well as red fir forests, especially those bounded by manzanita. Fungi are a favorite of this species and it will dig many small holes looking for truffles and other hypogeous fungi. The Lodgepole is named after a tree and likes to climb them, sometimes over 40 feet above the ground. This "friendly" subspecies has been collected at Angora Lakes, Susie Lake, Gilmore Lake, Lake of the Woods and Upper Velma Lake—usually below 8,500 feet.

Long-eared Chipmunk, *Tamias quadrimaculatus* (Gray)

8–10 inches   Plate 46.

I am both embarrassed and proud to say that this is the only chipmunk I feel somewhat confident that I have truly identified around Fallen Leaf—actually on the dining room deck at Stanford Sierra Camp. I then learned it is the only species of chipmunk that had not been collected here in the early 1900s... The conspicuous white patches behind the long ears and indistinct body stripes (brown/cream vs. black/white) are diagnostic field marks. (The face has more strongly contrasting stripes than the body.) Still, it may take an extra cup of coffee and a few more minutes of observation to become 99-percent sure of your identification.

These are denizens of the mixed conifer belt and can be found up to about 7,500 feet in our watershed. The museum specimen this species was first described from was taken from near Michigan Bluff, CA—just 40 miles west of Lake Tahoe.

Allen's (Shadow) Chipmunk, *Tamias senex senex* (JA Allen)

8–10 inches

Allen's is the dullest and grayest (most shadowy) of our three chipmunks. Its ear patches are less white and not as conspicuous as the Long-eared. Like the Lodgepole Chipmunk, this species is also a tree-climber and really likes fungi: look for many truffle-hunting pits in red fir forests and surrounding brush. The original type specimen of this species was collected at Donner Pass (northwest of Lake Tahoe) and numerous specimens have been collected near Glen Alpine Creek. Found in upper montane forests below 9,000 feet.

This species was recently separated from Townsend's Chipmunk based on—you guessed it—penis bone morphology. This is pretty funny because of our culture's general taboo against talking about such things, but it actually is the best correlation we have between genetics and morphology. (I'm sure you'll agree that trying to tell chipmunks apart based on something like their stripe thickness or shade of brown is frustratingly futile!)

Dr. Joel Asaph Allen (1838–1921) led the first expedition organized by the American Museum of Natural History and became their curator of birds and mammals in 1885. He was with Harvard's Museum of Comparative Zoology in the 1860s and 1870s and was a founding member of the American Ornithologists Union, American Bison Society and National Audubon Society. Ironically, he reversed the tide of the "splitters" during his time by using trinomials (subspecies) instead of elevating each new variation discovered within a species to the status of a full species. He is famous for saying, "Specimens have too often been described instead of species," meaning that scientists were focusing too much on individual variation. (He may be rolling in his grave because this subspecies he described has been split from T. townsendii and is now a full species with its own subspecies!)

Note: This is not the same Allen who has a hummingbird named after him. That is Charles Andrew Allen (1841–1930), a collector who did extensive work in California.

Yellow-Pine Chipmunk, *Tamias amoenus monoensis* (JA Allen)

7–9 inches

Yellow Pine Chipmunks are not common on the west slope south of Donner Pass (the location of the type specimen taken in 1890), but they do occur below 7,000 feet in our open Jeffrey Pine forests. It is the smallest chipmunk likely to be found in our area and its rusty colors tend more toward yellow than the Lodgepole. The outermost black body stripe is most obvious in this species in comparison with the others.

Douglas's Squirrel (Chickaree), *Tamiasciurus douglasii* (Bachman)

11–13 inches   Plate 46.

This squirrel turns harmless green pine cones into heavy, Earth-bound missiles in the late summer. (If you happen to have a tall, cone-laden Jeffrey Pine near your tent or cabin, you may be wise to stay out from under it during August and September!) Douglas's Squirrels cut down huge numbers of nearly-ripe cones—before the cones mature, dry and open—and cache them at the bases of trees, logs or banks. One cache of almost 500 cones has been reported, but most caches are in the area of dozens. Sealed cones in these refrigerator-like sites can keep their seeds fresh for up to three years, although most are eaten the following winter. These piles of cones were commonly raided for their seeds when reforestation nurseries were being started.

Douglas's Squirrels are our only tree squirrel (not counting the strictly nocturnal flying squirrel) so they are easy to identify. In our watershed they have rusty-edged, creamy-white bellies, dark gray-brown backs, tiny tufts on their ears, light crescents above and below their eyes and bushy, 5-inch-long silver-tipped tails. (Their bellies are darker and rustier in the humid rainforests of the Pacific Northwest.) Generally, they look pretty cute—unless they are scolding you with their rapid, mechanical chatter. They also have a short call that starts out like a sharp, piercing bark and then drops and trails off—which they can repeat every few seconds for a very long time.

Feeding often takes place on exposed perches, such as on top of a log or stump, where the squirrel can watch for danger. These sites are easy to identify based on the midden of cone scales and drumstick-shaped Jeffrey Pine cone cores that litter the ground below. Mushrooms are often cached in the crotch of a branch to dry for storage.

Summer nests (dreys) can be balls of lichens, bark, leaves and twigs high in the canopy, but these squirrels find a tree cavity or old woodpecker hole to sleep in on winter nights. Active year-round, they are a common source of food for predators such as the Goshawk and Pine Marten, especially when most other rodents are hibernating. The genus translates as "storing (or chipmunk) shadow-tail," the first part for their hording habits (or small, chipmunk-like size) and the second for holding their tail over their back while resting or eating.

SUBFAMILY Pteromyinae

Northern Flying Squirrel, *Glaucomys sabrinus lascivus* (Shaw)

10–13 inches, including a 5–inch tail   Plate 46.

Northern Flying Squirrels are strictly nocturnal and therefore rarely seen, but are probably just as abundant as our Douglas's Squirrel and maybe more so in their preferred mature red fir forests. Collections of this species have been taken near both Glen Alpine Creek and Echo Lake.

On moonlit nights, listen for faint "thuds" as they alight on a trunk, followed by a quick scurrying to the opposite side. (Upon landing, they immediately move to the other side just in case a predator like a Spotted Owl is following them.) Keep an eye out for their light gray undersides—which look like paper towels gliding through the forest—steered by 5-inch-long, flat, furry tails. Their eyes are very large in proportion to their round head, dark and surrounded by dark "eyeliner" (as opposed to Douglas's, which has white eyeliner). Their back is a dark gray-brown.

Of course "flying" is a bit of a misnomer: they can only glide, with the help of a long fold of skin that extends from their ankles to their wrist, the patagium. Most glides are between 15 and 80 feet, but on rare occasions, going down-slope, flying squirrels have been recorded gliding 150–300 feet. (Glide angles average about 27 degrees.)

They will build dreys (spherical nests in the canopy), but seem to prefer woodpecker holes and other tree cavities. Northern Flying Squirrels specialize on fungi and lichen, but also eat seeds, fruit, insects, other small animals and carrion. These squirrels are also common visitors to bird feeders at night. Call notes have been variously described as low chucks or churrs, high-pitched squeaks and bird-like chirps. Like Douglas's, they are active throughout the winter and are generally solitary (but have been reported sleeping in shared cavities on cold winter days).

The genus translates as "bluish-gray mouse," possibly due to their silky, silvery underside. The specific epithet is a longer story: the type specimen was collected near the Severn River (in Ontario, Canada) that was named after the same river in England, which was named after the mythological river nymph Sabrinus by the Romans. Or maybe Shaw just had a girlfriend named Sabrina.

POCKET GOPHERS, Family *Geomyidae*

Mountain Pocket Gopher, *Thomomys monticola* (J. A. Allen)

7–9 inches   Plate 46.

Named for its fur-lined, external cheek pouches, this animal will quickly stuff these "pockets" with vegetation while perched at the opening of its tunnel. Once the pockets are full, it will quickly descend and plug the whole to eat in dark, solitary safety. These obvious plugs in a hole to the side of fans of excavated soil are a good way to identify a pocket gopher's hole.

This well-equipped digger spends most of its life underground and is rarely seen. Luckily, they leave "gopher cores" so we can see where they live. These are cylinders of dirt about two inches in diameter, sometimes branching, formed by gophers packing excavated dirt into snow tunnels along the surface all winter long.

Established older females can have burrow systems that cover an area equal to a good-sized house: 2,000 square feet. This large "home" is often shared by many other arthropods, amphibians and other small animals. The long claws on the forefeet are the main digging elements. However, the teeth are also used to snip roots or break apart hard clods and have a special flap of skin that seals off the mouth behind them to keep the dirt out. In another member of this genus, the ever-growing incisors have been documented to grow almost a foot a year—but are worn down just as quickly. Diet is mostly roots and bulbs, supplemented by above-ground vegetation in the summer.

Unlike moles, gophers still have to give birth through their extremely narrow pelvis. To facilitate this otherwise impossible feat, hormones are released during pregnancy that cause the connection at the pubic bones to dissolve—turning what used to be a real bottleneck into a nearly infinitely flexible valley.

The mounds of soil we see on the surface earn this genus its name, "heap-mouse." The specific epithet translates as "mountain-dweller"—it is only found in meadows above 5,000 feet. In 1910, 29 were collected in our area: 23 between Gilmore Lake and Mt. Tallac, 5 near the NE corner of Fallen Leaf Lake and one north of Heather Lake.

BEAVERS, Family *Castoridae*

Beaver, *Castor canadensis* (Kuhl)

3 feet long, including tail

© Barbara Gleason

Beavers are native to the Sierras, but only up to about 5,000 feet: Robert T. Orr's comprehensive *Mammals of Lake Tahoe* (published in 1949) does not even mention beavers. They have been introduced to higher elevations over the past 50 years and are now dramatically altering ecosystems up to 9,000 feet. Lily Lake and Taylor Creek are both good sites to observe the effects of this industrious introduced engineer. Our now-local variety is often referred to as the "Montana Flat-tailed Beaver."

Mice & Voles, Family *Muridae*

Deer Mouse, *Peromyscus maniculatus gambelii* (Baird)

3–4 inch body; 2–3 inch tail   Plate 46.

This species can be found from central Alaska to south of Mexico City. It is the most numerous and widespread mammal in the Sierras, California and North America. Deer Mice are brown on top (except young under three months old, which are a dark blue-gray), white underneath and have white feet. (Unlike the more uniformly colored European House Mouse, which we do not have here.) Adults have tails shorter than their body length (unlike the Brush Mouse).

Commonly found around human habitation, this is the species most likely to be caught in an old-fashioned mousetrap in our area. Mice (and their droppings) can carry a number of diseases (including Hantavirus as well as plague-laden fleas), so please handle them with care and try not to breathe (or wear a good filtering mask) while cleaning up after them.

With their large, black eyes and relatively big ears, Deer mice are pretty cute—even if they do chew holes in packs. (Don't leave food inside any bags left outside your tent at night!) Deer Mice are thought to be important predators of insect larvae as well as seeds and just about anything else they can find. Name translates as "little-handed booted-mouse," probably a reference to the white feet and dexterous hand-like forefeet.

Brush Mouse, *Peromyscus boylii boylii* (Baird)

3–4 inch body; 3 ½–4 ½ inch tail

This well-named mouse is most closely associated with woody debris, brush (especially huckleberry oak) and junipers up to about 8,000 feet. Not as numerous or commonly seen as the Deer Mouse, but probably present in our area (documented on the east side of Tahoe). This mouse is known for climbing trees and making nests in tree cavities or logs. The Brush Mouse eats insects, huckleberry oak acorns, mistletoe berries, juniper berries and other conifer seeds. Adults have tails longer than their body length (unlike Deer Mouse).

Baird named this species in honor of Dr. Charles Elisha Boyle (1821–1870). He was a public school teacher and then an M.D. who followed the Oregon Trail to the California gold rush. In 1850, he set up a medical practice in Placerville and sent many specimens from El Dorado County to the Smithsonian (mostly reptiles & amphibians—the Foothill Yellow-legged Frog, *Rana boylii*, is also named after him). He soon went on to build and sail a boat from San Francisco to Norfolk, Virginia via Cape Horn and was supposedly fluent in 32 languages. Boyle spent much of his time and practice taking care of people who were unable to pay him and therefore died relatively poor himself.

Bushy-tailed Woodrat, *Neotoma cinerea* (Ord)

14–18 inches, including a 5–7 inch tail

A true "pack rat," the piled-stick nests of this species often contain curious assemblages of shiny objects. Woodrats are also called "trade rat" because they will sometimes set down a less desirable object to pick up another—effectively trading, for example, a bottle cap for your quarter. Some theorize this behavior is related to their apparent urge to continually bring home sticks to add their nest.

Throughout our area, woodrats usually build their stick nests deep in rocky crevices and mark them with musky secretions. The genus translates as "new-cutter" because this genus of rodents was discovered relatively recently (early 1800s).

VOLES, Subfamily *Arvicolinae*

The term "vole" comes from the Swedish word, *voll*, meaning "field" and is short for field-mouse, or (as we say) meadow-mouse. These busy little furballs are active around the clock, all year long and are important prey items for hawks, owls, coyotes, weasels and many other predators. This may be one reason why they achieve sexual maturity in a matter of weeks and most voles have two litters each summer of 4–9 young per litter—the female being impregnated for a second time within just a few weeks of giving birth. The lemmings also belong to this subfamily and are famous for their incredible rates of reproduction farther north. Unlike mice, voles are strictly herbivorous. In the late fall, voles can be surprisingly approachable as they single-mindedly stuff their cheeks with vegetation to store for the winter.

Montane Vole, *Microtus montanus* (Peale)

6–7 inches total length   Plate 46.

The Montane or Mountain Vole is common in wet meadows at almost every elevation in our area. This species is probably responsible for 90% of our vole runways (or surface tunnels under the grass blades) in grassy areas (Long-tailed Voles are more free-living and do not create runways as often). The tail is only about 1½–2 inches long (less than 1/3 of the body length).

Long-tailed Vole, *Microtus longicaudus sierrae* (Merriam)

7–8 inches total length

The Long-tailed Vole is our most versatile, widespread species and can even be found in dry forested or brushy areas although they seem to prefer streamside vegetation. The tail is long (2–3 inches or more) and more than a third of its body length. Unlike most voles, runways are not commonly used by this species and they are usually only active at night. Two specimens were collected near Lower Velma Lake in 1926.

Western Heather Vole, *Phenacomys intermedius* (Merriam)

5–6 inches total length

This species is extremely rare in our area and has only been historically recorded in the Tahoe Basin at two locations: near Pyramid Peak and near Echo Lake. It is now suspected to be extirpated in the Tahoe Basin, but it was never abundant. Heather Voles could very well still be living quiet, nearly nocturnal lives under red heather near timberline in our area. Previously called the Gray Lemming Mouse, this species is indeed on the grayer side of brown and has a short, inch-long tail.

JUMPING MICE, Family *Zapodidae*

Western Jumping Mouse, *Zapus princeps pacificus* (J A Allen)

8–9 inches total length

With a nearly naked tail about one and a half times the length of its body, this mouse is strikingly different from the rest of our mice species. The body is only slightly larger than a deer mouse, but the hind legs are very long and can propel this rodent 2–3 feet in a single bound (hence the long tail for balancing). Our jumping mice are most commonly found along streams and wet meadows all the way up to timberline and are normally nocturnal. Two were collected near Glen Alpine Creek in 1921. Hibernation begins early—in September—and may last for over eight months. (Unlike most mice, which do not hibernate at all.)

PORCUPINES, Suborder *Hystricomorpha*, Family *Erethizonidae*

Porcupine, *Erethizon dorsatum* (Linnaeus)

2–3 feet long   Plate 46.

Commonly seen late at night along Fallen Leaf Road, this well-protected rodent specializes in eating the inner cambium layer of trees. Although they cannot really "throw" their quills (modified stiff, hollow hairs), they can thrash their short tail about in defense. The quills are barbed and will continue to work their way into—and sometimes through—any animal unfortunate enough to get stuck with one. Perhaps because of its "irritating or angry back" (as the scientific name translates), this pigeon-toed mammal rarely accelerates beyond a slow waddle.

Fishers are one of the few predators that regularly feed on porcupines and their current rarity may be a significant contributor towards increasing porcupine populations. Fishers have been re-introduced to many areas (where they were extirpated by trapping) specifically to control porcupines. These large, quick weasels use their speed to dodge the thrashing tail and circle around to deliver multiple bites to the porcupine's unprotected face. Mountain lions follow a similar strategy but prefer to prey on deer when possible.

"Pine pigs" (the name is actually from the Latin *porcus*, pig and *spinus*, spine or thorn) or "porkies" do seem to prefer pines, but will eat the inner bark of just about any woody plant. Because of this diet, their scat can resemble the inch-long sawdust pellets now used in some heating stoves or can be shaped like a kidney bean or cashew. Scat can pile up at the entrance to their dens, usually in rocky ledges, crevices or cliffs. Occasionally they will also take a rest on a high tree branch. Porcupines eat more herbaceous vegetation in the spring and are reported to have a fondness for mistletoe.

Perhaps because of their high survival rate, porcupines only have one young each year. Don't worry: the spines are soft at birth and harden after they dry.

CARNIVORES, Order *Carnivora*
Suborder *Fissipedia*
Family *Canidae*, Dogs

Coyote, *Canis latrans* (Say)

    4 feet long   Plate 47.

The "trickster" of many Native American legends is also legendary for its ability to persist and even thrive despite the many challenges humans have provided. Most commonly seen in the lower elevations around Fallen Leaf, the coyote is far-ranging and could be encountered anywhere. Opportunistic omnivores, coyotes will eat just about any small animal as well as large amounts of berries, other fruits and grass in season.

Most active at night, coyotes are heard howling, yipping or barking more often than they are seen. With the **Sierra Nevada Red Fox** (*Vulpes vulpes necator*) and **Wolf** (*Canis lupus*) apparently extirpated from the Tahoe Basin, the coyote is now our only wild representative of this family. (Red foxes were historically reported near the Velma Lakes.) The scientific name translates as "barking dog" and the common name comes from the Aztec word, *coyotl*, which shares the same meaning.

BEARS, Family *Ursidae*

Sierra Nevada Black Bear
Ursus americanus californiensis (Pallus) *Plate 47.*

Although not always black, this is now our only bear. (The **Grizzly Bear**, *Ursus arctos*, ironically only survives in California as a drawing on our state flag.) Black bears are not nearly as large or as aggressive as grizzlies, but should be treated with respect nevertheless—especially if a mother has cubs around. A wild bear will usually flee from a shouting and arm-waving human, but not always. Unfortunately, bears are most commonly encountered around Fallen Leaf Lake where people are not responsibly storing their garbage. In our area, bears are rarely encountered above 8,500 feet and are most common below 7,500 feet.

Our largest mammal prefers to feed primarily on grasses, berries, nuts, bulbs and other plant food. The black bear will supplement this with opportunistic hunting of small animals, yellow jacket nests, bee hives, spawning fish and carrion.

One to three young are born every other year, with females reaching maturity between 3 and 8 years of age. This reproductive rate is the lowest of any mammal. Like the weasels, bears mate in the early summer but delay implantation of the fertilized embryo for four months in order to give birth in the late winter.

Black bears can build up almost 5 inches of fat for what can be a six-month uninterrupted hibernation. They prepare a comfortable den with bedding, curl up and lower their body temperature to 88 degrees. In this state, their heart rate can be as slow as eight beats per minute and their waste is miraculously recycled so well they can go all winter without defecating or urinating. They will emerge in the spring having lost 15-30 percent of their weight (females who give birth in the late winter and nurse the young in the den can lose as much as 40 percent).

RACCOON, Family *Procyonidae*

Raccoon, *Procyon lotor* (Linnaeus)

2–3 feet

© Barbara Gleason

This well-known ring-tailed masked bandit is much less common in our area than in nearby suburban zones, but it is possible to see it at our lower elevations, especially near water or carelessly secured garbage cans. On June 22, 1947, Robert T. Orr reported raccoon tracks a mile southeast of the Velma Lakes at an elevation of 8,500 feet—one of the highest recorded sightings. Raccoons favor hollow snags for sleeping in during the day, but also seem to be happy in the crawl spaces under homes or decks.

Raccoons are like people in many ways: their forepaws leave prints which look like they were left by a small human hand, their vocalizations have been compared to screaming babies and they have enough dexterity to open a doorknob. They are also opportunistic omnivores, favoring small animals of all kinds, fruits and eggs when available. True to their name (*lotor* means "washer"), they are usually found near water and will sometimes wet their food before eating it (although this "washing" behavior is more common in captivity than in the wild). *Procyon* means "before the dog," a reference to its dog-like appearance.

WEASELS, Family *Mustelidae*

This family is characterized by five toes on every foot, well-developed scent glands, relatively short legs and elongated bodies. The **Wolverine** (*Gulo gulo*) is the only member of this family officially presumed extirpated in our area.

WEASELS, Subfamily *Mustelinae*

The various species of weasels in this subfamily all have similar long, cylindrical bodies. The differences are basically just size, behavior and habitat preferences. Male weasels can be nearly twice the size of females, possibly to take advantage of different size prey or simply to compete for mates. Their long narrow bodies dissipate heat rapidly and can necessitate consuming over a third of their body weight in a day. Most weasels mate within ten days of giving birth but delay implantation of the fertilized embryo for 10–11 months. The delay enables the month-long period of active gestation to be made in late winter and young are born in the early spring.

This group contains most of our "fur-bearing" species, a reference to their historic importance as sources of human clothing (Fisher pelts are very similar to Siberian sable and command the highest price). Weasels usually dispatch their prey with a powerful bite to the base of the skull. Quick, agile, incredibly ferocious and able to subdue prey larger than themselves, weasels are sometimes referred to as "dynamite with legs."

From largest to smallest, for comparison—descriptions follow:

SPECIES	TOTAL LENGTH
Fisher, *Martes pennanti (pacificus)*	2 ½–3 ½ feet
Marten, *Martes americana sierrae*	about 2 feet
Mink, *Mustela vison*	1 ½–2 feet
Long-tailed Weasel, *Mustela frenata nevadensis*	12–18 inches
Short-tailed Weasel (Ermine), *Mustela erminea muricus*	7–12 inches

Fisher, *Martes pennanti (pacificus)* (Erxleben)

2 ½–3 ½ feet total length

Fishers have always been relatively rare, but are now even more so because of their preference for mature old-growth forests. They were detected only a few times near Lake Tahoe by the early 1900's. Extensive monitoring efforts throughout California from 1989 to 1994 failed to document any Fishers in the central and northern Sierras; the southern Sierra Nevada population is an Endangered Species candidate based on its current isolation. Fishers eat a wide variety of smaller animals such as snowshoe hares, squirrels and many other rodents, and porcupines—by choice (see Porcupine). Fisher stomachs can even safely soften and pass quills. Fishers have retractable claws and can rotate their ankles 180 degrees to facilitate running up and down trees. Fishers have very dark brown fur (becoming grizzled around the head with age) and a 14–17-inch tail: much longer than a Marten's.

The origin of the common name is debatable, but it is agreed that it is *not* because this species is known for catching fish. *Fichet* is the French term for the pelt of the related European pole-cat (*Mustela putorius*) and may have been used by the first French fur trappers in North America. It may also have the same root as "vicious," perhaps from the Dutch, *visse*, meaning "nasty"—either due to their Tasmanian-devil-like dispositions, or their smelly musky secretions. Robert T. Orr logically argued that *Pekan*, a Native American name, may be the most appropriate. Johann Erxleben described the species in 1777 based on a 1771 account from Thomas Pennant (1726–1798), a famous Welsh naturalist and traveler.

Some experts place the West Coast (Pacific) Fishers in their own subspecies, *pacificus*. The Fisher is a State & Federal Species of Concern.

Marten, *Martes americana sierrae* (Turton)
   about 2 feet total length

Martens (a.k.a. Pine Martens) are the largest weasels confirmed to be living in our area, often above 7,000 feet. A full dozen were easily taken (due to their innate curiosity) from near the Velma Lakes area in the early 1900s. They are usually a rich cinnamon brown (but can range from buff to nearly black) with a lighter face, darker tail and irregular orange patches on their upper chest and throat. Martens are the most arboreal of weasels and prey on tree squirrels, voles and birds of red fir forests in the winter but eagerly pursue a variety of rodents and pikas on rocky talus slopes during the summer.

The common name and genus is from an Old French term. Some experts contend that, based on new genetic evidence, our martens (those found in the southwestern part of its range, from California through western British Columbia) should be returned to full species status as *M. caurina*.

Mink, *Mustela vison* (Schreber)
   1 ½–2 feet total length

The most aquatic of our weasels, mink have dark, chocolaty-brown waterproof coats (sometimes with spots of white under the chin) and webbed feet. These adaptations enable this weasel to dive to depths over 12 feet deep and swim underwater for almost a hundred feet at a time. Mink are most commonly found in our lower elevations along the margins of larger creeks and lakes.

Mink eat just about anything: crayfish, amphibians, fish, snakes, birds, eggs, rabbits, muskrats and many other small animals (even if they are larger than a mink). There is at least one report of a mink that attacked a duck and held on even as it took to flight—waiting until the duck tired and was forced to land before finishing it off.

The common name is from the Swedish word *maenk*, meaning "the stinker," after the supposedly even-worse-than-skunk smell produced by its scent glands. *Mustela* is from a Roman name and *vison* is an Old French name of the European species.

Long-tailed Weasel, *Mustela frenata nevadensis* (Hall)
   12–18 inches total length   Plate 47.

Short-tailed Weasel, *Mustela erminea muricus* (Bangs)
   7–12 inches total length

These two species are our smallest weasels. The Long-tailed (tail is 4 ½–6 ½ inches long) is by far the most widespread, occurring in a wide variety of habitats from Canada to Peru (two were collected between Gilmore Lake and Mt. Tallac in 1910). The Short-tailed (tail is 2 ½–3 ½ inches long) is a circumpolar species that is present in small numbers at our higher elevations (although one was collected at Fallen Leaf Lake in 1919). The Long-tailed is a medium brown above and yellow below (frenata means "bridled"—the yellow often extends up around the base of the chin); the Short-tailed is more contrasting: dark brown above and creamy-white below.

Long-tailed Weasels hunt meadows, rockslides and forests for rodents, lagomorphs, birds and other small animals. Short-tailed Weasels appear to specialize on voles in high altitude meadows, but also take a variety of other mice and similarly-sized animals. Both are perfectly built to pursue their prey through burrows, between rocks or under snow.

In our area, both of these species molt into a white winter pelage with black-tipped tails (the black tip possibly attracting attention to their most expendable part). These black tips are what appear as spots in the white trim of a stereotypical drawing of a medieval king's robe (i.e. Old King Cole). When white, both species are referred to as "ermine" ("Armenian") by furriers and it is actually the Long-tailed that is most often made into "ermine" coats—because it takes fewer of them.

The type specimen (the individual animal the species was described from) of *Mustela erminea muricus* was taken near Echo Lakes in 1899.

OTTERS, Subfamily *Lutrinae*

River Otter, *Lutra canadensis* (Schreber)
   about 3 ½ feet total length

Otters are very rarely seen in our watershed, but have been recorded in the Tahoe Basin and could find their way up Taylor Creek.

BADGER, Subfamily *Taxidiinae*

Badger, *Taxidea taxus* (Schreber)
   about 2 feet total length   Plate 47.

Born to dig, this large weasel has a powerful flattened body, broad muscular shoulders and sharp claws that can approach two inches in length.

These adaptations are for quickly digging out prey such as ground squirrels and other burrowing animals, but badgers can also dig to escape, too: fully disappearing below ground in just over a minute.

Badgers prefer to inhabit grasslands with plentiful burrowing mammals and easy-to-dig soil, so they are relatively rare in our area, but could be encountered at any elevation. Their large, flattened oval holes and characteristic claw marks are often the only indication of their presence—they are most active at night. Like skunks, badgers will often den up for extended periods of rest in the winter but do not officially hibernate. The scientific name is derived from the Roman name.

SKUNKS, Subfamily *Mephitinae*

Striped Skunk, *Mephitis mephitis* (Schreber)
   about 2 feet total length   Plate 47.

Many people can identify this infamous weasel by smell alone. The powerful scent glands of this family have been refined to maximize both distance (over ten feet) and accuracy (they aim for the eyes) in this species. Skunks will usually warn its possible target by first stamping its feet and then arching its tail over its back before spraying. The "active ingredient," N-butyl mercaptan, causes temporary blindness and a severe burning sensation upon contact with mucous membranes—in addition to the nausea-inducing sulfur-based smell.

Small holes can litter the surface of the ground where skunks have been digging for beetle grubs or other insect larvae at night. Skunks also have a fondness for yellow jacket larvae for which they will happily dig out ground nests and endure many stings. Although insects make up the majority of their diet, they are true omnivores and eat a wide variety of foods including small animals, eggs, fruit and other plant foods. Skunks are not common and are usually encountered only in the lower elevations of our area.

Unlike most weasels, skunks will be largely inactive and sleep during most of the winter (they do not strictly hibernate because their body temperature does not drop). Great-horned owls are famous for preying on skunks (owls can't smell very well) and their nests can often be smelled before they are seen.

Mephitis is defined in Webster's as Latin for "a harmful, bad-smelling vapor from the earth, as the exhalation from decomposing organic matter or poisonous gas from a mine"—an accurate name worthy of repetition.

Western Spotted Skunks (*Spilogale putorius gracilis* or *S. gracilis*) have been documented in the Tahoe Basin, but only infrequently and usually on the drier, brushier Nevada side.

CATS, Family *Felidae*

Note: "lumpers"—as opposed to "splitters"—argue that both our cats, along with domestic cats, should be in the genus *Felis*.

Bobcat, *Lynx rufus* (Schreber)

about 3 feet long *Plate 47.*

Named after their stubby little tails, bobcats are common and widespread in North America. The young of both bobcats and cougars have black spots. However, unlike cougars, adult bobcats retain many of their spots, especially on the lower half of their body. Bobcats resemble their larger, more northerly relatives, the Lynx, but Lynx have never been documented in California. Bobcats specialize on small rodents, rabbits and birds such as quail. On rare occasions, they are capable of killing a deer if it is handicapped by deep snow, age or injury. These small cats could be seen anywhere in our area, but are most likely to be found at lower elevations.

Mountain Lion (Cougar), *Puma concolor* (Linnaeus)

6–8 feet, including a 2–3 foot tail *Plate 47.*

The most widespread mammal in the New World, *Puma concolor* ranges from Canada to Patagonia. Rarely seen in our area, cougars are much more common in the middle elevations of the west slope, where their primary prey are also more common and can support a male's need for up to one deer per week. Females average about 90 pounds and males average about 150 pounds.

Cougars are not long-distance runners, but they are incredible sprinters and jumpers. They hunt by stalking or ambushing prey, leaping distances of up to 25 feet. The distance between a lion's canines is almost an exact fit to the width of a deer's cervical vertebra and facilitates a quick and clean severing of the spinal column.

Mountain lion kills are neatly eviscerated, with the stomach and intestines set aside and nutritious organs (i.e. liver, heart, kidneys) consumed first. This butchering technique greatly slows the rate of decomposition, which is important since kills are usually covered with leaves and consumed, twenty pounds at a time, over a period of several days. Like other cats, mountain lions generally cover their scat. Mountain lion prints are huge (3 inches across), round and clawless.

This species is variously known as mountain lion, cougar, puma or panther. "Cougar" comes from multiple botched translations (via Portuguese) of the Native Amazonian Tupi name, *susuarana*, meaning "deer-like," after its coloring. "Puma" is the Native Peruvian Quechua name for this "mighty magical animal." Various other Native American tribal names for this species contain superlative references such as lord, god, father, big, greatest, silent, etc. Panther is derived from the Greek and Latin words used to refer to African leopards, especially uniformly colored melanistic (black) ones.

UNGULATES (even-toed) Order *Artiodactyla*;
Ruminates, Suborder *Ruminantia*
DEER, Family *Cervidae*

Mule Deer, *Odocoileus hemionus* (Rafinesque)

4 ½–5 ½ feet   Plate 47.

Mule Deer are most common in our area in the summer when they move upslope, mainly from the east side of the Sierra, although some may remain at our lower elevations year-round. During the winter, our deer generally prefer to stay in areas which receive less than a foot and a half of snow so they can move about and find food more easily. Although they will graze, deer are primarily browsers and prefer just about any kind of shrub to grass.

Mountain lions are their main predator, although coyotes, bears, golden eagles and bobcats will take young fawns or infirm individuals if they have the chance. Fawns are left hidden while mother deer feed, relying on their spotted camouflage and relative lack of smell to keep them hidden from predators. However, mothers will aggressively defend fawns from predators as large as bobcats and coyotes. Resting fawns are often mistakenly "rescued" by well-meaning humans, but mother deer probably define it as "kidnapping"—please leave them alone! Spots on fawns gradually fade until they are completely replaced by the first winter coat in the fall.

Mule deer are so named because of their very large ears. The scientific name translates as "hollow-toothed half-ass" (where ass means a donkey- or mule-like member of the horse family).

FISHES

CLASS *Osteichthyes*, bony fishes
ORDER *Cypriniformes*, minnows, suckers & carp

FAMILY *Cyprinidae*, minnows

Siphateles (Gila) bicolor	Tui chub
Richardsonius egregius	Lahontan redside shiner
Rhinichthys osculus	Speckled dace

FAMILY *Catostomidae*, suckers

Catostomus tahoensis	Tahoe sucker

ORDER *Salmoniformes*, salmon & trout

FAMILY *Salmonidae*, salmon & trout

Prosopium williamsoni	Mountain whitefish
Oncorhynchus clarki henshawi	Lahontan cutthroat trout
Oncorhynchus mykiss	Rainbow trout*
Oncorhynchus mykiss aguabonita	Golden trout*
Oncorhynchus nerka kennerlyi	Kokanee* (ssp. of sockeye salmon)
Salmo trutta	Brown trout*
Salvelinus fontinalis	Brook trout*
Salvelinus namaycush	Mackinaw, lake trout*

ORDER *Scorpaenniformes*, sculpins (& scorpionfishes, rockfishes)

FAMILY *Cottidae*, sculpins

Cottus beldingi	Paiute sculpin

Other species introduced to the Tahoe Basin, but not commonly found in our watershed:

Carassis auratus	Goldfish*
Cyprinus carpio	Common carp*
Gambusia affinis	Mosquito fish*
Ictalurus nebulosis	Brown bullhead catfish*
Lepomis macrochirus	Bluegill sunfish*
Macropterus salmoides	Largemouth bass*
Micropterus dolomieui	Smallmouth bass*
Notemigonus crysoleucas	Golden shiner*
Pomoxis annularis	White crappie*
Pomoxis nigromaculatus	Black crappie*

Failed introductions to the Tahoe Basin:

Oncorhynchus tshawytscha	Chinook salmon*
Salmo salar	Atlantic salmon*
Thamallus arcticus	Arctic grayling*
Coregonus clupeaformis	Lake whitefish*

*introduced species

UNDERWATER:
Lake Tahoe and Fallen Leaf Lake

By Rebecca Chaplin

This section will discuss three different important water-related issues in the Tahoe area. The first is a description of the fish community in Lake Tahoe and Fallen Leaf Lake, how it has been altered by humans, and what restorations efforts are being made. The second is a discussion of jelly balls, submerged trees and other research. The third is an analysis of human impact on Lake Tahoe (and other lakes, where relevant) and of the ecosystem services provided by wetlands.

Fishes of Lake Tahoe and Fallen Leaf Lake

Before the turn of the 20th century, Lake Tahoe and Fallen Leaf Lake were thought to be an inexhaustible resource for the Lahontan Cutthroat Trout. While their brethren were mining for silver in the hills to the east, many settlers in the Tahoe area made their fortune catching these fish, which could weight over 20 or even 30 ponds. They were considered a delicacy in their time and were sent down by the truckload to the Palace Hotel in San Francisco to be served fresh the next day. The Cutthroat population held out surprisingly long considering the excessive fishing pressure to which they were subjected, but in the early 1900s, they proved their exhaustibility. The Lahontan Cutthroat was fished to local extinction.

> **Backcountry Fish Communities**
> *While Taylor Creek joins Lake Tahoe and Fallen Leaf Lake, enabling the fish inhabiting Tahoe to migrate to the waters of Fallen Leaf (an easier feat before the dam was put in), the lakes in the backcountry are isolated by waterfalls. All trout found in Desolation Wilderness lakes were introduced. Native aquatic species continue to suffer because of the presence of these alien predators.*

In the past century the composition of the fish communities of Fallen Leaf Lake and Lake Tahoe have changed considerably, but this next century may see the return of the Cutthroat to the area. After the Cutthroat's extinction, the Department of Fish & Game introduced many other types of sport fish to its place. None of them were native. Among them were: the Brown Trout, from Germany; the Rainbow Trout, a closer transplant from Pacific coastal streams; the Kokanee Salmon, a landlocked version of the Pacific Ocean-dwelling Sockeye; and the Mackinaw (also known as the Lake Trout), from the Great Lakes. In recent years, as non-native and invasive species began to be seen as undesirable, efforts have been undertaken to return native fish to Lake Tahoe. The Department of Fish & Game teamed with the U.S. Fish & Wildlife Service and the Tahoe Research Group to determine whether it would be possible to reintroduce the Lahontan Cutthroat Trout. Using Fallen Leaf Lake as a microcosm in which to study the Cutthroat's reestablishment, these groups planted thousands of fish during the summers of 2002 and 2003 to determine which sizes fared best. They have been carefully monitoring the success of these fish in hopes of gaining insight into what it would take to restore the Cutthroat on the much larger scale of Tahoe.

Why do we care about returning a native fish to Lake Tahoe, anyway? When we have such an array of environmental problems to choose from in today's complex world, why spend precious conservation dollars on bringing back a fish most people have never heard of? While some may make moral arguments about the responsibility to leave things in their "natural" state, the groups attempting the restoration probably found the potential ecosystem effects of nonnative species a more compelling reason. The Cutthroat was a top predator, and top predators have important roles in regulating the populations of the rest of the ecosystem. When a top predator is lost, or replaced by another that regulates those populations slightly differently, dramatic changes can be expected in the structure of the ecosystem. Ecosystem structure is often tied to ecosystem function, and changes in the former can often be reflected in the latter. The Mackinaw has become the top predator for Lake Tahoe and Fallen Leaf Lake in the absence of the Cutthroat. An important difference between these two fish is that the Cutthroat inhabited more of the surface waters, whereas the Mackinaw lives in much deeper waters. A Cutthroat would therefore rarely have come across a bottom dwelling fish such as the Tahoe Sucker, but the Mackinaw feed on them regularly. The Tahoe Sucker is an herbivorous fish, and is thought to be a major driving force behind the clarity of Lake Tahoe by keeping algae populations in check. In what is known as a trophic cascade, the introduction of a predator that decreases the Tahoe Sucker population would have an indirectly positive effect on the algae populations. This may be an additional contributing factor to the eutrophication problem discussed in the next section of this chapter. The decline in abundance of Tahoe Suckers is tightly correlated with the decline in clarity in Lake Tahoe. The argument for returning native species as a means of restoring the ecosystem function is of course highly dependent on those native species achieving dominance over the non-natives. While it is unknown whether the Cutthroat, once established, will be able to out-compete the Mackinaw, it is hoped that because the Cutthroat has a few million more years of evolution in this region under its belt than the Mackinaw, it will rise to dominance once again.

> **Un-extincting the Cutthroat**
> *Even if you decide it's the desirable thing to do, how do you reverse extinction? The Cutthroat hung on in a few tributaries to the Truckee River and in Pyramid Lake, and scientists found strains most genetically similar to the populations that lived in Tahoe and Fallen Leaf and bred them in a fish hatchery. How did they determine the genetics of an extinct population? DNA samples were taken from a fortuitous archive source: fish mounted on mantelpieces that had been caught in Tahoe before the population went extinct!*

Keeping Tahoe Blue

The lakes surrounding us are some of the clearest in the world, but these pristine waters have become threatened in the last 50 years. Inlaid in the granite basin of Tahoe, these lakes have historically received very little sediment and very few nutrients from run-off, maintaining the remarkable clarity to which they owe their beauty. Lake Tahoe in particular has been admired for this reason, and has drawn tourists since before Congress established the Lake Tahoe Forest Reserve in 1899. Beyond its inherent aesthetic value, clarity is an important indicator for the health of the lake ecosystem. In the 1950s the visibility in Lake Tahoe was 130 feet, but has been dropping by a few feet a year, and reached an all time low of 60 feet in 1996. This decline in clarity is due to a process called eutrophication, the stimulation of phytoplankton growth from an increase in nutrient availability.

Eutrophication has dangerous consequences for lake ecosystems. Between 1960 and 1980 the amount of primary production in Lake Tahoe more than doubled. This may sound like it would benefit the lake ecosystem. After all, on land, more plants mean more food for the animals.

> **Eutrophication Hits Home**
> *The green scum that collects on many ponds is the effect of eutrophication. Camp's own Witch's Pond suffered from this slimy green variety of eutrophication and the fish stocked in the pond couldn't survive long in the oxygen-depleted water before the aerator was installed. The appearance needn't be so drastic for there to be a substantial effect, however; a change in color from blue to green as the water grows more cloudy is an indication that our lake ecosystems may be compromised.*

However, eutrophication causes a decrease in the dissolved oxygen available for fish to breathe, and if the case is extreme enough, the oxygen levels may drop below what is necessary to sustain most aquatic life. How can this be, when plants make oxygen? Shouldn't increasing phytoplankton abundance directly increase oxygen supply? This may well be true if a lake were just a thin layer with oxygen-producing phytoplankton spread across it. However, the phytoplankton tends to aggregate toward the surface, where the sunlight is maximized, and they do produce oxygen there. But when they die, they sink, and are decomposed by organisms on the bottom that consume oxygen. Therefore, an increase in phytoplankton at the surface means a proportional decrease of oxygen at the bottom.

How does eutrophication happen?

Lakes are extremely limited by nitrogen and especially phosphorus, much more so than terrestrial ecosystems. When these nutrients are delivered to the lake system, phytoplankton growth takes off. As a natural process, a lake will undergo eutrophication and eventually fill into a bog and then a meadow as sediments carrying nutrients are gradually added to the lake by the streams. Depending on the depth of the lake and sediment load, this process could take hundreds or many thousands of years. As our lakes in the Sierras (especially Tahoe and Fallen Leaf) tend to be very deep and the amount of sediment carried away by rivers running over bare granite is minimal, natural eutrophication is not detectable on a human timescale. The changes we have witnessed in Lake Tahoe over the past century have been a result of eutrophication acceleration by humans.

The first step toward improving the situation in Lake Tahoe was to identify the problem. Anthropogenic nutrients causing eutrophication can come from a number of sources. One predictable origin is from fertilizers, since they were after all designed to stimulate plant growth. The problem with the fertilizers we apply is that tend to be incredibly mobile nutrients, which is why we end up having to apply so much. All the nutrients that get washed away have to go somewhere, and will collect in watersheds or, ultimately, the ocean. The agricultural run-off carried by the Mississippi River is responsible for enormous phytoplankton blooms in the Gulf of Mexico, resulting in what is known as the "dead zone," an area of thousands of square miles that is so low in oxygen no fish can live there. On a smaller scale, the fertilizers people apply to their gardens and lawns may be the cause of unusual algal growth in their local lake. Luckily, there is no agricultural activity around Tahoe and expansive lawns are hard to come by, so this possibility can be mostly discounted. Turning our attention to a more likely culprit, sewage was thought to have leaked into the lake during the 1960s and 70s. As the lake clarity deteriorated, the League to Save Lake Tahoe was formed to raise public awareness about the issue with their "Keep Tahoe Blue" campaign, spurring the Environmental Protection Agency to build an advanced sewage treatment plant that would remove nitrates and phosphates from the water. Still, eutrophication continued, and in the end the main source of the nutrients was determined to be the soils themselves. As construction escalated around Lake Tahoe, soils were disrupted and erosion was accelerated, delivering nitrogen and phosphorus to the lake at an unprecedented rate. In the 1980s a moratorium was placed on development around Lake Tahoe, despite tremendous protest on part of the commercial interests in the area. There are other causes and consequences of sedimentation, but these will be discussed in the final section of this chapter.

> **Ecosystem Services: A New York Watershed Example**
> *In a similar situation to Tahoe's, New York was facing a multi-billion dollar plan to build a water filtration plant that would cost millions of dollars annually to maintain. By utilizing ecosystem services instead, spending a few million dollars to purchase the watershed and restore wetlands around the area, the state avoided having to build the plant and enjoyed the additional benefit of having many more recreational areas for walkers and bird watchers.*

The clarity has begun to improve since 1996, probably largely attributable to the cessation of development, but assisted by wetland restoration efforts. Much of the development, most notably in the Tahoe Keys area, involved filling in and paving over wetlands. Wetlands perform an important ecosystem service of filtering water, serving as a natural treatment plant. As water slowly percolates through the soils of the wetland, nutrients are absorbed (along with any heavy metals or other pollutants the water may be carrying, which isn't favorable for the health of the wetland but further illustrates its filtering capacity). The water exiting the wetland is purified in much the same way it would be had it gone through an elaborate filtration plant. The Tahoe Keys, which used to be wetlands, had long performed this service for Lake Tahoe, making the already pure alpine waters even cleaner. Even once development started muddying those waters, the wetlands would serve as a buffer against environmental degradation to a certain extent, had the development not been situated on the wetlands themselves. Even as the Tahoe planners were building their expensive sewage treatment plant, they were destroying their only natural means of eutrophication mitigation. As the notion of ecosystem services performed by wetlands became more widely accepted in recent years, The League to Save Lake Tahoe and other conservation agencies began acquiring developed lakeshore property to restore to wetland. The value of such property makes acquisition difficult for non-profit organizations, so progress has understandably been slow, but results to date look hopeful.

The Jelly Balls and Submerged Trees of Fallen Leaf Lake

Perhaps the most exciting research the University of Nevada, Reno, has undertaken on Fallen Leaf Lake involves the discovery of a forest of underwater trees. The bottom of the lake is littered with trees and pieces of trees that have fallen in over time that never decompose because the cold temperature of the alpine water inhibits such microbial activity. A few years ago, however, Dr. John Kleppe discovered a tree that was standing straight up from the bottom and, when he investigated further, found that the tree appeared to still be rooted. Through the use of a remotely operated vehicle to scan the bottom of the lake, Dr. Kleppe and his team have subsequently found almost a dozen more trees rooted in the ground under a hundred feet of water. (The trees are not at the very deepest bottom of the lake, which is rumored to be over 400 feet deep, but are at a level that could have been a prehistoric shoreline.) The most amazing aspect of these underwater trees is that they still have bark on them. If you've walked through a forest with fallen trees before, you may have noticed that the bark is the first thing to rot off, usually after only a few years. The water that drowned these trees under Fallen Leaf Lake not only rose fast enough to preserve them standing up (rather than rotting out their roots first until they fell over), it rose so fast that even the bark was preserved. What kind of a flood could account for the lake level rising that rapidly?

Using ice core data from the period in which these trees died (they all carbon date to about 1200 years ago), we learn that the global climate during that time was shifting from a severe 200–year drought to a wet period. Though local climate patterns for this period are unknown, it is possible that they more or less followed global patterns and the Sierras experienced a regime change from dry to wet. Still, it would take a pretty dramatic flood to drown these 80 foot trees fast enough to preserve them as they have been, and no such trees have been found in other lakes in the area, including Lake Tahoe. What's so special about Fallen Leaf Lake?

The answer lies in the watershed to lake area ratio. An area of 16 square miles in the backcountry drains into Fallen Leaf Lake, which covers just two square miles. This means that a foot of precipitation in the backcountry would raise the level of the lake eight feet. Tahoe, by comparison has a watershed to lake area ratio of just 2:1. The level of Lake Tahoe also rose during this period, but not as quickly or dramatically as Fallen Leaf Lake.

These trees now offer the only existing record of climate for the Tahoe area for the period they lived through 1200 years ago. By examining the rings, scientists can tell how fast the trees grew, and from that they can infer how the environment in which the trees were growing changed over the years of the trees' lifetimes. While isotope ratios in ocean sediments and in ice cores at the poles or from permanent glaciers give a general idea of temperature and precipitation of different eras, local climate records are trickier to piece together. Often researchers must rely on pollen deposits in lake sediments to tell them what types of plants lived in the area as a way of estimating the environmental conditions of ancient eras. These trees offer much more concrete data. Why do we care what the climate in Tahoe was like 1200 years ago, or at any period in history other than this one? In order to understand how our climate may change in future years, it helps to know how it already has. And while we may have decent data to predict trends on a global scale, the changes most likely to affect us personally are those that operate on the local scale.

Additionally, these underwater trees can serve as a natural fire record, since scars from where the trees were burned can be detected and the years between burns can be estimated simply by counting the number of rings between scars. This could prove to be an invaluable tool to forest managers as they try to determine what a natural fire regime would look like for the Tahoe area. This is especially important since we have gotten so far off track that it's hard to define what "natural" means anymore.

The final discovery related to finding the trees started out as a side-note and now has taken on a research momentum of its own. Clinging to the trunks of some of the trees were what appeared to be jellyfish in their sessile phase of life. For a few months, scientists were buzzing with the excitement of what they thought may be the largest freshwater jellyfish on record. Further investigation by Dr. Gary Williams at the California Academy of Sciences has revealed that these "jellyfish" are in fact an unknown species of cryptomonad or chloromonad protists: colonial unicellular organisms.

Their research continues...

With the potential to inform fire management and climate research, as well the association with the discovery of what may be a new species, the trees under Fallen Leaf Lake are believed by Dr. Kleppe and his crew to be of national (or even international) significance. Researchers from Russia studying at the Tahoe-Baikal Institute made a special trip out to Fallen Leaf Lake in the summer of 2003 just to see the trees for themselves. Counselors have made up plenty of stories for Campers over the years about what lurks beneath the surface of Fallen Leaf; now there's more fodder for Camp folklore, and in this case, truth is as exciting as fiction!

Chaplin spoke with Dr. Kleppe and his assistant, Grant Adams, to get firsthand details on the Fallen Leaf Research, and interviewed several people from the Forest Service in South Lake Tahoe to obtain the Forest and Fire Management statistics.

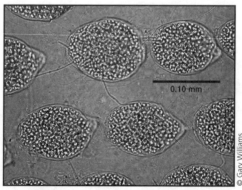

Magnified protists from a slice of jelly ball.

Fallen Leaf Lake Research
Lake Health

The University of Nevada, Reno (UNR) has taken particular interest in monitoring and exploring Fallen Leaf Lake, primarily because one of its professors, Dr. John Kleppe, lives on the lake. UNR has promoted a citizen monitoring program on lake health. Camp was fortunate enough to tap into their resources, and as part of Naturalist programming for the summer of 2002 and 2003, guests learned how to take measurements to assess water quality in Fallen Leaf Lake. This included measuring clarity and testing nutrient and dissolved levels, techniques used in monitoring the eutrophication described previously. Camp's water monitoring program also addressed other potential threats to lake health that have not received as much attention from conservation agencies in the area.

One of these threats is lake acidification. Acid rain can be a problem wherever nitrous oxides and sulfur oxides are emitted, through the burning of coal or combustion of gasoline by cars; these oxides form acidic compounds with moisture in the air and can then acidify the environment in which they are ultimately deposited. Prevailing winds from the Bay Area and Sacramento are a cause for concern that pollution produced there will be deposited here. Ordinarily acid deposition will be buffered to a large extent by the cation exchange capacity of the soils. Essentially, what makes acid so corrosive is the abundance of highly reactive hydrogen ions, and soil particles, especially soils high in clay content like those around Stanford, are quite effective at absorbing most of those hydrogen ions. (Of course, if the acidification is serious enough, the buffering capacity of soils can be overwhelmed.) In the Sierras, however, since most of the soils originate from granitic bedrock, they cannot perform this function. Granite is composed of very inert compounds that do not react with hydrogen ions and thus will not buffer against acidity. Any acid deposition that occurs in the Sierras can be expected to find its way immediately to streams and lakes.

Acid lakes are disastrous for aquatic life, as you might expect (though not because the acid burns the flesh off of aquatic organism or anything sensational like that). Fish respond to acidic conditions by secreting a mucus to protect against the corrosiveness. The side-effect of this mucus unfortunately is that it clogs their gills and prevents them from acquiring enough oxygen. Eventually the fish will die from suffocation. Fortunately, our lakes remain pristine in this aspect, at a solidly neutral pH, but it's a good idea to remain vigilant. This is why citizen monitoring is so important; building a baseline of data to be able to recognize future changes requires a sustained effort—one more easily achieved through dedicated citizens invested in the health of their environment than scientists whose funding may be unreliable.

Another threat to lake and stream ecosystems is sedimentation resulting from erosion. Humans increase sedimentation rates in a number of ways. Dams slow the natural flow of water and cause suspended particles to be deposited where they would otherwise be carried downstream. Harvesting timber, especially on a hillside, can destabilize the topsoil and remove sheltering vegetation. Construction projects expose unprotected soils which easily wash away. Tahoe has experienced all three of these phenomena. Nearly all streams flowing into Lake Tahoe are dammed, presumably to maintain an artificially constant water source for property owners with summer homes. While most of the public lands are protected from clear-cutting, many development projects around Tahoe, including but not limited to alpine ski resorts, result in clearing wide gaps in the forest. While a moratorium has been placed on building around Lake Tahoe's shorelines, property values around the area continue to escalate and the erosion resulting from development finds its way to nearby streams that ultimately lead to the Tahoe watershed.

Why is sedimentation a cause for environmental concern, other than the reasons we've already discussed pertaining to eutrophication? When particles are suspended in water, they absorb more heat from sunlight than does perfectly clear water. When there is enough sediment in the water, the temperature can rise dramatically. An increase in water temperature can affect physiology directly, causing heat stress or shock in many aquatic organisms; it also works indirectly to impact their respiration, since warmer water holds less dissolved oxygen. This problem has been well documented in many streams in Northern California where aggressive timber harvesting is commonly practiced. It is thought that the Coho Salmon that run in these streams owe their current endangered status at least in part to increased sedimentation rates raising the temperature of the streams. Measuring temperature in lakes and streams around Tahoe provides yet another baseline to which to compare future data, and will help identify whether potential future changes in dissolved oxygen are more directly attributable to the effects of eutrophication or sedimentation directly.

Monitoring temperature also aided in preliminary research for the reintroduction of the Cutthroat discussed in the previous section. UNR used data taken by Camp to determine when and where the thermocline formed in Fallen Leaf Lake. The thermocline is a division in lakes that separates a warm surface layer from a colder, denser bottom layer. It forms during the summer months because the sunlight warms the surface waters and when the freshly melted snow runoff that feeds the lake encounters this substantially warmer water, it immediately sinks beneath this water. (Fun physics fact: all else being equal, colder temperature means greater density.)

The stratification created by the thermocline has biological consequences, since it may determine which part of the water column different species inhabit and thus whether they will encounter each other. Biologists overseeing the Cutthroat introduction were interested in information about the thermocline because they knew that the Cutthroat's natural habitat was the top 25 or so feet of the lake, while the Mackinaw, native to the brisk waters of the Great Lakes, required cold temperatures year round and would therefore not be likely to venture above the thermocline. If they waited to plant their Cutthroats until after the thermocline had formed and exceeded a depth of about 25 feet, the young fish might stand a fighting chance. It was hoped that by the time the thermocline broke down in the fall the Cutthroats would have become acclimated enough to their environment to be able to avoid predation or perhaps would even have grown enough to have achieved a size refuge. Cutthroat can eventually get as big as Mackinaw, but the biologists were using the thermocline to protect these fish through the vulnerable period immediately following the planting. Initial results indicate that the Cutthroats still suffered some mortality in the stomach of the Mackinaw, but not nearly as much as was expected. This is an example of the interdisciplinary nature of environmental problem solving, integrating physical science with ecology.

—Rebecca Chaplin

GLOSSARY

achene. A dry, one-seeded, indehiscent fruit derived from a one-chambered ovary with the ovary wall closely enveloping the seed. (i.e., an unshelled sunflower seed)

acuminate. Having a tapering point, the sides of which are concave. (see Illustrated Glossary, Leaf Tips)

acute. Having a sharp-pointed tip with convex or straight sides which join at less than 90 degrees. (see Illustrated Glossary, Leaf Tips)

alien. Not native or naturally occuring; introduced (usually through human-related activity); exotic.

alpine. Above timberline (high altitudes or latitudes where trees can no longer grow upright).

alternate. Occuring singly (one per node) at different levels along an axis, usually changing sides. (see Illustrated Glossary, Leaf Arrangements)

annual. Completing the entire life cycle in a single year or growing season. (opposite of perennial) anther. The part of the stamen which produces pollen, usually located at the tip of the filament.

axil. The upper angle created between a main stem and a leaf or branch.

axillary. Arising from or positioned in an axil.

banner. The uppermost (usually largest) petal of a typical pea flower (Family Fabaceae). (see Illustrated Glossary, Pea Flower Parts)

basal. At the base or bottom of a plant, often referring to leaves in a circular rosette near the ground.

berry. Fleshy fruit derived from a single pistil with one to several seeds not encased in stones. (i.e. a blueberry or tomato)

biennial. Completing the entire life cycle in two years, normally flowering only in the second year.

blade. The expanded, often flattened, portion of a leaf. (see Illustrated Glossary, Leaf Parts)

bloom. White powdery-waxy coating.

bract. Small leaf-like structure, usually at the base of a flower, inflorescence, or leaf bundle.

bud. Embryonic or incompletely developed shoot, leaf, or flower, generally axillary or at the tip of a stem.

bulb. Underground stem and the fleshy leaves that surround it. (i.e. onion, garlic)

burl. A gnarled, knotty, woody growth, usually capable of sprouting. (esp. of manzanita, briar, or redwood)

burry. Sound quality that is not quite raspy, gutteral, or buzzy, but definitely not a pure, clear note; a rough, vibrating voice (esp. in reference to bird songs or calls).

call. A short, year-round vocalization made by both male and female birds. (contrast with *song*)

calyx. Collective term for sepals. (see Illustrated Glossary, General Flower Parts)

cambium. A layer of cells in stems and roots which produce other cells; commonly used to refer to the sugar-conducting layer directly under the bark of trees (phloem). (see phloem, xylem)

capsule. Dry, many-seeded fruit formed from one pistil, usually dehiscent.

catkin. Spike-like inflorescence of unisexual flowers, often pendant, staminate, and inconspicuous.

cauline. Along stem; not basal. (esp. leaves)

compound. 1. Composed of two or more parts, as in leaves. (i.e. pinnate or ternate, see Illustrated Glossary, Leaf Blade Composition) 2. Repeated structural pattern. (i.e. spike of spikelets)

congeneric. A species which shares the same genus with another.

coprophagy. The practice of re-ingesting fecal pellets after their first run through in order to maximize the nutrition and water extracted from the originally ingested food. Common in Lagomorphs (rabbits, hares & pikas).

cordate. Heart-shaped.

corolla. Collective term for petals.

cotyledon. Seed-leaf, often modified to store food for use during germination and the first to appear; the green part(s) on "sprouts." (see also monocot and dicot).

crepuscular. Most active at dawn and dusk. (not quite nocturnal, but not quite diurnal)

cyme. A branched inflorescence (often flat-topped) in which the central or uppermost flower opens first, before the lowermost or peripheral flowers on any axis. (see panicle)

deciduous. Not remaining; falling off. Esp. referring to woody plants which shed their leaves seasonally.

dehiscent. Splitting open at maturity, esp. in reference to fruits opening to disperse their seeds.

dicot. Short for dicotyledon; the group of flowering plants which generally have two seed-leaves, flower parts in multiples of four or five, and net-veined leaves. (i.e. forget-me-nots, buttercups, cherries, oaks) (see cotyledon, monocot)

dioecious. [die-ee-shus] Species with unisexual flowers (staminate and pistillate; male and female) on separate plants; any individual plant having either staminate or pistillate flowers, but not both. (i.e. Meadow Rue, Gingko) (see monoecious)

disk flower. The small tubular flowers found in the flat, sometimes dark, circular center of the compound head of some species in the Sunflower Family (Asteraceae). (see Illustrated Glossary, Sunflower Parts)

diurnal. Active during the day. (opposite of nocturnal)

drupe. A fleshy fruit in which the single seed is encased in a woody endocarp or hardened "stone" (a.k.a. pit). (i.e. plum, cherry, peach)

ecology. 1. The relationships between living organisms and their environment, including the physical environment as well as other organisms. 2. The scientific study of (1).

ecosystem. The general physical environmental factors (climate, topography, soil, moisture, etc) together with communities of living organisms (plants, animals, fungi, microbes, etc) of a given region which combine to make a functional, recognizable, and **virtually self-supporting ecological unit**. (i.e. alpine, foothill chaparral, coastal redwood forest). [This definition is a general one: several more detailed definitions exist and are continually debated. Although the "ecosystem-based" approach to biological conservation is generally agreed to be the "best," a single, accepted definition for "ecosystem" itself does not exist.]

elliptic. Shape of an ellipse or flattened circle. (see Illustrated Glossary, Leaf Shapes)

emarginate. Notched at the tip. (i.e. Prunus emarginata)

endemic. Native and restricted to a well-defined geographic area.

entire. Smooth; not serrate. (see Illustrated Glossary, Leaf Margins)

evergreen. Always having green leaves; a plant which retains its leaves for more than one season and does not lose all its leaves at once.

exserted. Protruding out of and beyond a surrounding structure (esp. referring to when stamens exceed petals).

extant. Surviving today; in existence. (opposite of extinct, extirpated)
extinct. Not surviving; not alive anywhere in the world.
extirpated. Not surviving within a defined geographic area; locally extinct, but usually existing elswhere.
fertile. Reproductive; having sexual parts.
filament. The stalk portion of the stamen that supports the anther. (see Illustrated Glossary, General Flower Parts)
fledge. To leave the nest, usually having grown flight feathers, esp. in reference to baby birds.
fledgling. Bird that has recently fledged.
genus. A taxonomic level of organization between Family and Species; a group of closely related species; first word of the two-parted scientific name for a species (see specific epithet).
habitat. Natural setting, plant community, ecosystem, or environment in which an organism lives.
head. A tight clustering of several non-stalked flowers, often mistaken for a single flower. (i.e. a sunflower) (see disk flower, ray flower)
herb. Plant without woody tissues above the ground.
implantation. When referring to reproduction, the point at which the blastocyst imbeds itself in the nutrient-rich wall of the uterus. This marks a significant change: prior to this point, the fertilized egg is simply undergoing cell division; only after implantation do real growth and cell differentiation occur.
indehiscent. Not opening to distribute seeds, usually in reference to a fruit.
indigenous. Native; naturally occuring in a particular geographic region or ecosystem.
individual. A single organism of a species (as opposed to the whole species).
inflorescence. Cluster of flowers, usually used with reference to their arrangement on a plant.
intergrade. To vary from the traits typical of one species into the traits typical of another species through an almost continuous series of intermediate stages.
intraspecies. Within a species; between individuals of a single species.
involucre. Bracts partially joined together as a unit, often found underneath sunflowers and acorns.
keel. Central ridge, as in the bottom of a boat; esp. the two lower central petals of a pea flower that are fused together to form a curving, hollow ridge which houses the stamens and pistil. (see Illustrated Glossary, Pea Flower Parts)
lanceolate. Narrowly tapering from a medium-broad base towards an acute tip. (see Illustrated Glossary, Leaf Shapes)
leaflet. A single leaf-like unit of a compound leaf.
legume. 1. The pea-pod or bean-like fruit of a member of the Pea Family. 2. A member of the Pea Family, Fabaceae (previously Leguminosae).
ligulate flower. A bisexual flower with a strap-like or petaloid corolla found in
Sunflower Family heads composed entirely of these flowers, without any disk flowers. (similar in appearance to a ray flower, but having stamens as well) (i.e. chicory, dandelion, White Hawkweed)
linear. Long, narrow, with nearly parallel edges. (see Illustrated Glossary, Leaf Shapes)
lip. A flat lobe or perianth part, often the largest and lowest. (see Illustrated Glossary, Orchid Parts)
lobe. Bulge or expanded segment; free tips of otherwise fused structures, esp. corollas and leaves. (see Illustrated Glossary, Leaf Blade Composition)

margin. The edge, esp. used in reference to leaf or petal edges. (see Illustrated Glossary, Leaf Margins)

melanistic. Darkly colored (more of the pigment melanin than normal)

monocot. Short for monocotyledon; the group of flowering plants that have one seed-leaf, flower parts in multiples of three, and parallel-veined leaves. (i.e. lilies, iris, orchids, palms, grasses) (see cotyledon, dicot)

monogamy. Breeding system in which one female mates with one male. (opposite of polygamy)

monoecious. [mo-nee-shus] Species which have separate unisexual flowers (staminate and pistillate; male and female) on the same plant. (i.e. alders, oaks, maples) (see dioecious)

montane. Of the mountains; specifically the cool, moist ecological zone below timberline which is usually dominated by evergreen conifers.

mycorrhizal. Pertaining to fungal associations with plant roots.

native. Naturally occuring; not introduced directly or indirectly through human activity.

nocturnal. Active at night. (opposite of diurnal)

node. Position on a stem where another structure arises, often indicated by a bump, branch, or leaf.

ob-. Prefix indicating the inversion of a shape. (i.e. see Illustrated Glossary, Leaf Shapes: lanceolate vs. oblanceolate)

open. Not crowded together; opposite of tightly packed when referring to an inflorescence.

opposite. Positioned directly across from, esp. in reference to two leaves occurring at each node. (see Illustrated Glossary, Leaf Arrangements)

ornithology. The scientific study of birds.

ovary. The ovule-bearing portion of the pistil which develops into the fruit uponfertilization (at which point the ovules become seeds). (see Illustrated Glossary, General Flower Parts)

ovate. Roughly the shape of a chicken egg, large end down. (see Illustrated Glossary, Leaf Shapes)

palmate. Radiating outward from a common point, remotely resembling a hand (palm). (i.e. a maple or hemp leaf) (see Illustrated Glossary, Leaf Shapes)

panicle. Branched inflorescence (a compound raceme) in which the outer or lower flowers bloom first and the central or terminal flowers bloom afterwards. (see cyme)

papilionaceous. Pea-like, used to describe the typical flower shape of the Pea Family, Fabaceae. (see Illustrated Glossary, Pea Flower Parts)

pappus. The structures which replace the sepals of the Sunflower Family that assist in airborne seed-dispersal. (i.e. the white hair-like structures that help dandelion seeds float on the wind, the hairy "choke" parts of an artichoke) (see Illustrated Glossary, Sunflower Parts)

pedicel. Stalk of an individual flower within an inflorescence.

peduncle. Stalk of an inflorescence or single flower.

perennial. Living for many years, most often used in reference to non-woody plants that re-sprout from the same bulb, tuber, or underground stem year after year. (i.e. a tulip) (see annual)

perianth. Collective term for the calyx and corolla together, used especially when the two are similar, as in lilies or orchids. (see Illustrated Glossary, General Flower Parts)

persistent. Not separating from the plant; remaining attatched.

petal. A single segment of the corolla, usually flattened and colored to attract attention.

petiole. Stalk of a leaf, connecting blade to stem. (see Illustrated Glossary, Leaf Parts)

phloem. The outer vascular cell layer which conduct sugars from leaves to the roots. (see xylem)

pinnate. Positioned in two rows on the opposite side of an axis, especially referring to the placements of leaflets; short for pinnately compound. (see Illustrated Glossary, Leaf Blade Composition)

pistil. The "female" reproductive structure of a flower which includes the ovary, style, and stigma. (see Illustrated Glossary, General Flower Parts)

pistillate. Having only pistils ("female" reproductive parts); without stamens; unisexual.

pollen. Microgametophytes (which later produce sperm), produced in the anther.

pollination. The act of pollen making contact with the stigma; the precursor to fertilization.

polyandry. Breeding system in which a single female mates with more than one male. (see polygyny)

polygamy. Breeding system in which an individual mates with more than one other individual; either polyandry or polygyny. (opposite of monogamy)

polygyny. Breeding system in which a single male mates with more than one female. (see polyandry)

pome. Fleshy fruit of the Rose Family. (i.e. an apple)

prickle. Sharp-pointed projection derived from a plant's epidermis, as on a rose bush. (often incorrectly referred to as a "thorn")

raceme. Inflorescence with stalked flowers along a single axis, blooming from the bottom up.

ray flower. Marginal pistillate flowers with fused, strap-like corollas which appear as the "petals" of a sunflower-family head with disk flowers in the middle. (see Illustrated Glossary, Sunflower Parts; compare with ligulate flower)

rhizome. Underground stem from which "individual plants" sprout, usually running horizontally just below the soil surface. (i.e. horsetails)

riparian. Stream-side; having to do with rivers.

rosette. A circular group of leaves radiating out from a stem near ground level.

sagittate. Shape of an arrowhead. (see Illustrated Glossary, Leaf Shapes)

samara. A winged, indehiscent fruit. (i.e. from a maple tree)

seed. Mature fertilized ovule.

sepal. Leaf-like (or sometimes petal-like) strucure in the whorl below the petals. (see Illustrated Glossary, General Flower Parts)

serrate. Jagged, used here only as a general descriptive term for non-smooth leaf edges. (includes crenate, dentate, toothed, etc) (see Illustrated Glossary, Leaf Margins)

sessile. Not stalked, originating directly from a main stem.

shrub. A woody plant of short (normally well under 20 feet) stature, usually branched. A broad, non-specific term.

simple. One-parted; not compound. (see Illustrated Glossary, Leaf Blade Composition)

song. A vocalization made during the breeding season to attract mates and defend territory, usually done by males and more lengthy than a "call." (specifically with reference to birds)

species. The basic lowermost unit of classification; a group of organisms that can interbreed.

specific epithet. The second word in the two-parted scientific name of a species. (three-part names further specify which subspecies or variety the population corresponds to within a species)

spike. Inflorescence with sessile flowers along a single axis.
spine. Sharp-pointed projection derived from a leaf or part of a leaf. (i.e. a cactus)
spur. A hollow tubular perianth projection, often containing nectar.
stamen. The "male" reproductive structure of a flower, including filament and anther. (see Illustrated Glossary, General Flower Parts)
staminate. Having only stamens ("male" reproductive parts); without pistils; unisexual.
sterile. Without any functional reproductive structures; not fertile. (vegetative)
stigma. Pollen-receiving surface, usually found at the tip of the style - often sticky, lobed, or hairy. (see Illustrated Glossary, General Flower Parts)
stolon. Above-ground, horizontal creeping stem which roots at the nodes to form new plants. (i.e. strawberry plants, some lawn weeds)
stone. Hard inner ovary wall that protects the seed in a drupe; a pit. (i.e. a plum or peach pit)
style. Segment of the pistil between the stigma and ovary, often elongated or stalk-like. (see Illustrated Glossary, General Flower Parts)
subtend. To be positioned directly below.
talus. Basketball to boulder-sized rock fragments, falling from above to create a relatively stable accumulation of loosely stacked rock. (i.e. slopes of Cathedral Peak)
taxon. A category of organisms at any rank. (family, genus, species etc)
taxonomy. The systematic classification of organisms.
tepal. The term used to refer to a segment of the perianth when petals and sepals are difficult to distinguish from one another, as in lillies. (see Illsutrated Glossary, General Flower Parts)
ternate. Divided into three parts. (see Illustrated Glossary, Leaf Blade Composition)
thermoregulate. The ability to adjust or maintain body temperature.
thorn. Sharp projection derived from a branch.
tree. A tall (generally over ten feet), woody plant with a central trunk.
treeline. The imaginary line beyond which trees cease to grow upright—usually determined by elevation, latitude or soils.
type specimen. The original specimen or individual that was used to describe a species for the first time. Usually stored in a museum or herbarium for future reference.
umbel. Dome-shaped inflorescence formed by many pedicels radiating outward from the tip of a stem, also used for umbels of umbels (compound). (i.e. Queen Anne's Lace, Cow Parsnip)
understory. Below the upper canopy of a forest; underneath the taller trees.
unisexual. Having either staminate or pistillate flowers, not both; not a typical (bisexual) flower.
whorl. Three or more structures radiating out from a node. (see Illustrated Glossary, Leaf Arrangements) (Petals, sepals, and branches also come in whorls)
xylem. The inner vascular cell layer which conducts water and minerals from roots to leaves.

BIBLIOGRAPHY

GENERAL

Abbey, Edward. 1968. *Desert Solitaire: A Season in the Wilderness*. Ballentine Books, New York, NY.

Animal Diversity Web, http://animaldiversity.ummz.umich.edu/

Christopherson, Robert. 1994. *Geosystems*. Macmillan College Publishing Company, Inc, Englewood Cliffs, NJ.

Chronology, http://www.clt.astate.edu/aromero/History%20of%20Biology/CHRONO.HTM

Cutright, Paul Russell. 1969. *Lewis & Clark: Pioneering Naturalists*. University of Illinois Press, IL.

Krohne, David, Alvelais, Rachel, and Horne, Nina. 2000. *General Ecology*. Brooks Cole, Pacific Grove, CA.

Neufeldt, Victoria & D.B. Guralnik. 1988. *Webster's New World Dictionary, Third College Edition*. Simon & Schuster, New York, NY.

Packer, Nancy H. and John Timpane. 1989. *Writing Worth Reading*. St. Martin's Press, New York, NY.

Purves, William K. and G.L. Orians. 1987. *Life: The Science of Biology*. Sinauer Associates Inc, Sunderland, MA.

Soukhanov, Anne H, ed. 1984. *Webster's II New Riverside University Dictionary*. Houghton Mifflin Company, Boston, MA.

Welcome to the MVZ, http://mvz.berkeley.edu/

Zoonomen Nomenclature Resource Page, http://www.zoonomen.net/

REGIONAL

BerkeleyMapper Point Mapping Service, http://berkeleymapper.berkeley.edu/

Brown, Vinson & B. Black. 1996. *The Sierra Nevadan Wildlife Region*, Fourth Revised Edition. Naturegraph Publishers, Happy Camp, CA.

California Academy of Science, http://www.calacademy.org/index.html

California Academy of Science's Manzanita Project—donated photos via Calphoto—http://www.calacademy.org/research/library/manzanita/html/

CALIFORNIA'S PLANTS AND ANIMALS, http://www.dfg.ca.gov/

CalPhotos, http://elib.cs.berkeley.edu/photos/

Hubbard, Douglass H. 1970. *Yosemite*. Golden Press, New York, NY.

Journals of the Lewis and Clark Expedition
http://libtextcenter.unl.edu/lewisandclark/index.html

Matthews, Daniel. 1988. *Cascade-Olympic Natural History*. Raven Editions and Portland Audubon Society, Portland, OR.

Murphy, Dennis D. & Christopher M. Knopp, eds. 2000. *Lake Tahoe Watershed Assessement: Volumes I & II*. (Gen. Tech. Rep. PSW-GTR-176) Pacific Southwest Research Station, USDA Forest Service, Albany, CA.

NatureServe, Comprehensive Reports on Species, http://www.natureserve.org/

Powell, Jerry A. and C.L. Hogue. *California Insects*. (California Natural History Guides: 44) University of California Press, Berkeley, CA.

Schaffer, Jeffery P. 2003. *Desolation Wilderness and the South Lake Tahoe Basin*. Wilderness Press, Berkeley, CA.

Sierra Nevada Alliance - Sierra Scene - Sierra Wide,

http://www.sierranevadaalliance.org/sierrascene/profile.html?index=947195402_13304

Storer, Tracy L., R.L. Usinger & David Lukas. 2004. *Sierra Nevada Natural History*, Revised Edition. (California Natural History Guide #73) University of California Press, Berkeley, CA.

Tahoe Area Bibliography Search Results, http://www.tahoe.unr.edu/bibsearch.aspx?p_subj=%25

USDA Forest Service. 2000. *A Guide to the Desolation Wilderness*. (map) El Dorado National Forest & Lake Tahoe Basin Management Unit. San Francisco, CA.

NATIVE AMERICAN/ MEDICINAL or EDIBLE PLANTS

Downs, James F. 1966. *The Two Worlds of the Washo: An Indian Tribe of California and Nevada*. Holt, Reinhart, and Winston Inc, Orlando, FL.

Clarke, Charlotte B. 1977. *Edible and Useful Plants of California*. (California Natural History Guides: 41) University of California Press, Berkeley, CA.

Chatfield, Kimball. 1997. *Medicine From the Mountains*. Range of Light Publications, South Lake Tahoe, CA.

Duke, James A. 1992. *Handbook of Edible Weeds*. CRC Press Inc, Boca Raton, FL.

Heizer, Robert F. and A.B. Elsasser. 1980. *The Natural World of the California Indians*. (California Natural History Guides: 46) University of California Press, Berkeley, CA.

Kirk, Donald R. 1975. *Wild Edible Plants of Western North America*. Naturegraph Publishers, Happy Camp, CA.

Medicinal Herbs Online. http://www.egregore.com/herbs

Medicinal Value of Whole Foods. http://www.naturalways.com/medValFd.htm

Moore, Michael. 1979. *Medicinal Plants of the Mountain West*. Museum of New Mexico Press, Santa Fe, NM.

Ody, Penelope. 1993. *The Complete Medicinal Herbal*. Dorling Kindersley Ltd, London, England.

Wiltens, James. 1999. *Edible and Poisonous Plants of Northern California*. Wilderness Press. Berkeley, CA.

PLANTS

Arno, Stephen F. 1973. *Discovering Sierra Trees*. Yosemite Natural History Assoc., Sequoia Natural History Assc, and the National Park Service.

Bailey, L.H. 1933. *How Plants Get Their Names*. (Macmillan) Dover Publications Inc, Mineola, NY.

Blackwell, Laird R. 1997. *Wildflowers of the Tahoe Sierra*. Lone Pine Publishing, Redmond, WA.

Blackwell, Laird R. 2002. *Wildflowers of the Eastern Sierra*. Lone Pine Publishing, Renton, WA.

Brockman, C. Frank and R. Merrilees. 1968. *A Guide to Field Identification: Trees of North America*. Golden Press, New York, NY.

Calflora Database, http://www.calflora.org/

Christie, Christopher—donated photos via CalPhoto, http://elib.cs.berkeley.edu/photos/

California Plant Names Meanings and Derivations, http://www.calflora.net/botanicalnames/

Graf, Michael. 1999. *Plants of the Tahoe Basin: Flowering Plants, Trees & Ferns*. California Native Plant Society Press, Sacramento, CA.

Grillos, Steve J. 1966. *Ferns and Fern Allies of California*. (California Natural History Guides: 16) University of California Press, Berkeley, CA.

Harrington, H.D. and L.W. Durrell. 1957. *How to Identify Plants*. Swallow Press / University of Ohio Press, Athens, OH.

Hickman, James C., ed. 1993. *The Jepson Manual: Higher Plants of California*. (The AUTHORITY for plant names used in this book) University of California Press, Berkeley, CA.

Jensen, Edward C. and C.R. Ross. 1994. *Trees to Know in Oregon*. Oregon State University Extension Service and Oregon Department of Forestry, Corvallis, OR.

Legg, Kenneth. 1970. *Lake Tahoe Wildflowers, Also of the Central Sierra*. Naturegraph Publishers, Healdsburg, CA.

Mauseth, James D. 1991. *Botany: An Introduction to Plant Biology*. Saunders College Publishing, San Francisco, CA.

Matson, Steve—donated photos via CalPhoto, http://elib.cs.berkeley.edu/photos/

McMinn, Howard E. and Evelyn Maino. 1935. *An Illustrated Manual of Pacific Coast Trees*. University of California Press Ltd, Berkeley, CA.

Munz, Philip A. 2003. *Introduction to California Mountain Wildflowers*, Revised Edition. University of California Press, Berkeley, CA.

Munz, Phillip A. 1959. *A California Flora (and Supplement, 1973)*. University of California Press Ltd, Berkeley, CA.

Niehaus, Theodore F. & C. L. Ripper. 1976. *A Field Guide to Pacific States Wildflowers*. (Peterson Field Guides) Houghton Mifflin Company, Boston, MA.

Nilsson, Karen B. 1994. *A Wildflower by any other Name*. Yosemite Association, Yosemite National Park, CA.

Peterson, P. Victor and P.V.P. Jr. 1975. *Native Trees of the Sierra Nevada*. (California Natural History Guides: 36) University of California Press, Berkeley, CA.

Prince, Susan D.—donated her photos

Spellenberg, Richard. 1979. *The Audubon Society Field Guide to North American Wildflowers*. Alfred A. Knopf, New York, NY.

Thomas, John Hunter & D.R. Parnell. 1974. *Native Shrubs of the Sierra Nevada*. (California Natural History Guides: 44) University of California Press, Berkeley, CA.

Thomas, John Hunter. 1961. *Flora of the Santa Cruz Mountains of California: A Manual of the Vascular Plants*. Stanford University Press, Stanford, CA.

Weeden, Norman F. 1996. *A Sierra Nevada Flora*, Fourth Edition. Wilderness Press, Berkeley, CA.

Weise, Karen. 2000. *Sierra Nevada Wildflowers*. Falcon Publishing, Helena, MT.

AMPHIBIANS, REPTILES & FISHES

Amphibia Web, http://elib.cs.berkeley.edu/
Amphibians & Reptiles of Oregon, http://www.uoregon.edu/~titus/herp/
Autodax Feeding in Hydromantes platycephalus,
    http://autodax.net/hydromovie.html
Biographies of People Honored in the Herpetological Nomenclature, http://ebeltz.net/herps/
California Reptiles and Amphibians, http://www.californiaherps.com/
CNAH - Standard Common and Current Scientific Names,
    http://www.naherpetology.org/nameslist.asp?id=4
Corkran, Charlotte C. & Chris Thoms. 1996. *Amphibians of Oregon, Washington & British Columbia*. Lone Pine Publishing, Renton, WA.
Deban, Stephen M., http://autodax.net/index.html
Nafis, Gary—donated photos via his website, http://www.californiaherps.com/
Scientific and Common Names of Reptiles and Amphibians– Explained,
    http://ebeltz.net/herps/
St. John, Alan D. 2002. *Reptiles of the Northwest*. Lone Pine Publishing, Renton, WA.
Zim, Herbert S., H.H. Shoemaker & J.G. Irving. 1955. *Fishes: A Guide to Fresh and Saltwater Species*. Golden Press, New York, NY.

BIRDS

All About Birds, http://www.birds.cornell.edu/programs/AllAboutBirds/BirdGuide/
Allessio, Lori, Nancy Bish & Dave Iribarne. 1995. *Birds of the Lake Tahoe Basin*. (checklist) Eastern Sierra Interpretive Association/USDA Forest Service: LT-BMU, South Lake Tahoe, CA.
AOU - Check-list of North American Birds, http://www.aou.org/checklist/
Barrowclough, GF et. al. "Phylogeographic structure, gene flow and species status in Blue Grouse." *Molecular Ecology* (2004) 13, 1911-22.
Beedy, Edward C. and S.L. Granholm. 1985. *Discovering Sierra Birds*. Yosemite Natural History Assc, Sequoia Natural History Assc, and the National Park Service.
Bird Checklist Evolution, http://www.tbfn.net/chekpast.htm
Brooks, Allan. "On Dendragapus obscurus being separated into two groups." *Auk*, Vol. XLVI, p. 111-113. Jan. 1929.
Brown, Vinson, H.G. Weston, and Jerry Buzzell. 1986. *Handbook of California Birds*, Third Edition. Naturegraph Publishers, Happy Camp, CA.
Cardinal, David—homepage: http://www.cardinalphoto.com/ - donated photos
Choate, Ernest, A. & R.A. Paynter, Jr. 1985. *The Dictionary of American Bird Names*, Revised Edition. The Harvard Common Press, Boston, MA
Dowlan, Stephen, Editor, Oregon Birds. email: owlhooter@aol.com. Donated photos via CalPhoto, http://elib.cs.berkeley.edu/photos/
Ehrlich, Paul R., D.S. Dobkin & D. Wheye. 1988. *The Birder's Handbook: A Field Guide To the Natural History of North American Birds*. Simon & Schuster Inc, New York, NY.
Gleason, Dan & Gleason, Barbara. 2002. *Birds! From the Inside Out*, Third Edition, CraneDance Communications, Eugene, OR. http://www.cranedance.com
Golden Gate Audubon Society - Early Birds - Thomas Nutall,
    http://www.goldengateaudubon.org/birding/earlybirds/ThomasNutall.htm

Greer, Tom—email: tbphotos@comcast.net—donated photos via CalPhoto, http://elib.cs.berkeley.edu/photos/

Gross, Joyce—home page: http://hyla.cs.berkeley.edu/ - donated photos via CalPhoto, http://elib.cs.berkeley.edu/photos/

Holloway, Joel E. 2003. *Dictionary of Birds of the United States.* Timber Press, Portland, OR.

Laws, John Muir. 2004. *Sierra Birds: A Hiker's Guide.* California Academy of Sciences & Heyday Books, Berkeley, CA.

Orr, Robert T. and James Moffit. 1971. *Birds of the Lake Tahoe Region.* California Academy of Sciences, San Francisco, CA.

Paulson, Dennis. 1993. *Shorebirds of the Pacific Northwest.* University of British-Columbia Press, Vancouver, British Columbia.

Peterson, Roger Tory, ed. 1992. *A Field Guide To Western Bird Songs*, Second ed. (2 CDs by Cornell Laboratory of Ornithology / Interactive Audio) Houghton Mifflin Co, Boston, MA.

Scott, S.L., ed. 1987. *Field Guide to the Birds of North America*, Second Edition. National Geographic Society, Washington, D.C.

Sibley, David Allen. 2000. *The Sibley Guide to Birds.* Alfred A. Knopf, New York, NY.

Smith, James P. Jr. 1977. *Vascular Plant Families.* Mad River Press Inc, Eureka, CA.

Walton, Richard K. and R.W. Lawson. 1990. *Birding By Ear: Western.* (3 audio tapes by Peterson Field Guides) Houghton Mifflin Co, Boston, MA.

MAMMALS

American Martens, http://www.american-marten.com/

Animals, http://www.brrc.unr.edu/data/animal/vertebrates/mammallist.htm

ASM Mammals of California, http://www.mammalsociety.org/statelists/camammals.html

Biogeography of American Marten, http://bss.sfsu.edu/holzman/courses/Fall%2003%20project/Biogeography%20of%20American%20Marten.htm

California Ground Squirrel Info, http://www.etc-etc.com/sqrlinfo.htm

Cockrum, E. L. & Y. Petryszyn. 1994. *Mammals of California & Nevada.* Treasure Chest Publications, Tucson, AZ.

Deck, Dennis—donated photos via his tracking website Virtual Dirt Time, http://dirttime.ws/DirtTime.htm

Demboski, JR and JA Cook. "Phylogeny of the dusky shrew, *Sorex monticolus.*" *Molecular Ecology* (2001) 10, 1227-1240. (via http://www.csupomona.edu/~jrdemboski/monticolus.pdf)

Drew, Lisa W. *Creatures That Time Forgot: Mountain Beavers* - National Wildlife Magazine (via http://www.nwf.org/nationalwildlife/article.cfm?articleId=500)

Fisher Wild Things Unlimited Rare Carnivores, http://home.mcn.net/~wtu/fisher.html

Florida PantherNet - Official Education Site, http://www.panther.state.fl.us/handbook/natural/whatname.html

Vernes, Karl. "Gliding performance of the northern flying squirrel." *Journal of Mammalogy*: Vol. 82, No. 4, pp. 1026-1033.

Halfpenny, James C. & E.A. Biesiot. 1986. *A Field Guide to Mammal Tracking in North America.* Johnson Publishing Company, Boulder, CO.

Hartson, Tamara. 1999. *Squirrels of the West.* Lone Pine Publishing, Renton, WA.

Hester, Joy. *Belding's Ground Squirrel*. (via http://www.bio.davidson.edu/people/vecase/Behavior/Spring2003/Hester/introductionc.htm)

Holekamp, Dr. Kay E.'s Laboratory, http://hyenas.zoology.msu.edu/beldingi/

Ingles, Loyd G. 1965. *Mammals of the Pacific States: California, Oregon, and Washington*. Stanford University Press, Stanford, CA.

ISEC Canada, http://www.wildcatconservation.org/cats/factsheets/northamerica/bobcat/index.shtml

Lai, Chien-Hsun and Andrew T. Smith. "Keystone status of Plateau Pikas (Ochotona curzoniae): effect of control on biodiversity of native birds." in: *Conserving China's Biodiversity* (II) (PETER Johan Schei, WANG Sung and XIE Yan eds). China Environmental Science Press. Beijing. 222-230p. 1996. (via http://www.chinabiodiversity.com/shwdyx/technical-report-e/x-9e.htm)

Kucera, TE et. al. "Current distribution of the American Marten in California." *California Department of Fish and Game* 81(3): 96-103, 1995. (via http://www.dfg.ca.gov/hcpb/info/bm_research/bm_pdfrpts/95_12.pdf)

Larrison, Earl J. & Amy Fisher. 1976. *Mammals of the Northwest*. Seattle Audubon Society/Durham & Downey, Inc, Portland, OR.

Lefalophodon Joel Asaph Allen, http://www.nceas.ucsb.edu/~alroy/lefa/Allen.html

Mammals, http://www.dfg.ca.gov/whdab/html/lifehistmammal.html

Mammals of California, http://wfcb.ucdavis.edu/www/Faculty/Doug/California%20Mammals.htm

Mammals of the Lake Tahoe Basin, http://ceres.ca.gov/tcsf/tahoe-local/mammals.html

Marten&Weasel, http://srmwww.gov.bc.ca/risc/pubs/tebiodiv/marten/maweml20-03.htm

Mountain Beaver—Aplodontia, http://www.lewis-clark.org/content/content-article.asp?ArticleID=1948

Mountain Beaver (Aplodontia rufa), http://infowright.com/mtbeaver/

The Biogeography of, http://bss.sfsu.edu/holzman/courses/Fall%2003%20project/mtnbeaver.htm

Murie, Olaus J. 1974. *Animal Tracks*. (Peterson Field Guides) Houghton Mifflin Company, Boston, MA.

Northern Flying Squirrel (Glaucomys sabrinus), http://weaselhead.org/profile/index.php?s=567

NWRC - Clinton Hart Merriam, http://www.aphis.usda.gov/ws/nwrc/hx/merriam.html

Ochotona, http://www.funet.fi/pub/sci/bio/life/

Orr, Robert T. 1949. *Mammals of Lake Tahoe*. California Academy of Sciences, San Francisco, CA.

Rezendes, Paul. 1992. *Tracking & the Art of Seeing: How to Read Animal Tracks & Sign*. Camden House Publishing, Charlotte, VT.

Steele, Dale T. "An Ecological Survey of Endemic Mountain Beavers (Aplodontia rufa) in California 1979-1983." *California Department of Fish & Game*, WM-DAR #89-1. 1989.
(via http://www.dfg.ca.gov/hcpb/info/bm_research/bm_pdfrpts/89_14.pdf)

Sutton, DA & BD Patterson. "Geographic Variation of the Western Chipmunks." *Journal of Mammology*, 81(2): 299-316, 2000. (via http://fm1.fieldmuseum.org/aa/Files/patterso/J_Mamm_2000_chipmunks.pdf)

About the Author

Charles Quinn graduated from Stanford University in 1994 with a self-designed degree in Humans and Conservation Ecology through the Program in Human Biology. During his undergraduate years, he was a docent at Jasper Ridge Biological Preserve, volunteered at the San Mateo Outdoor Education Camp and participated in field studies on a variety of plants, birds, mammals and butterflies. Charlie spent all four summers as a member of the "staph" at Stanford Sierra Camp, mostly as naturalist. In Oregon, he has volunteered for Portland Audubon, creating a birding-by-ear tape for their Green City Data Program. He also volunteered for the Tualatin Riverkeepers and wrote a chapter for *Exploring the Tualatin River Basin*. After volunteering for The Nature Conservancy and the Oregon Natural Heritage Program as a hike leader and bird researcher, he was hired in 1995 to manage the Oregon chapter's Natural History Excursions program. He has staffed Stanford Family Adventures to Greece & Turkey and the Galapagos and continues to volunteer for the Stanford Alumni Association. Charlie currently works for The Nature Conservancy in Oregon as an associate director based in Eugene.

About the Contributing Author

Becky Chaplin is pursuing a PhD in Environmental Science, Policy and Management at the University of California, Berkeley. She studied Earth Systems at Stanford for her undergraduate and masters degrees, and worked as a naturalist at Stanford Sierra Camp during the summers of 2002 and 2003. Her experience there instilled in her a love of education and she plans to pursue a teaching career. She is currently undertaking research aimed at quantifying ecosystem services: assessing the value of natural habitat beyond that of extractive uses, to more formally recognize human dependence on ecological processes.

INDEX

A

Abies concolor, 2, pl. 1
  magnifica magnifica, 3, pl.1
Accipiter cooperii, 117
  gentilis, 117
  striatus, 117, pl. 33
Acer glabrum torreyi, 16, pl. 3
Achillea millefolium, 74, 85, pl. 23
Aconitum columbianum, 45, 82, pl. 10
Actitis macularius, 120, pl. 33
Adiantum aleuticum, 38, pl. 7
Aechmophorus clarkii, 112, pl. 31
  occidentalis, 112, pl. 31
Aegolius acadicus, , pl. 34
Agastache urticifolia, 45, pl. 11
Agelaius phoeniceus nevadensis, 161, pl. 43
Aix sponsa, pl. 28
Alder, Mountain, 15, pl. 3
  White, 15
Allium campanulatum, 55, 83, pl. 15
  validum, 55, 83 , pl. 15
Alnus incana tenuifolia, 15, pl. 3
  rhombifolia, 15
Alumroot, Pink, 51, pl. 13
Ambystoma macrodacylum sigillatum, 89, pl. 25
Amelanchier alnifolia pumila, 28, pl. 5
  utahensis, 28
Anas acuta, pl. 29
  americana, pl. 28
  clypeata, pl. 29
  crecca, pl. 29
  cyanoptera, pl. 29
  platyrhynchos, 107, pl. 28
  strepera, pl. 28
Anennaria media, 75, pl. 23
  rosea rosea, 55, pl. 15
Angelica, Brewer's, 72, pl. 22
Angelica brewerii, 72, pl. 22
Anser albifrons , pl. 20
Anthus rubescens, 149, pl. 40
Antennaria media, 75
Aphelocoma californica, 137, pl. 37
Aplodontia rufa californica, 178, pl. 45
Apocynum androsaemifolium, 51, pl. 13
Aquila chrysaetos, 118
Aquilegia formosa, 59, 80, pl. 16
Arabis holboelii, 68, pl. 20
Arceuthobium campylopodum, 77, pl. 24
Arctostaphylos nevadensis, 27, pl. 4
  patula, 27, 81, pl. 4
Ardea alba, 114, pl. 32
  herodias, 113, pl. 32
Arnica, 79
  Heartleaf, 66, pl. 19
Arnica cordifolia, 66, 79, pl. 19
Artemisia arbuscula, 28
  douglasiana, 67, pl. 20
  rothrockii, 28
  spiciformis, 28

  tridentata vaseyana, 28, pl. 5
Aspen, Quaking, 12
Aspidotis densa, 38, pl. 7
Aster, Western, 47, pl. 11
Aster occidentalis occidentalis, 47, pl. 11
Aythya affinis, pl. 29
  collaris, pl. 29
  marila, pl. 29
  valisineria, pl. 29
Athyrium alpestre americanum, 40
  filix-femina cyclosporum, 40, pl. 8

B

Badger, 196, pl. 47
Balsam-root, Arrow-leaved, 67, pl. 19
Balsamorhiza sagittata, 67, pl. 19
Bat, Big Brown, 174
  Brazilian free-tailed, 174
  Silver-haired, 174
  see also Myotis and Pipistrelle (bats)
Bear, (Sierra Nevada) Black, 192, pl. 47
Beaver, 187
Beetle, Fir Engraver, 3, 20
Bishop's Cap, Brewer's, 76, pl. 24
Blackbird, Brewer's, 162, pl. 43
  Red-winged, 161, pl. 43
  Yellow-headed, 161, pl. 43
Bluebird, Mountain, 147, pl. 40
  Western, 147, 160, pl. 40
Blue Elderberry, 30
Blue Flag, Western, 46, pl. 11
Boa, Rubber (Northern), 98, pl. 27
Bobcat, 198, pl. 47
Bog-Orchid, Green-flowered, 77, pl. 24
  White-flowered, 73, pl. 22
Borrelia birgdorferi, 97
Botrychium multifidum, 37, pl. 7
  simplex, 37
Branta canadensis moffitti, 107, pl. 28
Brickellbush, Large-flowered, 65, pl. 18
Brickellia grandifolia, 65, pl. 18
Bubo virginianus, 124, pl. 34
Bucephala albeola, pl. 30
  clangula, pl. 30
  islandica, pl. 30
Buckwheat, Naked, 71, pl. 21
Bufflehead, 107, pl. 30
Bufo boreas halophilus, 94, pl. 25
Bullfrog, 93, pl. 25
Bunting, Lazuli, 160, pl. 43
Buteo jamaicensis, 118, pl. 33
  regalis, 118
  swainsoni, 117
Buttercup, Plantain Leaf, 63, pl. 18

C

California Fuchsia, 52, 58
California Grass-of-Parnassus, 71
Calocedrus decurrens, 10, pl. 3
Calochortus leichtlinii, 68, 82, pl. 20
  minimus, 68, pl. 20

A Nature Guide to the Southwest Tahoe Basin

Calypte anna, 126, pl. 35
Calyptridium umbellatum, 56, pl. 15
Camas, 47, pl. 11
Camassia quamash, 47, pl. 11
Canis latrans, 191, pl. 47
  lupus, 192
Canvasback, 107, pl. 29
Carduelis pinus, 166, pl. 44
Carpodacus cassinii, 165, pl. 44
  purpureus, 165, pl. 44
Castilleja applegatei, 60, pl. 16
  miniata miniata, 60, pl. 16
Castor canadensis, 187
Catostomus tahoensis, 200
Cathartes aura, 115, pl. 32
Catharus guttatus, 148, pl. 40
  ustulatus, 148
Catherpes mexicanus, pl. 39
Ceanothus cordulatus, 26, pl. 4
  velutinus velutinus, 25, pl. 4
Certhia americana, 143, pl. 39
Ceryle alcyon, 127, pl. 35
Charadrius vociferous, 120, pl. 33
Charina bottae, 98, pl. 27
"cheeseburger" bird, 141
Cheilanthes gracillima, 39, pl. 7
Chen caerulescens, pl. 28
Cherry, Bitter, 29, pl. 5
Chickadee, Mountain, 141, pl. 38
Chlidonias niger, 122
Chinquapin, Bush, 25, pl. 4
Chipmunk, Allen's (Shadow), 183
  Least, 183
  Lodgepole, 183, pl. 46
  Long-eared, 183, pl. 46
  Yellow-Pine, 184
Choke-cherry, Western, 29, pl. 5
Chordeiles minor hesperis, 124, pl. 35
Chrysothamnus nauseosus, 66, pl. 19
Chrysolepis sempervirens, 25, pl. 4
Chub, Tui, 200
Cinclus mexicanus, 145, pl. 39
Cinquefoil, Graceful, 62, pl. 17
  Shrubby, 61, pl. 17
  Sticky, 62, pl. 17
Circaea alpina pacifica, 68, pl. 20
Circus cyaneus, 116, pl. 32, pl. 15
Cistothorus palustris, pl. 39
Cirsium andersonii, 56
Cliff-break, Bridge's, 38, pl. 7
Coccothraustes vespertinus brooksi, 167, pl. 44
Coffeeberry, Sierra, 26, pl. 4
Colaptes auratus collaris, 132, pl. 36
Columbine, 59, 80, pl. 16
Condor, California, 118
Contopus cooperi, 133
  sordidulus veliei, 133, pl. 36
Coot, American, 119, pl. 33
Corallorhiza maculata, 60, pl. 16
Coralroot, Spotted, 60, pl. 16
Cormorant, Double-crested, 113, pl. 32
Corn Lily, 80, pl. 23
Cornus sericea sericea, 31, pl. 6

  stolinifera, 31
Corvus brachyrhynchos, 139, pl. 38
  corax, 139, pl. 38
Cottontail, Nuttall's (Mountain), 177, pl. 45
Cottonwood, Black, 13
Cottus beldingi, 200
Cougar, 198, pl. 47
Coyote, 191, pl. 47
Cow Parsnip, 71, pl. 22
Cowbird, Brown-headed, 134, 136, 137, pl. 43
Creeper, Brown, 143, pl. 39
Creeping Snowberry, 54
Crossbill, Red, 166, pl. 44
Crow, American, 139, pl. 38
Crystopteris fragilis, 40
Crytogramma acrostichoides, 38, pl. 7
Currant, Sierra, 49, pl. 13
  Sticky, 50, pl. 13
Cyanocitta stelleri frontalis, 138, pl. 37
Cygnus columbianus, pl. 2

D

Dace, Speckled, 200
Daisy, Wandering, 47
Dandelion, 80
Death Camas, 47, 73, 81, pl. 22
Deer, Mule, 199, pl. 47
Delphinium glaucum, 44, pl. 10
  nuttallianum, 44, pl. 10
Dendragapus fuiginosus sierrae, 109
  obscurus sierrae, 108
Dendroica coronata auduboni, 151, pl. 41
  nigrescens, 152, pl. 41
  occidentalis, 152, pl. 41
  petechia, 151, pl. 41
  townsendi, 152, pl. 41
Dipper, American, 145, pl. 39
Dodecatheon jeffreyi, 53, pl. 14
Dogbane, Spreading, 51, pl. 13
Dogwood, American, 31
  Creek, 31, pl. 6
  Pacific, 31
  Red-osier, 31
  Silky, 31
Douglas-fir, 4, pl. 1
Dove, Mourning, 123, pl. 34
  Rock, 122
Dryocopus pileatus, 132
Duck, Ring-necked, 107, pl. 29
  Ruddy, 107, pl. 30
  Wood, 107, pl. 28

E

Eagle, Bald, 116, pl. 32
  Golden, 118, 119, pl. 33
Egret, Great, 114, pl. 32
  Snowy, pl. 32
Elderberry, Blue, 30, pl. 6
  Red, 30, pl. 6
Elephant's Head, 51, pl. 13
Elgaria coerulea palmeri, 98, pl. 26
Empidonax difficilis, 135, pl. 36
  hammondii, 135, pl. 36
  oberholseri, 135

trailii, 134, pl. 36
Epilobium angustifolia circumvagum, 47, pl. 12
    canum latifolia, 58, pl. 16
    glaberrimum glaberrimum, 48, pl. 12
    obcordatum, 48, pl. 12
Equisetum arvense, 39, 81, pl. 8
    hyemale affine, 39
Erethizon dorsatum, 190, pl. 46
Erigeron, Fleabane (see Daisy, Wandering)
Erigeron peregrinus callianthemus, 47
Erigonum nudum, 71, pl. 21
    umbellatum polyanthum, 64
Ermine, 194
Erysimum capitatum perrene, 61, pl. 17
Euphagus cyanocephalus, 162, pl. 43
Evening Primrose, Hooker's, 61, pl. 17

F

Falco sparverius, 119, pl. 33
Falcon, Peregrine, 119
    Prairie, 119
False Solomon's Seal. (see Solomon's Seal)
Felis concolor, 198, pl. 47
    rufus, 198
Fern, Alpine Lady, 40
    American Parsley, 38, pl. 7
    Bracken, 37, pl. 7
    Bridge's Cliff-Brake, 38, pl. 7
    Cliff, 40
    Five-finger, 38, pl. 7
    Fragile, 40
    Holly, 40
    Indian Dream, 38, pl. 7
    Kruckberg's Sword, 40
    Lace, 39, pl. 7
    Lady, 40, pl. 8
    Leather Grape-, 37, pl. 7
Fern allies, Horsetail, 81, pl. 8
Finch, Cassin's, 165, pl. 44
    Purple, 165, pl. 44
Fir, Red, 3, pl. 1
    White, 2, 36, pl. 1
Fir Engraver Beetle, 20
Fireweed, 47, pl. 12
Fireweed, Smooth-stemmed, 48, pl. 12
Fisher, 194
Flag, Western Blue, 46, pl. 11
Flax, Alpine Blue, 42, pl. 9
Flicker, Gilded, 132
    Northern, 132, pl. 36
Flycatcher, Dusky, 135
    Hammond's, 135, pl. 37
    Olive-sided, 133
    Pacific Slope, 135, pl. 37
    Willow, 134, 163, pl. 36
Flying Squirrel, Northern, 46, 185
Fox, Sierra Nevada Red, 192
Frog, Mountain (Sierra) Yellow-legged, 92, pl. 25
    Northern Leopard, 94
    Pacific Chorus, 91, pl. 25
Fuchsia, California, 52, 58, pl. 16
Fulica americana, 119, pl. 33

G

Gadwall, 107, pl. 28

Gavia immer, 110, pl. 31
Gentian, Explorer's, 42, pl. 9
Gentiana calycosa, 42, pl. 9
Gilia, Scarlet, 58, pl. 16
Glaucidium gnoma, 124, pl. 34
Glaucomys sabrinus lascivus, 185, pl. 46
Goldeneye, Barrow's, 107, pl. 30
    Common, 107, pl. 30
Goldenrod, Canada, 66, pl. 19
Goose, Canada, 106, 107, pl. 28
    Greater White-fronted, 107, pl. 28
    Snow, 107, pl. 28
Gooseberry, Sierra, 49, pl. 12
Gopher, pocket, 186, pl. 46
Goshawk, Northern, 117
Grape-Fern, Leather, 37, pl. 7
Grass-of-Parnassus, California, 71, pl. 21
Grebe, Clark's, 111, 112, pl. 31
    Eared, pl. 31
    Pied-billed, 111, pl. 31
    Red-necked, 112, pl. 31
    Western, 111, 112, pl. 31
Grosbeak, Black-headed, 148, 154, 155, 159, pl. 43
    Evening, 16, 167, pl. 44
    Pine, 164
    Rose-breasted, 160
Groundsel, Arrowleaf, 67, pl. 19
Grouse, Blue, 108, pl. 30
Gull, California, 121, pl. 33
    Herring, 121
    Ring-billed, 121, pl. 33
Gulo gulo, 193

H

Hackelia micrantha, 43, pl. 9
Haliaeetus leucocephalus, 116, pl. 32
Hare, Sierra Nevada Snowshoe, 176, pl. 45
    White-tailed, 177
Harrier, Northern, 116, pl. 32
Hawk, Cooper's, 117, 133
    Ferruginous, 115, 118
    Marsh, 116, pl. 32
    Red-tailed, 115, 117, 118, pl. 33
    Rough-legged, 115
    Sharp-shinned, 117, pl. 33
    Sparrow, 119, pl. 33
    Swainson's, 117
Hawkweed, White, 74, pl. 23
Heather, Red, 54, pl. 14
    White (Alpine), 54
Hemlock, Mountain, 4, pl. 1
Hemlock, Poison, 4
Heracleum lanatum, 71, pl. 22
Heron, Great Blue, 32, 113–114, pl. 32
Heuchera rubescens glandulosa, 51, pl. 13
Hieracium albiflorum, 75, pl. 23
Hirundo rustica, 140, pl. 38
Horsemint, Nettle-leaf, 45, pl. 11
Horsetail, Common, 39, 81, pl. 8
Hummingbird, Allen's, 127
    Anna's, 126, pl. 35
    Calliope, 126, pl. 35
    Rufous, 127, pl. 35
Hydromantes platycephalus, 89, pl. 25

Hystricopsylla schefferi, 179

I

Incense-cedar, 10, pl. 3
Indian Dream, 38, pl. 7
Ipomopsis aggregata, 58, pl. 16
Iris missouriensis, 46
Ivesia, Mousetail, 69, pl. 21
Ivesia santolinoides, 69, pl. 21
Ixoreus naevius, 149, pl. 40

J

Jay, Blue, 137
　Steller's, 137, 138, pl. 37
　Western Scrub-, 137, pl. 37
jelly balls, 206–208
Jewelflower, Mountain, 41, pl. 9
Jumping Mouse, Western, 190
Junco, Dark-eyed, 43, 159, 163, pl. 43
Junco hyemalis, 158, pl. 43
Juniper, 10, 11, 81, pl. 3
Juniperus communis, 81
　occidentalis, 81, pl. 3
　occidentalis australis, 11

K

Kalmia polifolia microphylla, 54, pl. 14
Kestrel, American, 119, pl. 33
Killdeer, 120, pl. 33
Kingfisher, Belted, 127, pl. 35
Kinglet, Golden-crowned, 145, pl. 39
　Ruby-crowned, 146, pl. 39
Kokanee, 200
Knotweed, Alpine, 71, pl. 21

L

Larkspur, Nuttall's, 44, pl. 10
　Rydberg's, 44, pl. 10
　Towering, 44, pl. 10
Larus argentatus, 121
　californicus, 121, pl. 33
　delawarensis, 121, pl. 33
Laurel, Alpine, 54, pl. 14
Leucostict atrata, 164
　tephrocotis dawsoni, 164
Lepidium denisflorum, 82
Lepus americanus tahoensis, 176, pl. 45
　townsendii, 177
Lilium parvum, 61, pl. 16
　washingtonianum, 74, pl. 23
Lily, Camas, 47, pl. 11
　Mariposa, 82, pl. 20
　Sierra Tiger, 61, pl. 16
　Washington, 74, pl. 23
Linanthus ciliatus, 50, pl. 13
Linum lewisii alpicola, 42, pl. 9
Lizard, Northern (Sierra) Alligator, 98, pl. 26
　Sagebrush, 97, pl. 26
　Western (Northwestern) Fence, 96, pl. 26
Loon, Common, 110, pl. 31
Lotus, Bird's-foot, 62, pl. 17
Lotus oblongifolius oblongifolius, 62, pl. 17
Lousewort, Dwarf, 77, pl. 24
Loxia curvirostra, 166, pl. 44
Lupine, 46
Lupinus spp., 46, pl. 11

Lutra canadensis, 196

M

Magpie, Black-billed, 137
　Yellow-billed, 137
Mallard, 106, 107, pl. 28
Manzanita, Greenleaf, 27, 81, pl. 4
　Pinemat, 27, pl. 4
Maple, Mountain, 16, pl. 3
Mariposa Lily, 82, pl. 20
　Leichtlin's, 68
Marmarota flaviventris flaviventris, 180, pl. 45
Marmot, Yellow-bellied, 180, pl. 45
Marten, (Pine), 194, 195
Martes americana sierrae, 194, 195
　caurina, possible species name, 195
　pennati (pacificus), 194
Meadowlark, Western, 161, pl. 43
Meadow-Rue, 75, pl. 24
Megascops kennicottii, pl. 34
Melanerpes lewis, 128, pl. 35
Melospiza lincolnii alticola, 42, pl. 42
　melodia, 157, pl. 42
Mephitis mephitis, 197, pl. 47
Merganser, Common, 106, 108, pl. 30
　Hooded, 107, 108
Mergus merganser, 108, pl. 30
Merlin, 119
Microtus longicaudus sierrae, 190
　montanus, 189, pl. 46
Mimulus breweri, 53, pl. 14
　guttatus, 63, pl. 17
　lewisii, 52, pl. 14
Miner's Pepper, 82
Mink, 194, 195
Mistletoe, Western Dwarf, 77, pl. 24
Mitella breweri, 76, pl. 24
Mole, Broad-footed, 173
Molothrus ater, 162, pl. 43
Monardella odoratissima pallida, 45, pl. 11
Monkeyflower, Brewer's, 53, pl. 14
　Lewis's, 52, pl. 14
　Mountain (see Seep-Spring Monkeyflower)
　Seep-Spring, 63, pl. 17
Monkshood, 45, 82, pl. 10
Moth, Pandora, 7
Mountain-ash, 29, pl. 6
Mountain Beaver (Boomer), (Sierra Nevada), 178, pl. 45
Mountain Lion, 198, pl. 47
Mountain Pride, 52, pl. 14
Mouse, Brush, 188
　Deer, 188, pl. 46
　Western Jumping, 190
Mugwort, 67, pl. 20
Mullein, Woolly, 64, pl. 18
Mustela erminea muricus, 194, 196
　frenata nevadensis, 194, 196, pl. 47
　vision, 194, 195
Myadestes townsendii townsendii, 147, pl. 40
Myotis, California, 174
　Fringed, 174
　Little Brown, 174
　Long-eared, 174

Yuma, 174
Myotis californicus californicus, 174
   evotis evotis, 174
   lucifugus carissima, 174
   thysanodes, 174
   yumanensis, 174

N

Neotoma cinerea, 189
Nettle, Stinging, 46, 76, 84, pl. 24
Night-Heron, Black-crowned, 114, pl. 32
Nighthawk, Common, 124, pl. 35
Nightshade, Enchanter's, 68, pl. 20
   Purple, 43, pl. 10
Nucifraga columbiana, 138, pl. 37
Nuphar polysepalum, 65
Nutcracker, Clark's, 9, 10, 138, pl. 37
Nuthatch, Pygmy, 142, pl. 39
   Red-breasted, 142, pl. 38
   White-breasted, 142, pl. 38
Nycticorax nycticorax, 114, pl. 32

O

Oak, Huckleberry, 14, 25, pl.4
Ochotona princeps muiri, 175, pl. 45
Odocoileus hemionus, 199, pl. 47
Oenothera elata hirsutissima, 61, pl. 17
Oncorhynchus clarki ehnshawi, 200
   mykiss, 200
   mykiss aguabonita, 200
   nerka kennerli, 200
Onion, Sierra, 55, 83, pl. 15
   Swamp, 55, 83, pl. 15
Oporornis tolmei tolmei, 153, pl. 41
Oreortyx pictus, 109
Orthilia secunda, 70, pl. 21
Osmorhiza occidentalis, 63, pl. 18
Osprey, 115, 116, pl. 32
Otter, River, 196
Ouzel, Water (see American Dipper)
Owl, Barn, 123
   Flammulated, 123
   Great Gray, 123
   Great Horned, 115, 124, 197, pl. 34
   Long-eared, 123
   Northern Pygmy-, 124, 148, pl. 34
   Northern Saw-whet, 123, 148, pl. 34
   Spotted, 123, 186, pl. 34
   Western Screech-, 123. Pl. 34
Oxyura jamaicensis, pl. 30

P

Paintbrush, Applegate's, 60, pl. 16
   Giant, 60, pl. 16
Pandion haliateus, 116, pl. 32
Parnassia californica, 71, pl. 21
Passerella iliaca megarhyncha, 156
Passerina amoena, 160, pl. 43
Patgioenas fasciata, 122, pl. 34
Pedicularis groenlandica, 51, pl. 13
   semibarbata, 77, pl. 20
Pelecanus erythrorhynchos, 112, pl. 31
Pelican, American White, 112, pl. 31
   Brown, 112
Pellaea bridgesii, 38, pl. 17
Pennyroyal, Mountain, 45, pl. 11

Penstemon, Hot Rock, 70, pl. 21
   Rydberg's, 44, pl. 10
   Showy, 44, pl. 10
Penstemon deustus pedicellatus, 70, pl. 21
   newberryi newberryi, 52, pl. 14
   rydbergii oreocharis, 44, pl. 10
   speciousus, 44, pl. 10
Perideridia parishii, 84
   parishii latifolia, 72, pl. 22
Peromyscus boylii bolylii, 188
   maniculatus gambelii, 188, pl. 46
Petrochelidon pyrrhonata, 141, pl. 38
Phacelia, Vari-leaved, 69, pl. 21
   Waterleaf, 43, pl. 9
Phacelia heterophylla virgata, 69, pl. 21
   hydrophylloides, 43, pl. 9
Phalaenoptilus nuttallii, 125, pl. 35
Phalocrocorax auritis, 113, pl. 32
Phenacomys intermedius, 190
Pheucticus melanocephalus, 159, pl. 43
Phlox, Spreading, 69
Phlox diffusa, 69
Phoebe, Black, 135, pl. 37
Phyllodoce breweri, 54, pl. 14
Picoides albolarvatus albolarvatus, 131, pl. 36
   arcticus, 131, pl. 36
   villosus, 130, pl. 36
Pigeon, Band-tailed, 122, pl. 34
   Rock, 122
Pika, 175-176, pl. 45
Pine, 82; Jeffrey, 6, pl. 42
   Lodgepole, 5, pl. 1
   Ponderosa, 7
   Sugar, 8, pl. 2
   Western White, 8, pl. 2
   Western Yellow, 7
   Whitebark, 9, pl. 2
Pine Drops, 57, pl. 15
Pinicola enucleator californicus, 164
Pinus albicaulis, 9, pl. 2
   contorta murrayana, 5, pl. 1
   jeffreyi, 6, pl. 2
   lambertiana, 8, pl. 2
   monticola, 8, pl. 2
   ponderosa, 7
   spp., 82
Pintail, Northern, 107, pl. 29
Pipilo chlorurus, 154, pl. 42
   maculatus, 155, pl. 42
Pipistrelle, Western, 174 (Bat)
Pipit, American, 149, pl. 40
Piranga ludoviciana, 154, pl. 42
Plantanthera leucostachys, 73, pl. 22
   sparsiflora, 77, pl. 24
Pocket Gopher, Mountain, 186, pl. 46
Podiceps auritus, pl. 31
   grisegna, pl. 31
   nigricollis, 111, pl. 31
Podilymbus podiceps, 111, pl. 31
Poecile gambeli abbreviatus, 141, pl. 38
Polygonum phytolaccifolium, 71, pl. 21
Polyporus amarus, 11
Polystichum kruckbergii, 40

lonchitis, 40
Ponderosa Pine, 7
Pond-Lily, Yellow, 65, pl. 18
Poorwill, Common, 124, 125, pl. 35
Populus balsamifera trichocarpa, 13
  tremuoides, 12
Porcupine, 190, pl. 46
Potentilla fruticosa, 61, pl. 17
  glandulosa, 62, pl. 17
  gracilis, 62, pl. 17
Prairie dogs, 176
Prettyface, 65, pl. 18
Procyon lotor, 193
Prosopium williamsoni, 200
protists, 208
Prunus emarginata, 29, pl. 5
  virginiana demissa, 29, pl. 5
Pseudacris (hyla) regilla, 91, pl. 25
Pseudotsuga menziesii, 4, pl. 1
Pteridium aquilinum pubescens, 37, pl. 7
Pterospora andromedea, 57, pl. 15
Pussy-toes, Alpine, 75, pl. 23
  Pink, 55, pl. 15
Pussypaws, 56, pl. 15
Pygmy-Owl, Northern, 124, 148, pl. 34
Pyrola, Pink, 50, pl. 13
Pyrola asarifolia asarifolia, 50, pl. 13
  picta, 70, pl. 21

Q

Quail, Mountain, 109, pl. 30
Quercus vaccinifolia, 25, pl. 4

R

Rabbitbrush, 66, pl. 19
Raccoon, 193
Rana catesbeiana, 93, pl. 25
  muscosa (sierrae?), 92, pl. 25
  pipiens, 94
Ranger's Buttons, 72, pl. 22
Ranunculus alismifolius, 63, pl. 18
Raven, Common, 139, pl. 38
Regulus calendula cineraceus, 146, pl. 39
  sattrapa, 145, pl. 39
Rhamnus rubra, 26, pl. 4
Rhinichthys osculus, 200
Ribes nevadense, 49, pl. 13
  roezlii roezlii, 49, pl. 12
  viscossimum, 50, pl. 13
Richarsonius egregius, 200
Robin, American, 148, 154, pl. 40
Rock-Brake, American (see American Parsley Fern)
rockchucks, 180
Rock Cress, 68, pl. 20
Rockfringe, 48, pl. 12
Rosa woodsii ultramontana, 48
Rose, Interior, 48
Rosy-Finch, Black, 164
  Gray-crowned, 164
Rubber Boa (Northern), 98
Rubus parviflorus, 69, 84, pl. 20
Rush, Common Scouring, 39

S

Sagebrush, Low, 28
  Mountain, 28, pl. 5
  Snow, 28
  Timberline, 28
Salamander, Mount Lyell, 89, pl. 25
  Long-toed, Southern , 89, pl. 25
Salix lucida, 85
  lucida lasiandra, 13
  scouleriana, 14
Salmo trutta, 200
Salpinctes, obsoletus, pl. 39
Salvelinus fontinalis, 200
Salvelinus namaycushk, 200
Sambucus mexicana, 30, pl. 6
  racemosa microbotrys, 30, pl. 6
Sandpiper, Spotted, 120, pl. 33
Sapsucker, Red-breasted, 130, pl. 36
  Red-naped, 130
  Williamson's, 129, pl. 35
Sarcodes sanguinea, 56, pl. 15
Sayornis nigricans, 136, pl. 37
Scapanus latimanus, 173
Scaup, Greater, 107, pl. 29
  Lesser, 107, pl. 29
Sceloporus graciosus gracilis, 97, pl. 26
  occidentalis occidentalis, 96, pl. 26
Screech-Owl, Western, 123, pl. 34
Scrub-Jay, Western, 137, pl. 37
Sculpin, Paiute, 200
Sedum, Rosy, 59, pl. 16
Sedum obtusatum, 83
  obtusatum obtusatum, 64, pl. 18
  roseum integrifolium, 59, pl. 16
Selasphorus rufus, 127, pl. 35
Senecio triangularis, 67, pl. 19
Sequoias, Giant, 10
Serviceberry, 28, pl. 5
Shiner, Lahontan redside, 200
Shooting Star, Sierra, 53, pl. 14
Shoveler, Northern, 107, pl. 29
Shrew, Dusky (Montane), 172
  Trowbridge's, 172
  Wandering (Vagrant), 172
  Water, 172
Sialia currucoides, 147, pl. 40
  mexicana, pl. 40
Siphateles (Gila) bicolor, 200
Siskin, Pine, 166, pl. 44
Sitta canadensis, 142,, pl. 38
  carolinensis aculeata, 142, pl. 38
  pygmaea, 143, pl. 39
Skunk, Striped, 197, pl. 47
  Western Spotted, 197
Smilicina racemosa, 73, pl. 23
  stellata, 73, pl. 23
Snake, Garter, Common (Valley), 100, pl. 27
  Garter, Sierra (Western Aquatic), 101–102, pl. 27
  Garter, Western Terrestrial (Mountain), 101, pl. 27
Snow Plant, 56, pl. 15
Snowberry, Creeping, 54, pl. 14
  Mountain, 53
Snowbrush, 25
Solanum xanti, 43, pl. 10

Solidago canadensis elongata, 66, pl. 19
Solitare, Townsend's, 147, pl. 40
Solomon's Seal, (Fat) False, 73, pl. 23
    Star (Slim) False, 73, pl. 23
Sorbus californica, 29, pl. 6
    scopulina, 29, pl. 6
Sorex monticolus obscurus, 172
    palustris navigator, 172
    trowbridgii mariposae, 172
    vagrans amoenus, 172
Sparrow, Black-throated, 155
    Brewer's, 156, 162, pl. 42
    Chipping, 155
    Fox, 155, 156
    Golden-crowned, 158, pl. 42
    Lark, 155
    Lincoln's, 157, pl. 42
    Rufous-crowned, 155
    Sage, 155
    Savannah, 155
    Song, 157, pl. 42
    Vesper, 155
    White-crowned, 158, pl. 42
    White-crowned, subspecies, 158
Speedwell, Alpine, 41, pl. 9
Spermophilus beecheyi sierrae, 181, pl. 45
    beldingi beldingi, 180, pl. 45
    lateralis chrysodeirus, 181, pl. 45
Sphenosciadium capitellatum, 72, pl. 22
Sphyrapicus ruber daggetti, 130, pl. 36
    nuchalis, 130
    thyroideus thyroideus, 129, pl. 35
Spilogale putorius gracilis, 197
Spirea, Mountain, 53, pl. 14
Spirea densiflora, 53, pl. 14
Spizella breweri, 156, pl. 42
    passerina arizonae, 155
Squirrel, Belding's Ground, 180, pl. 45
    California (Beechey) Ground, 181, pl. 45
    Douglas's (Chickaree), 7, 184, 185pl. 46
    Golden-mantled Ground, 117, 181, pl. 45
    Northern Flying, 185, pl. 46
Stellula calliope, 126, pl. 35
Sterna caspia, 121, pl. 34
    forsteri, 121, pl. 34
Sternella neglecta, 161, pl. 43
Stickseed, Small-flowered, 43, pl. 9
Streptanthus tortuosus var. *orbiculatus*, 42, pl. 9
Stonecrop, Sierra, 64, 83, pl. 18
Strix occidentalis, pl. 34
Sugar Pine, 8
Sulfur Flower, 64
Swallow, Barn, 140, pl. 38
    Cliff, 140, pl. 38
    Tree, 129, 140, pl. 38
    Violet-green, 140
Swan, Tundra, 107, pl. 28
Sweet Cicely, Western, 63, pl. 18
Swift, Black, 126
    Vaux's, 126
    White-throated, 126
Sylvilagus nuttallii, 177, pl. 45
Symphoricarpos mollis, 54
    rotundifolius var. *rotundifolius*, 53

T

Tachycineta bicolor, 140, pl. 28
Tamias amoenus monoensis, 184
    minimus, 183
    quadrimaculatus, 183, pl. 46
    senex senex, 183
    speciosus frater, 183, pl. 46
Tamiasciurus douglasii, 184, pl. 46
Tanager, Western, 153, pl. 42
Taraxacum officinale, 80
Taxidea taxus, 196, pl. 47
Teal, Cinnamon, 107, pl. 29
    Green-winged, 107, pl. 29
Tern, Black, 121, 122
    Caspian, 121, pl. 34
    Forster's, 121, pl. 34
Thalictrum fendleri fendleri, 75, pl. 24
Thamnophis couchii, 101, pl. 27
    elegans elegans, 101, pl. 27
    sirtalis fitchii, 100, pl. 27
Thimbleberry, 69, 84, pl. 20
Thistle, Anderson's, 56. Pl. 15
Thomomys monticola, 186, pl. 46
Thrush, Hermit, 148, pl. 40
    Swainson's, 148
    Varied, 148, pl. 40
Tiger Lily, Sierra, 61, pl. 16
Toad, Western, 94, pl. 25
    Yosemite, 91
Tobacco Brush, 25, pl. 4
Towhee. Green-tailed, 159, pl. 42
    Spotted, 155, pl. 42
Triteleia ixoides anilina, 65, pl. 18
Troglodytes aedon parkmanii, 144, pl. 39
Trout spp., 108, 200; Brook, 200
    Brown, 200
    Golden, 200
    Lahontan cutthroat, 200
    Lake, Mackinaw, 200
    Rainbow, 200
Tsuga mertensiana, 4, pl. 1
Tulip, Sierra Star, 68, pl. 20
Turdus migratorius propinquus, 148, pl. 40

U

Ursus americanus californiensis, 192, pl. 47
Urtica dioica, 84
    dioica holosericea, 76, pl. 24

V

Veratrum californicum, 74, 80, pl. 23
Verbascum thapsus, 64, pl. 18
Vermivora celata lutescens, 150, pl. 40
    ruficapilla, 150, pl. 41
Veronica wormskjoldii, 41, pl. 9
Viola macloskeyi, 72, pl. 22
    pinetorium pinetorium, 64, pl. 18
Violet, Macloskey's, 72, pl. 22
    Pine, 64, pl. 18
Vireo, Bell's, 163
    Blue-headed, 136
    Cassin's, 136, pl. 37
    Plumbeous, 136
    Solitary, 163

Warbling, 136, 163, pl. 37
Vireo cassinii, 136, pl. 37
    gilvus, 137, pl. 37
Vole, Long-tailed, 190
    Montane, 189, pl. 46
    Western Heather, 190
Vulpes vulpes, 192
Vulture, Turkey, 115, pl. 32
Vultures, American, 114–115

W

Wallflower, Sierra, 61, pl. 17
Warbler, Black-throated Gray, 151, pl. 41
    Hermit, 152, pl. 41
    MacGillivray's, 152, pl. 41
    Nashville, 150, 153, pl. 41
    Orange-crowned, 150, pl. 40
    Townsend's, 152, pl. 41
    Wilson's, 53, pl. 41
    Yellow, 151, 163, pl. 41
    Yellow-rumped, 151, pl. 41
Weasel, Long-tailed, 194, 196, pl. 47
    Short-tailed, 194, 196
Whip-poor-will, 125
Whisker Brush, 50, pl. 13
Whitefish, Mountain, 200
Whitethorn, Mountain, 26, pl. 4
Wigeon, American, 107, pl. 28
Willow, Scouler, 14
    Shining, 13
    spp., 85
Wilsonia pusilla chryseola, 153, pl. 41
Wintergreen, One-sided, 70, pl. 21
    White-veined, 70, pl. 21

Wolf, 192
Wolverine, 193
Wood-Pewee, Western, 36, 133
Woodpecker, American Three-toed, 131
    Black-backed, 131, pl. 36
    Downy, 131
    Gila, 130
    Hairy, 130, pl. 36
    Ivory-billed, 133
    Lewis's, 128, pl. 35
    Pileated, 132, pl. 36
    White-headed, 131, pl. 36
Woodrat, Bushy-tailed, 189
Woodsia scopulina, 40
Wren, Bewick's, 145
    Canyon, 144, pl. 39
    House, 144, pl. 39
    Marsh, 145, pl. 39
    Rock, 144, pl. 39
    Winter, 145

X

Xanthocephalus xanthocephalus, 161, pl. 43

Y

Yampah, Parish's, 72, 84, pl. 22
Yarrow, 74, 85, pl. 23
Yosemite Moonwort, 37

Z

Zapus princeps pacificus, 190
Zenaida macroura, 123, pl. 34
Zigadenus venenosus venenosus, 73, 81, pl. 22
Zonotrichia atricapilla, 158, pl. 42
    leucophrys oriantha, 158, pl. 42